William Playfair

The History of Jacobinism

Its Crimes, Cruelties and Perfidies: Vol. II.

William Playfair

The History of Jacobinism
Its Crimes, Cruelties and Perfidies: Vol. II.

ISBN/EAN: 9783337077389

Printed in Europe, USA, Canada, Australia, Japan

Cover: Foto ©ninafisch / pixelio.de

More available books at **www.hansebooks.com**

HISTORY

OF

JACOBINISM

THE

HISTORY OF JACOBINISM,

Its CRIMES, CRUELTIES and PERFIDIES:

COMPRISING

AN INQUIRY

Into the Manner of Disseminating, under the Appearance of

PHILOSOPHY AND VIRTUE,

PRINCIPLES

WHICH ARE EQUALLY SUBVERSIVE OF

ORDER, VIRTUE, RELIGION,
LIBERTY AND HAPPINESS.

BY WILLIAM PLAYFAIR.

With an Appendix,

BY PETER PORCUPINE,

Containing a History of the American Jacobins, commonly
denominated Democrats.

VOL. II.

" History, who keeps a durable record of all our acts, and exer-
" cifes her awful cenfure over *all forts of fovereigns*, will not forget
" thefe events."

BURKE.

PHILADELPHIA:

PRINTED FOR WILLIAM COBBETT, NORTH SECOND
STREET, OPPOSITE CHRIST CHURCH.
1796.

CONTENTS.

VOLUME II.

CHAP. I.

CONDUCT *of the chiefs of the revolt who were at the Hotel de Ville—Cruelties of the* 10th *of August—Decrees of that day—Insidious conduct towards the king and treachery to the nation—Manner in which Paris ruled despotically over France—Difficulties attending the establishment of a* FREE *republic in a large, populous, and old country—Comparison between the despotism of unlimited monarchy and republican despotism—Few instances of unlimited monarchies, and those confined to Asia and Africa—General reflections,*   *p.* 9.

CHAP. II.

Beginning of the reign of Robespierre—Robespierre vindicated against the revolutionists, the aristocrats, and the whole of mankind—The trial of the king—Probable motive—Vanity of democrats

C H A P. III.

C H A P. IV.

CHAP. V.

HISTORY

OF

JACOBINISM,

CHAP. I.

Conduct of the chiefs of the revolt who were at the Hotel de Ville—Cruelties of the 10th of August—Decrees of that day—Infidious conduct towards the king and treachery to the nation—Manner in which Paris ruled defpotically over France—Difficulties attending the eftablifhment of a FREE republic in a large, populous, and old country—Comparifon between the defpotifm of unlimited monarchy and republican defpotifm—Few inftances of unlimited monarchies, and thofe confined to Afia and Africa—General reflections.

THIS fecond period of the French revolution which now began, fhews in all its extent the misfortunes and crimes that refult from encouraging men to rebel againft legitimate authority. The reign of the people was now fairly eftablifhed, and the firft operation was to maffacre all the

Swifs guards who fell into their hands. Numbers,
were murdered and mutilated in detail, but the
large column which had been taken was conducted to the Hotel de Ville, and, according to the
cuftom (began with Bertier and Foulon two years
ago), they were all maffacred at the foot of the
ftairs, and in prefence of the felf-created, ufurping magiftrates. Thefe murders were all approved of and protected upon the great fcale, but
the affembly pretended to preach refpect to perfons and property, when any particular occafion
occurred that might fhew fomething like a regard
to juftice without deranging the main plan of ex-
terminating its enemies. As cruelty and humanity
are incompatible with each other, and cannot
lodge in the fame breaft, the affembly, the leaders
of the revolt, and thofe who conducted it, muft
drop all claim to one or other of thefe qualities,
and certainly it is not to that of cruelty; we are,
therefore, juftified in confidering the cafes in
which they deviated from their general line of
conduct, as unwilling facrifices made to the
fhrine of juftice and humanity, in order to blind
the fpectators with refpect to the extent of their
atrocities.

The new common council of Paris was now
become the executive power, with Petion at its
head and the rabble at its command; the affembly
having confented to act the part of a paffive inftrument, and to decree whatever the populace,
fet on by the municipality, demanded, all power
might be faid to be lodged in the mayor and his
conforts, who were the leaders of the Jacobin and
Cordelier clubs.

The

The municipal officers were formidable from their violence of difpofition, as well as from their great number; felected from the different quarters of Paris, they had fpies, connections, and enemies in every part of that large and populous city. A part of this number remained at the Hotel de Ville to deliberate and fend off orders, and the remainder were difpatched to fee them executed. The barriers had all been fhut at an early hour in the morning to prevent their victims from efcaping, as well as to prevent the departments of the kingdom from hearing the hiftory of what was going on till all fhould be finifhed. In this they imitated the firft leaders of the infurrection, who did precifely the fame things on the fourteenth of July; but as the democrats of former times were the ariftocrats of the prefent day, they were purfued with unrelenting vengeance, for they had been popular once, and might be formidable now.

M. de Clermont Tonnerre, one of the members of the firft deputation of the affembly at Verfailles to the infurgents of Paris, when the Baftile was taken, was the fecond victim after Mandat.* A number of *fufpected* perfons

had

---

* This gentleman had always profeffed very moderate principles, though he had encouraged *the beginning of the revolt*. He was feized by the populace near his own hotel, at a diftance from the Thuilleries. Every thing fhewed that he was not occupied in any fort of plot or confpiracy. He ufed his eloquence and his arguments in vain. When the people found that he defended himfelf from all blame, a blow was aimed at him, and the attempt to ward it off was a fufficient crime; he was then attacking the majefty of the nation, and was immediately immolated to its juftice. This is one of

the

had been imprifoned during the night only becaufe they were found walking the ftreets, and
becaufe fome of them had arms, a very natural
precaution in fuch times; and eleven out of
twenty-eight were barbaroufly murdered in order
to excite the people to acts of outrage and violence by the double feeling of fear and rage.   A
plot it was pretended had been difcovered, and the
heads of the pretended confpirators were carried
about on poles; this artifice had already been fo
often practifed, and in general fucceeded fo well,
that no doubt can be entertained of the defign
with which it was done.

The populace affembled through curiofity and
anxiety at firft, but had not taken any active part

the ten thoufand leffons given by the revolution to thofe who
for one moment think that infurrection can be a duty.   The
virtuous and moderate Clermont Tonnerre was more obnoxious to the anarchifts now, than the greateft ariftocrat had
been at the beginning of the revolution.

The perfons flopped in the night time were ftragglers,
who, through curiofity, or inquietude, could not ftay at
home; nothing could be proved againft them, nor was it attempted. They were chiefly young men, well dreffed, and fome
of them of wit and talents; they were, therefore, ariftocrats,
and that was enough, republican juftice and zeal required
nothing more for a pretence, and the real motive was to render the people mad with rage.   All this was done before the
attack of the Thuilleries commenced; and it is well known
that any violent excefs of this fort infpires a mob with anger
againft the military who are ftationed for the prefervation of
order; becaufe a crime committed leads to the fear of punifhment, therefore, defperation follows the fhedding of innocent
blood.   Befides this, heads carried on poles fhew the inhabitants that the mob has triumphed over law and order, and,
therefore, all thofe who go with the ftrongeft, became aiders
and abettors.

in

in the attack upon the Thuilleries, but when they faw thefe bloody trophies, and as foon as the unfortunate guard were conquered, they were ready to play their part in robbery and aflaffination.

The trick played off formerly to incenfe the people againft the governor of the Baftile was now employed againft the Swifs, and with a fimilar effect ;* they were purfued like wild beafts, and no mercy was given. Their mutilated carcaffes beftrewed the ftreets, and received the laft indignities that a complication of abominable, paffions could infpire into the minds of a corrupted and enraged populace.

The perpetrators of many of the infamies and horrors of the revolution are fkreened from the full extent of the anger and difguft which their atrocities would infpire, from the circumftance that THEY DO NOT ADMIT OF BEING REPEATED, *not to be repeated.* until all regard to modefty, and the feelings of humanity fhall be ftifled in the minds of other nations ; fhould fuch an unfortunate and miferable period ever come, then will Parifian refinement and the acts of the good people *(le bon peuple)* of France fhine forth in all their natural and original fplendour ; till then, we muft be contented to fay, that depraved imaginations were tortured to invent whatever it was poffible for favages void of every feeling of humanity to execute.

* It was faid that the Swifs had betrayed the people by an appearance of friendfhip and peace, and when they had made them approach, received them with a general difcharge of mufketry. Nothing was more **falfe.**

The

The porters of the gates of the Thuillerie garden, and who were as innocent of what had
paffed at the palace as if they had been an hundred miles diftant, were cruelly maffacred with
their wives and children. The menial fervants
of the palace, whofe misfortune it was to be
there, but who had not engaged in any refiftance, fhared the fate of the Swifs.* Cooks,
fcullions, man-fervants and maid-fervants, all
alike fell victims to the republican rage.

The affembly pretended to deliberate calmly,
and to govern France, while they took the moft
important refolutions at the command of the
mob, and no proteft has ever been entered
into againft the legality of the proceedings
[*Note* N.]

As foon as matters were a little quieted, cou-
riers were difpatchéd to all the provinces, which
were in expectation of fome great event, as in the
firft days of the revolution, and ready to receive
whatever impulfe might be given. There was
now, however a difference of the pofition of
men's minds; at the firft epoch, men were tired
of the oppreffions of a regular government, they
were now tired of the ten-fold greater evils of
anarchy. In the beginning, hope of being better
was the predominant paffion, it was now fear of
being worfe that reigned, and of confequence,
when the addrefs of the affembly arrived, obedience and refignation were ready; but the Jaco-

* Thefe laft might have efcaped if they had imagined
there was any danger for them, but they fell victims, like
many others, to the republicans, by not being able to conceive their danger.

bin

bin clubs fet to work, and foon procured addreffes of adhefion and congratulation on the
fall of that conftitution which they had all fo
eagerly and fo repeatedly fworn to maintain.—
Whether the villany of the leaders, or the pu-
fillanimity of the inhabitants at large was the
greateft, it is difficult to determine; but it cannot be doubted that both the two were im-
menfely great, and it is evident that the Parifian
leaders counted upon the obedient and fubmiffive
difpofition of the nation, becaufe the defire of
adhering to the conftitution had been recently
manifefted by a very great majority of the departments of the kingdom.

The leaders of the infurrection reafoned thus:
we are few, but we fhall perfuade a number of
the people whofe indigence renders them difcontented, to join us; when we are ten thoufand,
no force in Paris can oppofe us, and therefore all
Paris will join with us; when the deed fhall be
done, we fhall be all equally guilty, and therefore
Paris will maintain what has become her act and
deed. Paris is the center of the kingdom, and
the moft populous city; no one department will
venture to rife againft us; we fhall call upon them
for fupport feparately and in detail; they will
have no time to confult with each other, and
muft therefore be incapable of any fyftematic
oppofition. Add to this, by our fifteen thoufand
clubs, we can put the magiftrates of all France in
fear and in danger, fo that before the moment
for reflection or refiftance can come, they will be
obliged to declare themfelves in our favour;
fhould fome departments not do fo, we have
means eafily to reduce them to obedience, as
they can make no combined effort.

Such

Such was actually the reasoning of the Jacobin leaders at Paris, and the event has shewn that they were not deceived.

The great extent of France, and all communications from the distant quarters being carried on by means of correspondences in Paris, rendered it absolutely impossible to take any measures to counteract whatever the Parisians chose to do.

Those who think that republican freedom can be established over a large and populous country, are much mistaken. If there is one large city that serves as a center, then will it rule the whole; if there is no such large city, then will the republic divide itself into smaller fractions. Even America, which has so many advantages in its favour, will either in time separate into different republics, or it will lose its liberty.* We must be careful to make a distinction between a republican form of government and a free government;

---

* It is not impossible but that the new federal city which the Americans are building as a center for their government, at a distance from the sea, is begun with an intention to prevent the whole country from becoming the slave of a large capital, and as such, it is extremely wise. With respect to the probability of the American states separating, when they become populous, or losing their liberties, it must depend on circumstances which of the two will happen; but the one or the other must happen, and it will be lucky for them if they separate and thereby preserve their liberty. Fear is the thing that supports despotism under a republican form, and fear cannot be inspired except when there is a powerful body to give the impulse in such a way, that both the action and reaction shall have taken place before there is time for the different provinces to consult together. Until America becomes populous there is not any danger.

they

they may, and fometimes are united, but they are not always fo, though the republican forms have more the appearance of freedom than monarchical forms have.

Defpotifm in monarchy arifes from a general difpofition in the fubjects to obey, and in republics from a general difunion and difference of opinion amongft the citizens. The Roman government was called republican, until the time of the emperors; but it was an abufe of language to comprehend the Roman provinces under the name of a free republic. The free republican government only exifted at Rome, and a fmall portion of Italy. We may allow that the Roman citizens at a certain period were free, and that the freedom they enjoyed was under a republican form; but the free republic only extended to a fmall diftance. The defpotic republic extended over a great portion of Europe.

The republic of Athens was a free republic altogether, becaufe its territories were not of fuch an extent as to admit the chief city giving arbitrary laws to the reft.

What was the confequence of the former of thofe republics? Why, that Rome increafed to a moft enormous fize; that the wealth of all the provinces was continually extorted from the opprefled inhabitants, on purpofe to fupport the enormous expenfes of an enormous city; and whatever revolutions the parties in the capital effected, the whole of its fubjects were obliged blindly to obey. France obeys Paris in the fame manner; whether its inhabitants make a conftitution or deftroy one, it is the fame thing to the nation at large, they muft fubmit.

Paper Money   The invention of paper money has foftened the rigour of thofe contributions, under which induftry and capital have been laid to fupport the vices and the expenfes of government; but it will likewife be more terrible in the end than taxes, for the former robs the nation of all its capital, and encourages idlenefs, whereas the latter obliges men to be induftrious, and only robs them of part of the fruits of their induftry.

As republican forms by no means fecure freedom, though they affume its appearance, it would be a very ufeful thing to enter fully into an inquiry, whether republican defpotifm or monarchical defpotifm is the worft? The prejudices of mankind are in favour of republics perhaps, but it would be very eafy to prove, that people are much happier under mixed governments, than under a purely republican or monarchical form of government. It is at all events very certain, that the liberty of people under a republic depends upon the intereft of all being nearly the fame; now, great extent of territory, or thofe peculiar diftinctions, views, prejudices, and inte- *old Nations* refts, which are to be found *in all old nations*, prevent the poffibility of that unanimity and co-operation which are neceffary in order to procure happinefs under a republican form of government. America is extenfive, but in all other refpects is at prefent muchbetter fitted for a republican than a monarchical government, but it will become lefs fo as it grows older. It was a general notion in France, that that kingdom

was

was too extenfive for a republican form of government, but this was combated by the example of America; and in this cafe the Jacobins
quoted example, the leffons of which they had
fo continually neglected, and upon an occafion
where they could not with any propriety be applied.

Perhaps many people will think that we are
going too far in faying, that even a mixed government could not exift in France, on account
of its extent, population, and manners; but
fhould we be wrong, there are at leaft a great
many reafons that feem to fupport it. We muft
here enter our proteft againft the idea of fpeaking in favour of unlimited monarchy and arbitrary power or of any form that is not fo far republican that the people fhall have reprefentatives with fufficient power to controul the will
of the king; yet there are certainly cafes, where
a nation is unfortunately in a ftate where thofe
bleffings cannot be enjoyed; and it feems probable that the French nation is one example.

There are three forts of hereditary monarchical
governments. The one is, unlimited or uncontrouled monarchy, where there is no conftitutional act to fupport the rights of the fubject,
and where, of confequence, the will of the ruler
is fupreme, and regulates all.

The fecond fort of monarchical government
is, where there is a conftitutional act, or where
cuftom, natural juftice or precedent, and laws
already made, are a rule of conduct for the fovereign. This is pure but limited monarchy.

The

The third is that mixed government, where the people share in the power of making laws with the king, and where they have sufficient means of making the constitutional act be preserved from any infringement on his part.

Under the first of these governments, none but ignorant barbarians or slothful voluptuaries can exist; but as there does not exist in Europe an example of one, nor, probably, an advocate in favour of one, it is not necessary to enter into any consideration of its incompatibility with human happiness.*

The second sort of monarchy is the most universal, in every sense of the word; first, such governments exist, and have existed, at all times, the bulk of civilised nations have possessed such, and do now possess such; they may be very mild, and the people very happy under them, or they may be the reverse; and it is unlucky that a form of government, under which men may be happy, which is so universal and capable of such modifiations, has obtained the name of *arbitrary monarchy*, though that appellation cannot, with propriety, be applied but to the first sort of government of which we have been speaking.

* It is very extraordinary, that neither Goths, Vandals, nor any barbarous tribes, formerly in Europe, were governed by this sort of kingly power; nor was there any tribe of North American savages, yet Africa and Asia have produced many examples of this government, and all the Asiatic and African governments approach very nearly to this state of uncontrouled kingly power.

Republicans

Republicans are particularly apt to fall into the error of calling this limited monarchy arbitrary, and as the will conveys an idea of the deed, men are apt to think, that wretchedneſs is the lot of the ſubjects of all ſuch governments, though experience does not, by any means, vindicate or ſupport this opinion, which is founded upon the belief, that human nature is ſo depraved and perverted that rulers are always diſpoſed to exerciſe injuſtice and oppreſſion. This idea is wrong in itſelf, and the more inexcuſable in republicans, that all their ſyſtem of republican happineſs are founded upon the belief, that men are in general guided by good intention and a love of their country.

It may be ſaid, that when people have rights ariſing either from a compact made with the king, or ariſing from certain principles having been long adopted and followed, unleſs they have a method of defending thoſe principles againſt the power of the king, ſuch rights are a mere illuſion. This is true, in ſome degree, but by no means to its full extent.

To argue, that a king of Spain, for inſtance, becauſe he has no parliament ready in Madrid to refuſe the ſupplies, or diſband the army, will lay unneceſſary and oppreſſive taxes on the people, and declare war without provocation, is as unfair as to argue, that the houſe of commons will refuſe the annual ſupplies becauſe it has the power to do ſo. Thoſe who calculate either upon the total depravity of the human mind in kings, or perfect virtue in people, are equally miſtaken, as the hiſtory of mankind, from the earlieſt

earlieſt ages, proves beyond a diſpute; and as the revolution of France confirms: it therefore follows, that the government of a nation ſhould neither be founded upon the one nor the other of theſe principles, but ſhould be regulated by the ſituation and nature of the people to be governed.

In Rome, as long as the people preſerved themſelves from corruption of manners and principles, every conteſt between parties ended in favour of liberty; at a later period, when the ſituations of men and things were changed, every conteſt ended in favour of deſpotiſm. In France, hitherto every conteſt for liberty has ended as in the latter period of the Roman government; and in England, every conteſt has ended as in the former period: there muſt therefore be, probably, ſome ſtrong reaſons for this difference of reſults, where the motives ſeem to have been the ſame.*

It is not, probably, one ſimple cauſe, but a combination of ſeveral different cauſes, that have operated ſo hurtfully againſt French liberty. The

* · Unlimited monarchies are rare things, and even thoſe are not ſo terrible as people may imagine: a monarch, even in the worſt of cafes begins by making laws, and both his pride and indolence are concerned in adhering to them rather than in overturning them. The cruelties and oppreſſion of ſuch kings are rather on private and particular occaſions than upon a large ſcale; and it is to be recollected, that the ſupreme power of one chief, by puniſhing with promptitude and ſeverity, prevents a great many ſmaller oppreſſors from daring to exert their power; tyrants do not love rivals in atrocity, and therefore the worſt of them generally protect their ſubjects from all oppreſſion but their own.

ſize

fize of the country, and the variety of the wants, wifhes, and difpofitions of the people, certainly are of the number—The impatient vivacity, which rufhes too haftily to conclufions, and rejects thofe precautions which are neceffary to prevent men from ruining themfelves, feems, however, to be the principal one.

Another great caufe is in the vanity and exalted notions of the people in general, which makes them reject the leffons of experience, and liften to wild theories.

To thefe caufes may be added another ftill. The depraved ftate of morals, and the confequent miftruft that takes place between different parties, which prevents OPPOSITE POWERS FROM ACTING WITH UNITED EFFORTS FOR THE WELL-BEING OF THE STATE.* Contented with the means of defence, the different powers in the ftate in England make no attack upon each other's prerogatives; but in France we fee it was a perpetual war for many ages. The king trampled on the rights of the people by depriving them of their lawful reprefentatives, whilft he had the power to do fo; and no fooner had an uncommonly virtuous monarch reftored their rights

* We never find in England different parties exprefs themfelves as if they thought all their opponents in politics were men void of principle, and not to be trufted. We make in this country a diftinction between moral principle and political opinions. We fuppofe all men who form any oftenfible part of fociety, agree nearly as to the former, though they differ widely as to the latter. Nobody will accufe the chiefs of either party of wifhing to ruin England, but many may fuppofe that the meafures of one of the parties lead to ruin.

to the people, than he finds himself stripped of his own, with a tyranny and perseverance without example.

That the depraved state of morals was a very active cause we may learn from this, that when the revolution began, and the general run of the people had yet some attachment to principle, there were many attempts made to become free and happy; but after three years of anarchy had rooted up all respect to things hitherto held sacred, the revolution became UNLIMITED ANARCHY. All regard to law and natural or established rights were equally thrown aside, and there was less of what is properly called freedom than at any former period of French history.

If freedom is only to be obtained by balancing different powers against each other, as in England, the French seem to be incapable of possessing it long, from their want of moderation and confidence in each other, which will prevent them from acting together. And if freedom is to be obtained by a pure republican form of government, they seem to be equally incapable of possessing it, from the variety of their views and interests, the violence of their passions, and their want of purity of manners.

It is therefore, perhaps, more probable that France may enjoy liberty under limited, but unmixed monarchy, than under either a mixed, or a republican form; or, if ever freedom is enjoyed under the latter form, it will be when France shall be divided, and so diminished, that the city which is the centre of government will be no
longer

longer capable of exercifing arbitrary fway under the appearance of republican liberty.

Who is the man, or where is he, that would not prefer being under the government of one king, than under that of thofe infamous men, who ufurped the government, by placing themfelves at the head of the revolt on the 10th of Auguft? Had Robefpierre. Danton, Petion, or Talien, reigned alone and without controul from that period, we fhould not have feen France defolated and difgraced by the maffacres that fucceeded. It is certainly no great compliment paid to kings, when we fuppofe them to be upon an equality in point of virtue and humanity with thefe mifcreants; but it is a very great compliment to kingly government, when we affert that, even in the hands of fuch wretches, it would be preferable to a republic in a corrupted ftate of fociety.

What may tend a little to confirm us in the opinion that monarchy alone, and unmixed monarchy will beft fuit the fituation and character of the French nation, is, that moft of thofe who wifhed to fee a free government eftablifhed in France, and who aided to deftroy the former government, but who are equally averfe to anarchy as to flavery, are now of opinion that they were miftaken in thinking fuch a change could be effected in France by a national affembly, or by two houfes of parliament.

The law of juries upon the Englifh plan, which is one of the greateft bleffings a people can enjoy, was never put in practice in France, fo as to attain the end of juftice; the fame difpofition for intrigue, the fame want of patience and want of folid principles led the jurymen aftray, that had ruined the national affembly and the nation. In the different municipalities and in the adminiftration of the departments, men were oppreffed with all the expenfes of the ancient government, and vexed with all the fophifms and new-fangled principles of the revolution; fo that it does certainly appear, as at leaft being very problematical, whether the French can be happy under any other than monarchical government, and that not of the *unlimited* fort, but, at the fame time, *unmixed*.

We have been naturally led into thefe reflections at the time when the revolution changed its character, and when the refults of the firft principles laid down by the conftituent affembly were fully developed; it was on the 14th of July that the nation had eat of the fruit of the forbidden tree, but it was not till the 10th of Auguft that its nakednefs and wretchednefs were perceived. [*See Note* O.]

The triumph of the rabble was as complete over the burgeffes after the 10th of Auguft, as that of the burgeffes had been over the nobles two years before. Men were now glad to hide their epaulets and uniforms, as they had formerly been to hide their ftars and ribands; to be ragged, dirty, and difgufting, was the way to be honoured and refpected, and was indifpenfable to individual fafety; it was likewife the way to power and profit.

The

The Marſeillois and their aſſociates were perpetually in the club of Cordeliers. The Jacobin club for a few weeks was not quite upon
the level of the revolution,* and it was conſidered as rather being too ariſtocratical for about
eight or ten days ; not that this reproach could
be made with juſtice to the whole of the club,
but that it wanted to be purified of many of its
members who had formerly ſhewn too much moderation.

The manifeſto of the Duke of Brunſwick had
produced in Paris a very different effect from
what he expected; he had threatened when he
ought to have promiſed; and, as the attack of
the 10th had laid the Pariſians open to all the
vengeance which he could inflict, ſhould he ſuc-
ceed, the whole inhabitants joined in wiſhing to
have him repulſed. This operated a coalition of
parties, exactly as the fooliſh affair of the Prince
de Lambeſc had done at the beginning of the revolution, and its effects were as fatal and as
formidable to the adviſers of that imprudent
meaſure.

The friends of royalty in France were ſorry to
ſee their fortunes put into the hands of the King
of Pruſſia, who was not half ſo much intereſted
in the reſult of the affair as the Emperor of Germany. Pruſſia, it was evident, could not carry
on the war at its own expenſe, and it was too
remote from France to have any thing to fear
from an attack upon itſelf. Beſides, the court of

* _Au niveau de la revolution_, a Jacobin method for expreſſing their being ready to ſupport every violent meaſure.

Berlin

Berlin fwarmed with men who did not approve of the monarchical form of government which they were to fight for, and all of whom were the enemies of the Houfe of Auftria. This hatred pervaded the officers and the private men as well as the courtiers; fo that great fuccefs could not be expected; and what might, perhaps, have been obtained, was rendered impoffible by the effect of the manifefto.

It is difficult to conceive by what arguments the Duke of Brunfwick, at the head of only 80,000 men, could be perfuaded, or could perfuade himfelf, to fend a manifefto, in which he menaced a great kingdom, to the affiftance of whofe king he was coming, whilft that king and his family were in the power of the very people he menaced. Did the duke reafon from the former nature of the French nation, or from its prefent difpofition? The French were never cowards formerly, and lately they had been very bold and audacious. At all events, it muft be confidered as very dangerous to put fuch men in fear, and reduce them to defpair, when they had the king and his family in their power.

Had the peaceable and well-inclined citizens of Paris wifhed to difavow the affair of the 10th of Auguft, they durft not now venture to do it, becaufe it was neceffary to be unanimous amongft themfelves, in order to avert the evils from a foreign army with which they were threatened, and from which thofe moft averfe to the revolt of the 10th had the moft to fear. The revolutionifts who had nothing to lofe could quit Paris, and would certainly have done fo had the Pruffian
army

army advanced, they would have likewife carried
the king and his family with them; but the citizen who had a houfe and fome property, muft
have remained, and fubmitted to the laws and
punifhments which the conqueror might chufe to
order. And what could he expect? either to be
treated as guilty of traiteroufly aiding to attack
the palace, or bafely looking on. And who were
to be the judges? why, ftrangers who knew
nothing of the matter.

The violent efforts of the Parifians to ftir up
all France to repel the Pruffian army, was the
natural confequence of this imprudent and fatal
manifefto; and we muft lament, that, if the revolution has furnifhed little elfe on the fide of the
revolted but perfidy and crimes, on the part of
thofe who wifh to crufh it, we have feen little
elfe than blunders, originating in the total ignorance of what was going on in France, and the
ftate of the minds of the people.

The decrees rendered by the affembly on the
10th of Auguft, [*See Note* P.] fhew how readily
the affembly concurred in deftroying the conftitution, even upon the fuppofition that it did nothing more than concur.

The king's minifters were difmiffed, and replaced by Le Brun for foreign affairs; Danton,
that factious and violent republican, for the minifter of juftice; Monge, a teacher of navigation,
for the marine; Servan, who had been of the
Jacobin miniftry a few months before, for the
war minifter; and Claviere. Thefe men were to
fupply the place of the king in the new order of
things;

things; that is to fay, they were to be the executive power,* under, however, the controul of Roland, who had been minifter at the fame time with the other Jacobins, and had diftinguifhed himfelf by an infolent letter to his majefty.

The re-appearance of thefe actors upon the fcene fhews the connection between the plans previous to the 10th of Auguft, and after it. It at leaft fhows, that this revolution did not originate in the king, nor was it the fpontaneous effort of the people, fince thofe who were feen fo long ago preparing the way for it, now were immediately exalted by it to the firft offices in the nation. It is thus, that when a rebel prince, in

* Le Brun was editor of a newfpaper, and had been banifhed France, to which he had only ventured to return after the revolution had commenced, like many others of thofe who now held places of profit and importance. He has fince been guillotined.

Servan had been openly accufed by the popular deputy Lecointre of Verfailles, as a corrupt minifter who had accepted bribes. He has fince been guillotined.

Monge was the moft unexceptionable of them all with regard to his paft life, which was confined to attention to his bufinefs.

Danton had been an advocate for caufes determined by the cabinet council of the king, as our houfe of lords decides in England. He was one of the moft daring and cruel men in France.

Claviere was originally a merchant in Geneva; he had left it for the revolution there; then had gone to Ireland to fettle a colony, which he had foon left in order to job in the funds in Paris. He was a man of knowledge in feveral lines, but of a cruel and vindictive temper. He cut his throat in prifon, as Roland did on the high road near Rouen.

Africa

Africa, dethrones a fovereign, he is put in his place; the perfons who had been moft active in dethroning Louis XVI. now reigned in his ftead, under the name of the executive minifters.

Three years had been employed in France to render odious the characters of kings and queens, by collecting the crimes of thofe individual monarchs during many centuries, who had rendered themfelves juftly odious by abufing the power put into their hands. But the monarchs of the affembly, of the miniftry, and of the municipality, willing, perhaps, to fpare their hiftorians a fimilar trouble, began by exhibiting in a few months more crimes and horrors than the hiftorian would be able to relate, or the reader to remember.

We have already faid, that the nature of the cruelties exercifed prevented a regard to decency from calling down upon the perpetrators the full extent of the vengeance of mankind. It is equally true that their *multiplicity* prevents a complete detail; fo that we may fay, that both for enormity and extent their crimes furpafs defcription.

As, after the 10th of Auguft, one of the firft acts was to fupprefs all the royalift, or even the moderate newfpapers; as the liberty of the prefs, which had never been fully eftablifhed except for the violent faction, was now entirely at an end, we muft take the teftimony of levellers and anarchifts for the proofs of their own crimes; and we fhall fee that, though probably they do not go nearly to the extent that truth would require, yet they go far enough for the purpofe of convincing us that no government was ever fo cruel, fo unjuft, juſt, nor ſo treacherous, as that of the leaders of this ſecond revolution.

Cambon, in a ſpeech to the national conven- tion, in November following, ſays :*

Cambon

" Witneſs myſelf to many facts, I think it " neceſſary to ſpeak of them, that the convention " may avoid what the legiſlative aſſembly ſuffer- " ed.   An enemy to kings, I embraced with ea- " ger joy the revolution of 1789, which brought " on the fall of kings.   When I arrived in Paris, " I perceived that a ſecond revolution was ne- " ceſſary to conſummate the fall of kings.   That " revolution was effected, not by thoſe who pre- " tend to have effected it, but by the legiſlative " body, which diſbanded the guard of conſpi- " rators of the king, which had ſuppreſſed the " ſtaff officers of the Pariſian guards, and order- " ed the Swiſs regiments to be diſmiſſed ; and " which had ſent away the regular troops from " Paris, in order that the people might have " nothing to fear.   The palace of the Thuilleries " felt the blow, and ſhut up its garden.   The " legiſlative body, always revolutionary, ſaid ; " ' You ſhut up your garden—well, we will " open it ;' and the garden was opened, in ſpite " of the tyrant who had ſhut it.   That meaſure " ſeemed contemptible but it was revolutionary. " The Pariſian, enemy of royalty, ſaw that all " obſtacles were removed, and he overturned " royalty ; the agitators, ſeeing government diſ- " organiſed, began to attack the legiſlative body.

Garden of the Thuilleries ſhut. opened by the Aſſem- bly.

Agitators

* Cambon—This is the financier who regulated all the finances until Barrere's expulſion from the aſſembly.

" They

" They wifhed to turn the revolution to their
" own advantage. From that time, *there are no*
" *horrors of which the legiflative body was not a*
" *witnefs.* From that time, the legiflative body
" was obliged to beg, not the people, which
" does not need fuch prayers, but the agitators,
" who wanted to maflacre and deftroy all. La
" Croix was obliged to go upon his knees to
" ftop their fury. The legiflative body fuffered
" much. The palace wanted to attack fuccef-
" fively all thofe who defended liberty. It fail-
" ed, becaufe the legiflative body was refolved
" to fave liberty. The legiflative body thought,
" that a revolution ought to be the act of the
" whole nation, and decreed, that 20,000 men
" fhould arrive in Paris. Defpotifm faw this
" with affright; it thought, that 20,000 men
" added to the Parifians might eftablifh and
" maintain order. Unfortunately, thofe 20,000
" men did not arrive, for they would have faved
" us from the anarchy that has reigned fince the
" 10th of Auguft. The 2d of September I was
" greatly grieved. If we had then taken pof-
" feffion of the municipal force, anarchy would
" have been prevented. I approve of the revo-
" lution of the 10th of Auguft."

M. Cambon, who preferved his credit with
the convention longer than Robefpierre himfelf,
here avows the plan laid to dethrone the king,
by fending away his guards, &c. as we have endeavoured already to explain. He accufes, neverthelefs, the palace of attacking, fucceffively,
all thofe who wanted to defend liberty. Both
cannot be true. The firft affertion is proved by
the decrees of the affembly, the fecond is with-

out any fhadow of proof; therefore there is no
hefitation which of the two deferves moft credit.

M. Cambon next declares, that intriguers
wifhed to profit by the revolution, and opprefs
the affembly of which he was a member; and
from that time there were no horrors to which
the affembly was not a witnefs. But who were
thofe intriguers? why he explains this by faying, if the municipality had been broke, all anarchy would have been prevented; it follows
then, as clearly as any truth can follow, that
the municipality which conducted the 10th of
Auguft, of which he approved, conducted the
fubfequent horrors; that is to fay, M. Cambon
approved of horrors, and called them patriotifm
and virtue, when directed againft the court;
but the fame were horrors of the moft terrible
fort, the moment that the prefident of the affembly was obliged to go down upon his knees to
avert them from the affembly.

This has been the uniform method in which
the revolutionifts have viewed the revolution; as
long as pillage, maffacre, and revolt, were employed againft their enemies, it was virtue; but
the moment it turned towards themfelves, it was
the greateft and moft execrable horror; fo that
he who writes about the crimes and cruelties of
the Jacobins only differs with themfelves in refpect to the commencement of the horrors, but
not about their exiftence; in this all agree; and
it is very lucky, that their condemnation coming from their own mouths, there is no room to
difpute about its juftice.

The

The heroes and patriots of the 10th of Auguſt, the virtuous mayor, Danton, and his aſſociates, and Talien, the moderate Talien, conducted the horrors of which Cambon complains; Robeſpierre, Barrere, Collet d'Herbois, and the demigod Marat, were likewiſe of the party on both occaſions. The fact is, that the perpetrators of both were exactly the ſame, as Cambon, without intending it, plainly ſhews; but as the maſſacres of which we are going to ſpeak preſently, could find no excuſe whatever, whereas that of the 10th of Auguſt, by the aid of falſity and fiction, could be a little diminiſhed, it was found convenient to throw the former upon the ſhoulders of another ſet of anarchiſts who were leſs known, or who were contented to divide the dangers and the crimes in the way that would be moſt advantageous to their abominable cauſe.

As ſoon as the addreſs to the departments was diſpatched, and the people, literally tired with killing and pillaging, had become a little more tranquil, the aſſembly voted a ſum of money to the families of thoſe who had fallen on the 10th of Auguſt, and alſo decreed a public funeral ceremony, in order to ſhew that honour to the victims of revolt that ſo ſacred a duty required.

To this decree, of which the intention was certainly bad, as it tended to render honourable what was infamous, ſucceeded the crueleſt and the moſt unjuſt decree that ever tyrant made.

The

The aſſembly, after decreeing the urgency of the caſe,* decrees,

Art. I. All thoſe eccleſiaſtics, who have not taken the oaths required, or who have retracted and perſiſted in their retraction, are ordered in eight days to quit the limits of their reſpective departments, and in fifteen days the kingdom; this delay to be counted from the publication of the preſent decree.

Art. II. Conſiſts of rules for executing the above article.

Art. III. Thoſe who do not obey the preſent decree ſhall be baniſhed *à la Guyanne Françaiſe.*—[Here follows the manner of executing this article].

Art. IV. Thoſe who leave the kingdom in a voluntary manner, are to have neither penſion nor revenue, but are to receive three livres for every ten leagues of the journey to the frontiers.†

Art. V. Every eccleſiaſtic, who ſhall remain after he has declared that he will go, or who ſhall return, ſhall be condemned to ten years impriſonment.

Art. VI. All other eccleſiaſtics, who were not obliged by law to take the oath, whether regular

* Decreeing urgency was the method adopted when they wanted to be unſhackled by law, juſtice, humanity, or any former decrees.

† Equal to an Engliſh penny per mile.

or

or fecular priefts, clerks, or lay-brothers, without exception, fhall be fubjected to the above decrees, whenever by any exterior acts they fhall have occafioned any troubles, or *when fix houfekeepers in the department fhall* demand their banifhment.

Art. VII. Rules for executing the above decrees.

Art. VIII. Infirm priefts and thofe above fixty years of age, are excepted.

Art. IX. The ecclefiaftics excepted, fhall be affembled in the chief town of each department, in a houfe of which the municipality fhall have the infpection and the police.

The three remaining articles are to regulate the execution of the decree, which is the moft cruel and unjuft that ever was pronounced. The ftranger who reads it, will imagine that he perceives a ray of humanity acrofs the injuftice, when he fees the eighth article, which makes an exception in favour of the aged and the infirm; but this was only a ray of cowardice and cruelty; thofe aged and infirm, as we fhall foon fee, were referved for the maffacres and flaughters which have fince that time taken place at Paris, at Nantz, and through the whole kingdom, and which have ferved to heap opprobrium on the French nation that perpetrated or permitted them.

It was this terrible decree which is fo fhameful to the French nation that afforded England the opportunity of diftinguifhing itfelf above all other nations

nations for generofity and liberality of fentiment, by receiving with compaffion, and fupporting with liberality the exiled priefts, who, in the end of that year, arrived in fuch numbers from the perfecutions of their favage countrymen.

The victims of the defpotifm of Louis the Fourteenth, when he revoked the edict of Nantz, were well received, but they brought with them arts, induftry, and capital ; they were of our own religion, yet our generofity towards them, then, was juftly celebrated. The latter inftance of Englifh generofity deferves fo much the greater praife, that it was entirely without any intereft, that it was to men of a different religion, and has been more extenfive and much longer conti-nued.*

This decree was followed by others in rapid fucceffion, which not being urgent, prove how far

* It might with great propriety be recommended to the emigrants to keep up a better police amongft themfelves than they do. Many have fignified that France was more noble and more generous to the followers of James the Second of England, than to give them only two Louis a month ; do thefe ungrateful ignorants know that James the Second had few followers, and moft of them excellent foldiers, who ferved Louis the Fourteenth well? It is to the emigrants themfelves to prevent fuch fcandalous ingratitude from be-ing manifefted ; and it is recommended to thofe worthy characters who have been placed at the head of the office for affifting lay emigrants, to be circumfpect in how they ap-ply money that is deftined for the helplefs, and not for thofe who keep chambermaids and valets. There are no valets allowed to a decayed Englifh gentleman.—This hint is meant in juftice to the deferving emigrants, and to the En-glifh nation, which pays.—It is to be prefumed that it would be ufelefs to fay any more on this fubject. This ad-vice is for the advantage of thofe to whom it was addreffed.

the

the affembly meant to adhere to its proteftation of
not augmenting its own power.

The deftruction of all the ftatues of bronze, to
be converted into cannon; the annihilation of all
claims for indemnity, for fuch feudal rights as
the conftituent affembly had thought required
any; the divifion of wafte lands and the fuppreffion of the order of merit of St. Louis, were
decreed; and to complete the catalogue the divifion and fale of the lands of all the emigrants
followed.

Such decrees, admitting their juftice, ought
to have been left to the convention, if the legiflative affembly had wifhed not to extend its own
power.

The regulations for calling a convention of the
people were then next made; and as it had always been their method to put practice and principles in oppofition to each other, it was ordered
by thefe regulations that the primary affemblies
fhould have no power to name their reprefentatives at the convention, they fhould only have
power to chufe electors, who fhould affemble and
chufe reprefentatives. This, which if the word
national convention has any fixed meaning, is
totally incompatible with fuch meaning, gave a
double fcope for intrigue. The Jacobin emiffaries had the double chance of gaining the pre-
ponderance in the primary affemblies, and in the
electoral affembly.

The French nation had been all alive after the
14th of July; hope had re-animated order which
infur-

infurrection had deftroyed ; but after the 10th of Auguft, there was no hope to effect fuch reanimation, and accordingly the elections were conducted by only a fmall portion of the nation, and thofe of the moft profligate and wicked. The convention has fairly fhewn by its own conduct, what fpirit reigned amongft the electors.

To thefe decrees foon fucceeded activity of execution, and it was pretty well underftood, that as the decree againft emigrants, and for dividing their lands, was an excellent expedient for enriching the nation, it would be well to *increafe the number of emigrants*, or punifh thofe who did not emigrate, in fuch a manner as to put an end to the ancient race of proprietors in France.

For this purpofe, arrefts and vifits in private houfes to difcover fufpected perfons were inftituted, under the infpection of the bloody municipality. The fection of Paris, which had but a few weeks before fhewn their attachment to the conftitution and to royalty, now fhewed great alacrity in executing thofe decrees of arreft upon fufpicion. There were two hundred and eighty members of the Hotel de Ville, about fix hundred officers belonging to the fections, and moft of them men whofe names and manner of figning, as well as whofe perfons were unknown in Paris. As all thofe were active in accufing, figning orders for arrefts, and executing thofe orders, the number of perfons who were feized was very great. In this confufion, all fort of regard to truth in the accufations was out of the queftion, as being totally impoffible to be afcertained. Private vengeace did a great deal, and the defire of

pillage

pillage ftill more. The members of the fections having become the agents of the principal leaders, through fear, the whole of the national guards, with only a very few exceptions, were juft as completely at the orders of the Brigands, as they had ever been at thofe of Bailly and La Fayette; with this difference, that from willing foldiers who fometimes fpoke their mind, they were become obedient flaves, who durft not even inquire into the motives of their mafters.

It was refolved, according to the French cuftom, to organife arreftation; thofe who had organifed revolt and anarchy, might eafily expect fuccefs in fo fimple an operation as that of arrefting a few thoufands of individuals, who being feparated, could make no refiftance.

Under the pretence of fearching for concealed arms, all the citizens, except thofe who were to be employed by the municipality, were ordered to remain at home, the barriers were fhut, and armed men were ftationed at all the corners of the ftreets; about one o'clock in the morning the fearch began, by patroles of men with pikes, compofed of hair-dreffers, and workmen of the loweft clafs, under the orders of commiffaries of the fections, who were little better than themfelves.* This organization of imprifonment produced

* A good picture of this has been given by M. Peltier, in his *Dernier Tableaux de Paris*, printed in London for the author, it is as follows: " At ten o'clock at night, " groups of foldiers, placed at the angles of all the ftreets, " arrefted whoever was yet found ftraying about. Two " hours had not yet been fufficient for thofe who fought a " place of fecrecy and furety againft the formidable inquifi-

duced a confiderable number of victims, although the precautions taken to efcape were proportioned to the vengeance which thofe who might be taken had to fear.

Parties had fo often changed their mafters in Paris, that it was difficult to fay who was fafe, or who was not. The degraded Parifians, by continually obeying the voice of the ftrongeft party, had alternately been the dupes of all, and few people could be certain whether or not they were fafe; and thofe whofe public conduct could ftand the teft, had their private enemies to fear.

As the prifons were now nearly filled with victims, it was thought proper to prepare for the cruel fcene, which the men of the 10th of Auguft were determined to act.

It would be ufelefs to give the names of the perfons who prefided at thefe maffacres, becaufe they were almoft all unheard of till then, and moft

" tion. The hufband fled from his wife, and the father
" from his children, whom he preffed to his bofom, thinking
" it was for the laft time. Every one thinks himfelf accu-
" fed; every one fears that amongft their vifitors will be
" found an enemy or a fpy, or a fervant who will difcover
" his place of refuge. One flies to the moft diftant quarter
" of the city; here one is received, there one is repulfed,
" and the fatal moment which approaches, doubles the in-
" quietude and anxiety. Decency is in a degree violated
" by friendfhip; here the brother fhares the bed of his fifter,
" and there chaftity and virtue implore an afylum from vice;
" and many, whofe lives had been without a ftain, feek fe-
" curity under the curtains of proftitution. Every where
" perfons and property are concealed; every where the in-
" terrupted founds of the muffled hammer are heard ftriking
" with a flow and fearful ftroke."

of them have never been heard of fince; but as
fome of them were known, and fome ftill endeavour to pafs upon the world for men of philofophy and humanity, they deferve to be noticed.

Petion, Manuel, and Danton had long laboured together in bringing about the fecond revolution, by their manœuvres at the Hotel de
Ville. Marat, in the club of the Cordeliers, with
Huguenin (the fame who had addreffed the king
with infolence on the 20th of June) Panis, Offelin,
and Talien.

Robefpierre, Vigaud, Panis, Bourdon, l'Huill-
hier, of the Jacobin club, and Chabot, Merlin,
and Baziere, of the legiflative affembly and Jacobin club. It was with the affiftance, however,
of many more, that thefe leaders effected their
cruel purpofe. Agents and principals there are
fuppofed to have been about nine hundred active
perfons. Some thoufands, who by a wicked and
cruel difpofition, were led occafionally to aid in
the oppreffions and arrefts, but not directly in the
murders; and the whole city of Paris, confifting
of about one hundred thoufand able bodied men,
looked bafely on.

The ufual art of exciting an alarm was employed to frighten the people at large, as well as
the national affembly.

When the affembly had difcovered that the
municipality was going on fo faft with arrefts,
and that fome of its members were amongft the
number arrefted; and when it had reafon, as M.
Cambon declared afterwards, to fear that its own
fafety

safety was threatened, it broke the municipality.*
On the 30th the municipality fat and deliberated,
and on the 31ft, Petion, the beloved, the virtuous
Petion, whom they had not ventured to difgrace
along with the other members, arrived at the head
of a deputation, and *coolly menaced the affembly* with
an infurrection if they did not annul the decree.
Talien delivered a difcourfe, which propofed
plans of a conciliation of parties, and of a new organization of the municipality, fo that the affembly was under the neceffity of leaving its decree
without execution.†

So much for the fyftem of terror with refpect
to the affembly, which was threatened with the
people; with refpect to the people, they were
threatened with the Duke of Brunfwick and the
King of Pruffia, and Danton, the chief of the
band of confpirators, by promifes and threats,

---

* How different to break the municipality now, from
the flattery beftowed on Petion the firft day of the revolt,
who was the conductor of the municipality. It is plain,
when the affembly was guilty of fuch adulation to Petion, as
is contained in the decree of the 10th of Auguft, they were
ignorant that they were giving themfelves a mafter; or if
they were not, the influence of fear was fo great, that it
overbalanced the danger that was to be apprehended from
the power of Petion.

† Huguenin, who was prefident of the municipality, being fent for, not becaufe he had caufed three thoufand refpectable and innocent perfons to be arrefted, but becaufe
he attempted to arreft, or rather had fummoned to appear,
a clerk belonging to Briffot's newfpaper office, declared to
the affembly that the municipality had unlimited powers,
that it was the reprefentative of the fovereign of Paris.——It
would be difficult to conceive an overthrow of order, authority, and right more complete than what was exhibited
at this time.

procured

procured from the affembly on the 2d of September, a decree that walking commiffaries fhould be named to execute the will and fecond the good intentions of the executive power, and to aid him to fave the country; and that whoever refufed to give up his arms, or to ferve in the army, fhould be declared a traitor to his country, and punifhed with death, and alfo that an addrefs to the people fhould be publifhed.

Danton was no fooner furnifhed with thofe powers, than the ambulating commiffaries were named, the barriers were fhut, and the municipality publifhed the following proclamation:

" Citizens, the enemy is at the gates of Paris,
" Verdon can only hold out eight days, let us
" affemble quickly at the Champ de Mars, and
" there form an army of 60,000 men to march
" againft the enemy."

The tocfin was founded, and the cannon of alarm fired, and the maffacre ready to begin; but till a pretext is found for the firft murder, the people are not fufficiently animated to fecond the fury of their chiefs; it is therefore neceffary to find a pretext for beginning, and then all the difficulty is over.

People were difpatched into all quarters of Paris to perfuade the curious and the idle, that as the prifons were full of ariftocrats and fufpected perfons, and that neceffity obliged the majority of the inhabitants to march againft the enemy, it would be dangerous to leave their wives and children to be maffacred by the ariftocrats,

tocrats, who had a defign to efcape from prifon, and deliver up the town to pillage, and all
the horrors of which ariftocrats are fuppofed
capable.

Whilft a general terror was thus inftantaneoufly fpread through the city, while the tocfin
was founding, and every thing wore the appearance of the greateft danger, different bands of affaffins, but none of them very numerous, and
all of them headed by fome of the Marfeillois,
went to different prifons.

Several carriages, leaving Paris with fome of
the priefts who were exiled by the unjuft decree
we have already feen, were ftopt at the gates,
and carried back to the abbey prifon, and the
convent of Carmelites, which was alfo employed
as a prifon. As the laft of thefe unfortunate men
were defcending, one of the affaffins pretended
that *he faw them making figns to the other prifoners*,
and that a general mutiny was intended; immediately all of them, to the number of about twenty, were maffacred.

The noife of this immediately fpread through
Paris, and ferved as the fignal for beginning the
work of carnage; it was the proof that the affaffins were not oppofed by the national guards,
and from that inftant the audacity of thofe who
were employed to fhed innocent blood was without refiftance or controul.

In the convent of the Carmelites were above
three hundred clergymen, againft not one of
whom was there any accufation, and of whom
many

many were diftinguifhed for learning, piety, and good actions.

The Archbifhop of Arles, the Bifhop of Beauvais, and the Bifhop of Saintes, whofe Chriftian virtues were well known, were the firft to fall beneath the fwords of the affaffins.* The active affaffins were few in number, and the national guards who were at the gates, were more numerous than they.

The maffacre was in the garden of the convent, adjoining to which was the chapel; there the unfortunate victims were fired upon as if they had been wild beafts in the foreft, and when their affaffins were fatiated with that mode of cruelty, they were all forced to enter into the chapel, from which the murderers brought them out one by one, and put to death in the garden.

Two hundred and forty-four innocent men were in this manner maffacred, before eight o'clock of the Sunday evening, by a handful of murderers, and the cowardly national guards

---

* The murderers on their arrival called out for the Archbifhop of Arles, whom they did not know, and whom none of his companions in misfortune would point out.—When at laft they difcovered him, one of them cried out—" So, you " you are the Archbifhop of Arles?" " Yes, gentlemen, I " am—" Ah, wretch, it is then you who fhed the blood of " the patriots of Arles."—" No, gentlemen, I never fhed " any blood, nor did harm to any man in my life."— " Well, then, I fhall fhew you how I can fhed your's," and at the inftant he ftruck the venerable prelate on the forehead with his fabre; this murder was foon completed with pikes and bayonets.

flood

ſtood looking on.*   [*Note 2.*] The maſſacre at the Abbey priſon was ſuſpended after the twenty prieſts who had been ſtopped at the barriers, but re-commenced about an hour after with the murder of the Swiſs officers, who were ſhut up there ſince the 10th of Auguſt, and whoſe crimes, in the opinion of the people, were too well proved already to need any further inquiry.

The loyal Swiſs being diſpatched, the other priſoners who were very numerous and of all claſſes and conditions, underwent a ſort of trial before a dozen judges named by the municipality.   The firſt and chief care of this bloody tribunal was to demand the effects of the priſoners: their interrogat was ſhort, and the execution inſtantaneous and cruel.   Thoſe who were condemned (and very few were not) upon ſuſpicion, or for being related to ſuſpected perſons, were cut down with ſabres by the furious murderers at the door, amidſt the cries of *Vive la liberte, vive la republique.*

The number of aſſaſſins was inconſiderable here, as at the convent of Carmelites, but the circumſtances are ſo extraordinary, and give ſo terrible a proof of the ferocity and depravity of the

---

* There were, by all accounts, even thoſe of the party which wanted to make all Paris ſhare in the guilt of the maſſacre, not above an hundred aſſaſſins ; thoſe, it has been proved, were paid, and it is certain that Manuel, the right-hand man of the mayor at that time, had three days before ſignified in very plain terms what was to be expected. As for the national guards, there were three times as many of them as there were of the aſſaſſins, they are at liberty to chuſe between the character of inhuman cowardly ſoldiers or wicked accomplices.

French

French nation, that the relation fo interefting, and undoubtedly true, of M. de St. Meard, formerly a captain in the regiment de roi, one of the prifoners, merits a particular attention. [*Note* R.] This gentleman was an ariftocrat, and had been a privileged one, but he was alfo an amiable and reafonable one. Many people were maffacred neverthelefs, who had been lefs active than St. Meard againft the revolution, but who had not his prefence of mind to convert their oppofition to the conftitution into true patriotifm, which, it is clear, thofe who overturned the conftitution muft have confidered it to be.*

Maillard, the fame who had conducted the expedition to Verfailles on the 4th of October, 1789, was prefident of this tribunal, as Huguenin, who conducted that to the Thuilleries on the 20th of June, 1792, was at the municipality; fo that the road to power and importance in this new order of things, was precifely that infurrection of which the firft philofophers of the revolution vaunted fo much.

As it is not of fo much importance to know, in what manner the flames confume an edifice, as to know in what manner it was fet on fire, and to afcertain the refult of the deftruction, it is neceffary to feize all thofe circumftances which fhew the connection between the firft principles and the laft exceffes. They are eafily to be feen by

* St. Meard does not, probably, venture to give the real reafon for his delivery. It is probable, that the tribunal wifhed to let fome one efcape, who, by publifhing his trial, might fhew, that they did not put the prifoners to death without judgment, and St. Meard was the proper man.

a thoufand inftances, and therefore it is that La Fayette, Necker, and the firft inftigators of the revolution, are confidered as more dangerous men than Maillard and Huguenin.

The bonds of fociety muft already be broken, when fuch men as the two prefidents of the maffacre are capable of doing much mifchief. In any regular government they could but commit a theft or a murder, and be fent to the gallows; but thofe who, aided by a good reputation, rank in life and friends, employ themfelves in loofening the bonds of fociety, are really dangerous to the whole; and fo dangerous, that unlefs a method is difcovered, of protecting free governments from the attacks of FACTIOUS PHILO-SOPHERS, POLITICAL DIVINES, and REFORMING PHILANTHROPISTS, free government will become impoffible: the rights of men, the reveries of Rouffeau, the fophifms of Seyes, led to the bloody tribunal of which we have been fpeaking, and to which we muft yet with reluctance return.

One hundred and eighty prifoners were maffacred in the Abbey, amongft whom were many ecclefiaftics and gentlemen of unblemifhed character, and againft none of whom was there any known accufation; fixty-five were difmiffed, and about an equal number difappeared whofe fate is uncertain; in all above 300 innocent perfons.

The maffacre of the Conciergerie of the Palais de Juftice, where the tribunal was actually fitting, and employed in judging Major Bachman, of the Swifs guards, began nearly at the fame time with
that

that of the Abbey St. Germain. Eight Swifs officers who were to have been tried, and other prifoners who were waiting their judgments, fome of which latter were probably guilty, to the number of eighty-five in all, were maffacred without form of procefs.

Two hundred prifoners,* at the prifon of the Great Chatelet, fhared the fame fate with thofe already mentioned. Many of thefe were confined upon fufpicion of forgery, or of paffing falfe affignats, others for crimes of a private nature, but none of them had been tried or condemned.

Seventy-three condemned felons, who were to be fent to the gallies, were imprifoned in a cloifter,† and there they were maffacred: this ferved as a proof, for Petion and the other inftigators of the whole, that the hatred of the people for crimes and criminals was the prime motive of action.

---

* Amongft thefe prifoners was a woman who formerly fold flowers, and who, in a fit of jealoufy, had mutilated her lover, one of the revolted French guards, in a very barbarous and fhameful manner. She had been condemned, but obtained a refpite for fome time. The rage of the murderers was redoubled on feeing the woman who had thus murdered one of their companions; fhe was tied to a ftake, her feet nailed to the ground, her breafts cut off with a fabre, and then tortured with lighted torches and pointed inftruments, in a more cruel and brutal manner than it would be fit to defcribe, or than any of the North American Indians treat their prifoners. This was the refult of three years experience in the art of cruelty.

† The cloifter St. Bernard.

The

The maffacre of forty-five unfortunate women of the town, at the hofpital or work-houfe of the Salpetriere, furnifhed another argument for the virtuous mayor and his noble accomplices in favour of the juft vengeance of the people ! ! !

The maffacre at the Bicetre, which was both a prifon and an hofpital, where the guilty, the fick, the wounded, and thofe in a deranged ftate of mind, were fhut up together, was the longeft and the moft dreadful of all. This began when the others were finifhed.

As the great number of the prifoners and the certainty of their fate infpired them with the defire of refifting, and with fome hopes of fuccefs, though in irons, they prepared for defence. The affailants brought cannons charged with grape fhot to the attack, and, in the midft of fiaughter and brutal infult, fired upon the prifoners confined in the courts as they ran from one fide to the other to avoid deftruction. They fhouted applaufe at the number of miferables who fell at one difcharge, and when they thought they were fufficiently diminifhed, the remainder were fhot with fmall arms by way of amufement.

This infernal carnage lafted a week, night and day without interruption ; and the number of victims certainly exceeded four-thoufand, but many are of opinion they were nearer to fix thoufand.

Petion appeared towards the end of this terrible fcene, but was not well received by the murderers. They had began the work for his pleafure,

fure, and they determined to finifh it for their own. It was thus Petion had arrived on the 20th of June to compliment the people on the *calm dignity* with which they had infulted the king; he now arrived, that on a future day he might exclaim againft thofe maffacres, fhould it be convenient; and the murderers feem to have been aware of his defign, by the rough manner in which he was received. That ftrangers and pofterity may never hefitate a moment in joining in this opinion, it may be well to know that the *mayor's palace* was fo near to two of the prifons, that the cries of the dying could be diftinctly heard from it, and that it was in the centre between all the other prifons, fo that in twenty minutes he might have tranfported himfelf, with the armed force which was at his command, to any one of the fcenes of flaughter.*

The maffacre at the prifon of the Hotel de la Force had been begun on the fecond of the month; but a few only were that day deftroyed. Two municipal officers, Hebert and l'Huillier, prefided there nearly in the fame manner as Maillard did at the Abbey.

It was in this prifon that the Princefs de Lamballe, and the other attendants on the queen were confined. A municipal officer had thought proper to leave that princefs there, when the evening before he had delivered twenty-four women, amongft whom were feveral of the queen's attendants.

* On the 27th of Auguft, when the affembly fufpended the municipality, the armed force of Paris was placed at the difpofal of M. Petion.

about

About eight o'clock in the morning of the third, this princefs, whofe only crime was that of an unconquerable and fincere attachment to her royal miftrefs, and her hatred equally unconquerable to the murderer of her hufband, the Duke of Orleans, was called up by two national guards, who compelled her to defcend, in order that fhe might be transferred to another prifon, though her death was determined on, and took place in lefs than half an hour after.*

It

* When the princefs arrived at the bloody tribunal fhe was almoft deprived of her fenfes, and had twice fainted away with the cries of the dying, and the horrible appearance of the murderers covered with blood. She was interrogated as follows :

Judge. Who are you ?
Princefs. Maria Louifa, Princefs of Savoy.
Judge. What is your employment ?
Princefs. Superintendant of the queen's houfhold.
Judge. Are you acquainted with the plots of the court on the 10th of Auguft ?
Princefs. I know not if there were any plots on the 10th of Auguft ; but I am certain I knew of none.
Judge. Take the oath of liberty and equality, and of hatred to the king, to the queen, and to royalty.
Princefs. I will readily take the two firft, but I cannot take the laft ; it is not in my heart.
A perfon who was there faid in her ear, fwear, or you are a dead woman. The princefs lifted up her eyes without faying a word, and went towards the door. The prefident gave the ufual fign for immediate execution *(qu'on elargiffe la prifoniere)* and in an inftant fhe was affaffinated with fabres, pikes, and bayonets. Her cloaths were ftripped off, and the naked body expofed to the moft abominable infults. After laying for feveral hours as a fpectacle to the curious, and a fport to the inhuman rabble, it was cut in pieces. The head was carried on a pole to the temple, and expofed to the view of the royal prifoners, who expected the fame fate. The king was compelled to approach the window and look at it : the
queen

It is generally believed, that this princefs could have purchafed her life on no other terms than that of fabricating charges againft the queen; but that, on fuch conditions, fhe would not only have been fafe, but under the particular protection of the affaffins. And if human nature is difgraced and degraded by the unexampled rage, brutal and beaftly fury of her murders, it is ennobled by the virtuous firmnefs of a devoted woman, under one of the moft terrible circumftances which can be conceived.

The total number of perfons who fuffered at the Hotel de la Force was 164.

To the maffacres already related muft be added that of the prifoners fent for from Orleans at the fame time, on pretence of conducting them to Paris. Thofe prifoners fent there on fufpicion for crimes of high treafon, or fedition, or incivifm, or for being attached to the ancient monarchy, had not been judged with that rapidity that fuited the prefent ftate of the revolution. The high court of Orleans, as it was called, had been organized, and the judges named, when the revolution was not quite fo far advanced in its progrefs towards liberty and equality; and, being at a diftance from Paris, the judges had not been able to keep pace with the Jacobin club, to which they had belonged, fo that it was fufpected the accufed might efcape punifhment.

queen and Madame Elizabeth had fainted away. The Duke of Orleans gave a dinner to fome Englifh democrats that day, and he was gratified with the fight of this bloody trophy juft before they fet down to table.

It

It would be ufelefs to relate the perfidious manner in which they were feized at Orleans, and conducted to Verfailles, there to be maffa- cred in the prefence of the national guards and municipal officers, without any attempt being made to fave them.

The revolution had now taken fo horrible and fo decided a turn; the different rulers, whether Girondifts or Mountaineers,* were all fo evi- dently culpable, and fo deeply immerfed in guilt, that there is neither room nor occafion for any difpute about the difference of culpability. It might do for themfelves to make diftinctions and to claim one action as patriotifm, and blame another as oppreffion and injuftice; but we muft confefs that, except to themfelves, no fuch dif- tinctions are apparent.

It would be ufelefs to fatigue ourfelves by fol- lowing out the manœuvres of the leading parties, in order to conceal their participation; that would be fuppofing a poffibility of doubt, concerning their guilt, when there can be none.† All that

can

* It was by this latter name that the moft violent party was diftinguifhed.

† The whole number maffacred from the 2nd of Sep- tember till the 9th, is very nearly as under :

At the hofpital of the Carmelites and St. Furmer	244
the abbey of St. Germain, - - -	180
the cloifter of the Bernardins - - -	73
the Conciergerie - - - - -	85
the hofpital of Saltpetriere - - -,	45
the prifon of the Chatelet - - -	214
the hotel de la Force - - - -	164
	1005

can be admitted is, that there were some individuals who co-operated more through fear than
through guilt; but that there is any difference
of criminality amongst the leaders, we must absolutely deny, when the public force was ten times
more than sufficient to have prevented the maffacres from beginning, or to have stopped them in
the firft hour when begun.

If there was any one more decidedly culpable
than the others, it feems to have been Danton;
he was more active in this than Robefpierre or
Briffot, yet Robefpierre has been confidered fince
as the *ne plus ultra* of cruelty; fo that we are at
laft obliged to confefs that their criminality is
without dimenfion, fince it eludes all effort to
meafure it.

Let us turn away from thefe dreadful fcenes a
moment, and confider the language of Roland,
who, as firft minifter, might have made an effort to ftop this bloody career. Roland, who
was the chief of the party, which affected to
blame thefe exceffes: from his letter we fhall fee
that it was to the continuation of infurrection and
infubordination that he attributed all this. The
whole of the letter is long, and much of it con-
fifts of profeffion of faith, and a regard to confcience, which, if it had fpoke very loudly, would

		1005
Verfailles, the prifoners from Orleans	-	- 47
		1052
Suppofed to be maffacred at the Bicetre	-	4000
At the loweft		5052

have told him that he fhould have been protecting his fellow creatures, and exacting obedience
to the law, in preference to writing long letters
on the 4th of September; but the following
phrafes are complete, without any thing added or
taken away that may alter their meaning.

" I know that revolutions are not to be calcu-
" lated by common rules; but I know likewife,
" that the power which makes them ought foon
" to arrange itfelf under obedience to the law, if
" total deftruction is not intended. The anger
" of the people and the movement of infurrec-
" tion are comparable to the action of a torrent,
" which overturns obftacles which no other pow-
" er is able to deftroy, but of which the over-
" fpreading will carry far and wide the ravage
" and devaftation, if it does not foon return to
" its ufual courfe. The day of the 10th of Au-
" guft it is evident was neceffary; without it we
" fhould have been loft; the court had prepar-
" ed long before to complete its treafons, by
" fpreading the ftandard of death over Paris, and
" to reign by fear. The fentiment of the peo-
" ple, always juft and ready when its opinion is
" not corrupted, has averted the treafon, and
" turned it againft the confpirators.

" It is in the nature of things, and of the hu-
" man heart, that victory fhould be followed by
" a certain degree of excefs; the fea, agitated by
" a tempeft, roars after the tempeft is over, but
" every thing has its bounds, where it ought at
" laft to be terminated.

" If

" If diforganization becomes a matter of habit
" and cuftom; if men, zealous, but without
" knowledge and fkill, pretend to mix perpe-
" tually with adminiftration, and to ftop its
" courfe if fupported by fome popular favour,
" obtained by a great degree of ardour, and
" maintained by a ftill greater facility of making
" harangues, they fpread abroad, miftruft and
" fow calumny and accufation, excite fury, and
" dictate profcriptions—the government is then
" only a fhadow, it is nothing, and a good man
" fhould retire from the helm of affairs, which
" he can no longer guide, and which is intend-
" ed for action, and not for fhow."

No declaration againft anarchy can be plainer
than this, M. Bailly or La Fayette could not
have fpoken better, and it is precifely what Briffot faid, fix months after, when he began to lofe
fight of the capital, and to approach the Tarpeian rock. To make a diftinction amongft the
men who approve of infurrection, is an abfurdity; they all agree perfectly in the principles, and
only vary in the application, and that variation
has only a regard to themfelves. The enemy
who attacks and batters down a city, when he is
once in poffeffion of the place, builds up its houfes, and repairs the fortifications; and fo would
thofe who patronize revolt wifh to do, but they
fhould not liken revolt, when fupported by principle, to a river that is to return to its bed; it
fhould be likened to a fire that never ceafes till
all is confumed. Have not all thofe who have
witneffed the revolution, feen that the habit of
revolt was fubverfive of order, law, and liberty,
as Roland fays? and is it not evident, that what
men

men are taught to confider as a duty, is very likely to become a habit with *good* citizens? Why
then, inftead of preaching eternally againft revolt carried too far, and continued too long, do
not they at once declare that revolt is illegal, and
in place of being a duty, is a crime? This is the
language evidently that ought to be fpoken but
each one willing to referve to himfelf and friends
the privilege of revolting, when to them it feems
proper, refufes to make this declaration, and
each one has in the end fallen a facrifice to this
terrible article of the declaration of rights.

Since the deftruction of the conftitution, and
the cruelties which we have feen infurrection and
anarchy produce, the Jacobins in other countries, who have not yet got the upper hand,
have changed their batteries; they pretend to
difapprove of the crimes, but they ftill preferve
their attachment to thofe principles which laid
the foundation, and paved the way for them;
but let them not think they are to impofe upon
fociety by fo flimfy a device. Petion faid, that
if the patriots perfecuted thofe who did not wear
red caps, that the ariftocrats would put them on
too, and pafs for republicans, and he was probably very right. We muft pay the fame attention to the Jacobins, who finding it is totally
impoffible not to join in condemning the horrors
lately committed in France, are as loud on that
fubject as any body elfe; it is not, therefore,
by that, that they are to be known, but by
their invariable endeavours to create difcontent,
and after that, quietly and calmly, under the
cloak of patriotifm and philanthropy, excite infurrection, or at leaft, by degrees, undermine

regular

regular government, fo as to bring on infurrection.

It was in this fituation of the capital, that the
elections for the national convention began ; and
without doubt, it was with an intention to fhew
the whole nation what fort of reprefentatives it
would be fafe for them to chufe, that the members of the municipality fent a circular addrefs to
all the other municipalities in the kingdom.*
The

---

* The letter of the municipality runs thus:
" Brothers and Friends,

" A terrible confpiracy having been entered into by the
" court to deftroy all the patriots in the French empire, in
" which plot a great number of the members of the national
" affembly were concerned, obliged the common council of
" the city of Paris to have recourfe to the power of the peo-
" ple, in order to fave the nation. Nothing has been ne-
" glected by us, and the affembly itfelf has rendered honour-
" able teftimony of our conduct. But who would have
" thought, after that, that new confpiracies, not lefs atro-
" cious, were planned in filence ; they broke out at the mo-
" ment when the national affembly, forgetting the merits of
" the municipality, was going to diffolve it as a reward for
" its civifm. At that news, public clamours arofe from all
" parts, and made the affembly feel the urgent neceffity of
" uniting itfelf with the people, and reftoring the munici-
" pality to its former power.

" Proud of having thus obtained fully the national confi-
" dence, which we fhall always ftrive to deferve more and
" more ; placed in the centre of all the confpiracies, we
" fhall not be fully fatisfied with our conduct until we fhall
" have obtained your approbation, the object of all our
" views, and which we fhall not think ourfelves certain of
" poffeffing, until all the departments fhall have fanctioned
" the meafures which we have taken to fave the nation.

" Profeffing the pureft principles of the moft perfect equa-
" lity. defiring no other privilege than that of being the
fuft

The atrocity is equal to any thing that is to be found in hiſtory, both for the falſities it contains, and for the ſentiments, if they can be called by that name.

It is perfectly evident by this letter, which was circulated under the counter-ſign of Danton,

" firſt to immolate ourſelves for the good of our country,
" we ſhall be ready to put ourſelves on a level with the
" ſmalleſt municipality of the ſtate, the moment that our
" country ſhall have nothing more to fear from the multi-
" tudes of ferocious enemies who approach the capital.

" We, the commons of Paris, haſten to inform our bro-
" thers and friends of all the departments, that a part of
" the ferocious conſpirators detained in the priſons, has been
" put to death by the people, *an act of juſtice* which appear-
" ed to them indiſpenſable to keep in awe thoſe legions of
" traitors who are concealed within our walls, at the mo-
" ment when the patriots were about to march againſt the
" enemy and without doubt the whole nation will adopt the
" meaſure, after ſo long a train of treaſons have conducted
" us to the borders of the abyſs, which was ſo neceſſary for
" the public ſafety, and that every Frenchman will cry out
" with the Pariſians, let us march againſt the enemy, but do
" not let us leave behind us traitors who will murder our
" wives and children.   Friends and Brothers, we expect
" that ſome of you will come to our aſſiſtance, and help us
" to repulſe the numerous legions of tyrants who have ſworn
" the deſtruction of the French.   We ſhall jointly ſave our
" country, and we ſhall owe you the praiſe of having ſaved
" it from the brink of ruin.

(" Signed,)

" The adminiſtrators of the committee of public
" ſafety, and the adminiſtrators adjoined, Pier-
" re Duplain, Panis, Serjent, l'Infant, Jour-
" daill, Marat l'ami du peuple, de Torgas, le
" Clerc, Dufortre, Celly, conſtituted by the
" commons of Paris, and ſitting at the houſe
" of the Mayor of Paris."

the

the minifter of juftice, that the intention of its writers was to procure the approbation of the whole nation, to the maffacres which they avowed, and to make fimilar meafures to be adopted, as they plainly exprefs themfelves ; giving for a reafon, the neceffity of protecting their wives and children from having their throats cut by the prifoners in the different jails.

At this time there were more than feventy thoufand fufpected perfons in the different prifons in France, and the Jacobin club wrote to all its correfpondents, to fecond this purification, as they called it, of the kingdom.

The addrefs from the national affembly, and this from the municipality and Jacobin club, were circulated all through the kingdom, and it was under the impreffions which fuch productions were capable of infpiring, that the affemblies were held for chufing the reprefentatives for the national convention.

We fee how the fame arts have all along been practifed to prevent the proprietors and lovers of peace from affifting at elections. The fans culottes, or rabble had completely triumphed, and they proclaimed in one breath their fanguinary victory and their fanguinary intentions ; fo that moderate men hid their heads, and the convention was chofen of the vileft, the moft defpicable, and moft defperate men in the kingdom.

The robberies which were committed during all thefe arrefts and murders, are eafily to be conceived ; the numbers whom fear and danger
drove

drove out of the country were immenſe, and the municipal officers and members of the Jacobin club who gave them, or procured for them paſſports, enriched themſelves by the exaction of enormous ſums, and the nation by the forfeiture of the eſtates of thoſe who fled.* Certainly thoſe emigrants who left France under ſuch circumſtances, are not to be accuſed either of want of courage or want of loyalty; France was no longer habitable for any but brigands, and it is only matter of wonder that ſo few emigrated.

While all theſe things were going on, M. Claviere, placed at the head of the contributions, only for the ſake of appearances, as no contributions were levied, ſet about laying other nations under contribution, by negociations upon the different changes in Europe.

Agents were ſent to London, Amſterdam, Madrid, and to every country, who had orders to negociate bills on Paris, payable (as all the world knows) in aſſignats. Thoſe bills being diſcounted in foreign countries, the value in *ſpecie was remitted to France*: when they became due, they were paid according to the courſe of exchange, but before this could be converted into gold or ſilver, a few aſſaſſins were hired to patrole the ſtreets, and threaten all thoſe who ſold gold

---

* Five thouſand pounds ſterling were frequenly given only for a paſſport, and many gave five hundred and leſſer ſums, ſo that the municipal officers who came into place, ſome of them without ſhoes, ſoon became rich.

or

or filver ;* three of thefe fellers loft their lives, and many were pillaged ; at other times, when the change was wanted, to be raifed on purpofe to draw new bills, Claviere fent men to offer more gold for fale than was wanted. This operation, which is eafily conceived by thofe who underftand any thing of the courfe of exchange, was called pumping the banks. A great part of the bankruptcies of 1793, in England, were occafioned by this operation, which had made gold fcarce in London ; and if an end had not been put to it by the war, or fome other caufe, there is no faying to what a pitch it might have been carried, for the merchants on the Change of London did not perceive the fnare ; and though they were aftonifhed at the courfe of exchange grew more favourable to France while the Duke of Brunfwick was marching to Paris, yet the hope of gaining by a quick operation, led them into fpeculations which muft have been very hurtful to many individuals, and were fraught with ruin to the nation.

It was about the fame time that the guard-meuble, containing all the jewels of the crown, was robbed by the patriots of the affembly ; and as the time was forefeen, when paper would no longer ferve to buy the neceffaries of life, which became every day more rare, every effort was made to heap up gold and filver in the mint.

* The gold and filver were fold by porters in the ftreets, fome of whom fold for their own account, but moft of them for monied men, who did not appear. Sometimes they were encouraged in this traffic, and fometimes chafed away. Some were even maffacred, and gold fell or rofe in price according to the rifk run by thefe men.

Had the nations of Europe taken any pains to ftudy the manœuvres of thefe revolutionary gentlemen, a great part of their plans would have been fruftrated; but no pains were taken by any nation: and if it had been poffible for the Girondift or Gafcon party to have kept infurrection under, fo as to let their plans have time fully to operate, matters would have been much worfe than they were with other nations.

It will be confidered, no doubt, as a very fingular circumftance, that though the conduct of the rulers of France was fuch as all men, fince the days of Nero and Caligula, have joined in condemning, yet, in every other nation in Europe, their agents were treated with a certain fort of diftinction by certain men, who pretend a greater love for juftice and of a pure conftitution, and a greater zeal for the welfare of the people, than any others. In England, M. Chauvelin, who had been fent as ambaffador by Louis XVI. became the charge d'affaire of Santerre, Panis, and Petion, and yet every door in England was not fhut againft him, for even fome friends of the people entered his door; and if an ill-conducted, and hitherto unfuccefsful but neceffary war, had not put an end to the intrigues, which the daring French agents were encouraged and feconded in here, we fhould, in all probability, long ere now have had a committee of brewers and blackguards fitting at the Manfion-houfe, and giving orders to arreft all rich and refpected perfons, to fhut up the Change, and maffacre all the prifoners in the jails of the kingdom. We have feen the refults of philofophical maxims, and we find, that the commanders of the maf-

facres

facres of September do not, on account of the innocent blood that they have fpilt, abate one degree of their claims to the title of patriots ; on the contrary they celebrate thofe horrors by new names invented for the purpofe, and interlard their addreffes to the people with the fame declaration of virtue, confcience, and purity of intention, that are to be found coming from the mouths of all patriots.*

* Sovereign juftice, the fovereign murderers, Septemberi-zers, purifying meafures.   Such were the names given by the *bravading* murderers to the crimes of their companions.

CHAP. II.

Beginning of the reign of Robefpierre—Robefpierre vindicated againft the revolutionifts, the ariftocrats, and the whole of mankind—The trial of the king—Probable motive—Vanity of democrats—Succefs of the republican armies—Condemnation and death of the king—New tumults in the convention, and fall of Briffot's party.

THE reign of terror was now begun, and all parties took a more or lefs active hand in it; but the revolutionifts themfelves were not purified; terror was not yet organifed and reduced to a fyftem, it was not completely fpread over the kingdom, it had only come to perfection in Paris, and it was to Robefpierre, that much calumniated man, that human nature, but above all, the French nation, has the obligation of reducing to method and fyftem, what all parties contended was right, but what they all alledged might fometimes be abufed. There is nothing like theory and fyftem for preventing abufe, and this Robefpierre, fo much feared during his life, and calumniated fince his death, perceiving, ftarted from the obfcurity in which he had for fome

time

time been,* to eftablifh upon a more regular and folid bafis the bleffings of liberty, equality, terror and the guillotine.

It might pleafe Briffot, Danton, Hebert, and all the other heads of parties, who were crufhed by Robefpierre, to declaim againft him. It may pleafe Talien, Collot d'Herbois, and Barrere, who have feen him fall in his turn under their power, to blame the conduct of Robefpierre.—The former, as well as the latter, had perfonal reafons, and were actuated by malice, but to a true revolutionary philanthropift, to a man who approves of the revolutionary meafures adopted in France, MAXIMILIAN ROBESPIERRE will feem not only a blamelefs but an illuftrious and diftinguifhed character.

Let us examine the claims of this man to the gratitude of the revolutionifts, and we fhall find that they are very great; he is now no more, he has now as many enemies as he formerly had flaves, but thofe who were never his flaves, are not obliged to be his enemies.

Robefpierre, as an inventor, has great merit; he firft thought of fixing a price, called the maximum, upon all articles ufeful in common life, that the poor might have them at a cheap price.

A philofopher had invented the guillotine out of mere humanity, and a philofophical affembly

* Robefpierre did not appear to take any *active* part in the maffacres of the 10th of Auguft.

Had

had decreed that it fhould be the inftrument of national juftice; but Robefpierre invented wheels to this machine, that the villages and country might partake of the blefling; he attached to it ambulant commiffaries and judges, who might adminifter juftice with as great promptitude as the facred inftrument inflicted punifhment.*— Thus were liberty and equality extended, and the meaneft peafant could now fee the philofophical inftrument of national vengeance and juftice in his own village.†

Had not riches been long confidered as a crime againft liberty and equality? and did not Robefpierre abolifh the bank, fhut up the Change, fequeftrate the India Company's magazines, and make it the crime of death for any citizen to be poffeffed of gold or filver? and did he not encourage the fervant to denounce his mafter, and the fon his father?

Had not the conftituent affembly in the fulnefs of its wifdom and philofophy decreed, that the hangman fhould be an active citizen, and be upon a par with the firft prince of the blood; that the king and the heir apparent alone fhould be

* A Frenchman faid, that though others had invented the revolution, Robefpierre fet it to regular mufic.

† Some ariftocrats think that Henry IV. whofe ambition was to fee every peafant in France have a pullet in his pot on Sunday, was a better fort of ambition; but fuch are greatly miftaken, for there is no difputing about taftes. In the barbarous days of the gallant Henry, the French cried, *Vive le roi et la bonne chere*; in the days of Robefpierre they cried out, *Vive la guillotine, vive la mort.* So each pleafed the nation in the way that fuited its tafte at the time.

fuperior

superior to him ? and did not the place of hangman become lucrative and honourable in the
time of Robespierre's power ? Have not virtuous
candidates for that office been seen canvassing for
votes, as we do at an election for a county member in England ? And might not this be said to
be the maximum of philosophy, and the mini-
mum of prejudice ? was it not a fair triumph of
the new principles over the old ridiculous notions ? and is there any thing so brilliant or so
great in the reign of the Emperor Augustus, so
boasted and so admired ? What are fine arts and
stately palaces compared to the perfection of the
human mind when it gets rid of human prejudice ?

Did not the aristocracy of rich merchants in
great cities offend the lovers of perfect equality ?
and did not Robespierre make war on all the rich
merchants and great towns of France ? Did not
Lyons, the populous, the wealthy, and the in-
dustrious, see its proud buildings levelled with
the ground ; and its inhabitants, who opposed
themselves to the system of equality and the destruction of property, put to flight, or to death,
by thousands at a time ? Did not the richest inhabitants of Bourdeaux, of Nantz, of Marseilles,
and of Strasburg, depose their wealth upon the
altar of the country in presence of the guillotine ?
and did not those who refused to part with their
property lose their lives ? and were not their wi-
dows and their children turned adrift to seek for
food and raiment where they could find it ?
After this who can complain of the revolutionary conduct of Robespierre, and of his love for
equality ? and who can accuse the man who had

the

the courage to put in practice what the others had only the courage to contrive?

But the merits of this great man exceed all that can be faid of him; did he not only invent the revolutionary government, that is to fay, contrived the means of giving permanency to the revolutionary meafures on the 10th of Auguft, and the maffacres of September? Did not he organife the revolutionary tribunal, which conducted on an average thirty people a day to the guillotine in Paris, and over all France many more? Did not he gratify the Parifian tafte, which was changed from that of plays and operas, to that of fhedding blood, by affording a public reprefentation *gratis* every day, where blood was fhed, and where the nation had the double enjoyment of contemplating the fufferings of the condemned, and reflecting on his forfeited riches, when the ragged fans culotte, that honourable character, exulted in the double enjoyment of national vengeance, and of being one of the heirs of the condemned victim?*

Did not Robefpierre compel, by the fyftem of terror, all the youth of the nation, to go and combat the combined defpots of Europe? and did he not eftablifh revolutionary armies, who,

---

* When thefe things are fairly confidered, all this looks more like a dream than a reality, and yet nothing is more true; Robefpierre ufed to fay, when he was told he was too fevere upon the rich with the guillotine, Let me alone, I am coining money. Three ftrokes of the guillotine were eftimated upon one occafion at twenty-two millions by Barrere, in a report to the convention. O France, it will be difficult to wipe away thofe ftains. Philofophy will never more have religion to reproach for the cruelties it has occafioned!

when

when equality and happinefs could not with all
its efforts be attained, *realifed equality in mifery,*
and fo brought the facred reign of equality
nearer to full perfection than it had ever before
been.

Was not kingly power difclaimed by the
French nation, and did not Robefpierre murder
the fovereign, his queen, and his fifter, and that
merely upon revolutionary principles, and without deigning to confult what ignorant fuperfti-
tious people in former times had confidered as
natural juftice or eftablifhed law? was not this
the laft triumph of your principles, and the true
end of your infurrections, and yet you have
dared to accufe him, to refift his will and to
blacken his memory?

If Robefpierre is fully cleared in the eyes of
revolutionary men of all countries, as he ought
to be let us fee what the ariftocrats have to fay
againft him? Ought not they alfo to paaife the
man who has avenged their caufe upon fo many
of their enemies? Can any lover of order blame
the man who purged the world of Danton, Fabre
d'Eglantine, and Camille de Moulins,* of Hebert, the atrocious Hebert, of the Duke of Orleans, of Briffot, Chabot, Merlin, and Bazire;
who difperfed the fanguinary minifters, Roland,
Le Brun, Claviere, and Servan: who condemned
Petion and his companion Manuel, Clootz the
Pruffian, and whole fquadrons of murdering

* Thefe two were Danton's fecretaries during the maffacres of September; they were afterwards members of the
convention.

philofophers ? During the reign of Robefpierre, did not Barnave fall, and would not every one of the firft inftigators to murder and pillage have fallen ? and did not Robefpiere, like Samfon, terrible in his death as he had been in his life, drag one hundred and forty-feven of the moft culpable citizens of Paris with him, after having done what was ftill of greater importance, carried revolutionary principles as far as they could go, and thereby changed the minds of men with refpect to their wifdom and juftice ? Did not Robefpierre fhew all reafonable men, that liberty and equality, on the French plan, was a mere chimera, a philofophical dream, and thereby prepare the way for returning reafon and peace ?*

Such are the obligations which the ariftocrats owe to Robefpierre for what he did ; but when it is confidered what he intended to have done ; when it is confidered that he had profcribed Barrere, Collot d'Herbois, and Talien, (the Adonis Talien, who was fo active at the maffacres of September) and all the remainder of the bloody tribe, and that he meant to have reigned alone, and have purged the world of all monfters but

* The fervices rendered by Robefpierre to the caufe of order, are far from being imaginary, he, in fact, fhewed the revolutionary fyftem in its full horror, and difgufted Jacobins with Jacobinifm ; fo that two things only now maintain the revolution, the firft in the difficulty of eftablifhing order, under a republican form, and the defire of keeping the lands of the emigrants, which, were kingly government to be reftored, would, they apprehended, be impoffible. Certain it is, that all France confeffes they have been fadly oppreffed, and that a great portion, at leaft of the country, is completely cured of *la maladie de* 1789.

felf

himfelf; muft you not allow, that for what he did,
what he was the caufe of being done, and what he
intended to do, Maximilian Robefpierre deferves
your thanks?*

The whole world fhould join in gratitude to
Robefpierre for his conduct during the laft month
of his life; when he found the moment was arrived when it was necefíary to overturn the convention, and to fix defpotifm on a terrible and folid bafis, he abandoned his poft in the convention, in the committees, and applied to the JA-
COBIN CLUB; it was from that, and that alone,
that he expected an energetic and effectual fupport; he has therefore eftablifhed beyond difpute,
what, indeed, the whole of the revolution has
confirmed, *that a political club, with affiliations
and correfpondences, and that claims the right of interfering in affairs of government, is the greateft enemy of the real freedom.* He has fhewn the ruin
and mifery in its full extent, to which men are
reduced by encouraging revolt; to add to his
other fervices, he has drawn down along with
him the ruin of the Jacobin club.

We have already faid, that the hiftory of the
Jacobins becomes lefs interefting as the revolution
advanced. We are now come to that period
where, as all men muft be nearly of one opinion
about the infamy of their manœuvres, their mi-
nute examination becomes lefs neceffary. We

* During the reign of Robefpierre, there were full as many revolutionifts guillotined as there were loyalifts, and it was
the chofen revolutionifts who excelled the others that he perfecuted the moft. They were friends in principles, but rivals in perfons.

fhall,

shall, therefore, in a rapid manner, follow them through the laft ftage of excefs and crime, which will ferve fully to fhew, that if infurrection is a facred duty, it is alfo one that is attended with very ferious confequences.

The repulfe of the Pruffian army gave the con-vention and the nation a little time to breathe, and this time was occupied by the convention in making a decree to excite the fubjects of all nations to revolt, in confidering the plans laid down by Briffot, Condorcet, and Clootz, for univerfal conqueft and an univerfal republic, and for bringing to the fcaffold the imprifoned monarch.* Audacity had now fucceeded to fear, and all nations were openly put at defiance.†   It is more than

---

* The cruelty of the nation in fhedding the blood of the king, had not the excufe alledged for the cruelties of Auguft and September, that of the fear of their enemies and the approach of the Pruffian army; on the contrary, during the trial of the king, the French armies were victorious, and had over-run Flanders and Brabant with an almoft unexampled degree of fuccefs. This is a proof, that if the French nation is cruel when in fear, it is no lefs fo when victorious; and this is the beft anfwer that can be given to thofe perfons, who affect to throw the blame of the cruel government of France upon the fear excited by combined powers.

† It was juft at the fame moment that all this was happening, that the Englifh friends of French liberty fent over two ambaffadors to prefent the convention with a congratulatory addrefs, and their foldiers with 2000 pairs of fhoes. It was at this time, that Meff. Paine and Prieftley were chofen members of the convention, and never was the fyftem of univerfal fraternity conceived by M. Clootz, or the deftruction of kingly government preached up by the different focieties, fo likely to be carried into effect: the maffacres of September had only whetted the appetite of thofe gentlemen, they had

than probable, that the vanity of ſhewing all Europe how little its menaces were regarded, cauſed the convention, without viſible motives, without any juſt reaſon, and even contrary to its apparent intereſt, to determine on the trial of one of the moſt innocent, moſt virtuous, and moſt unfortunate of kings. Such as know the audacious vanity of the Pariſian Jacobins, and their ferocity, will not be ſurpriſed at this. Time may, perhaps, unveil ſome other cauſe for the cruel deed, but until there is a certainty of the exiſtence of ſuch a cauſe, it is fair to aſſign that which is the moſt probable.

There is no doubt but that the republic might be conſidered by the convention as being more certain when the king ſhould no longer exiſt; but this is contradicted by the votes of a great number of determined republicans, who did not vote for death, but impriſonment or baniſhment.*

had ſmelt the blood acroſs the channel, and, as the poet Klopſtock ſaid, they longed to approach their victims, that they might with a dry eye contemplate the laſt convulſion, and indulge their ears with the laſt groan.

* The Gironde party was compoſed of the real republicans, the Mountain was compoſed of anarchiſts, and men who only wanting blood and pillage, had not any fixed notions about government at all; it was the Mountain that voted for the puniſhment of death; thoſe of the other parties, leſs ſanguinary, but likewiſe leſs bold, were induced to vote by the calculations about their own perſonal ſafety. The Mountain was with government as it was with religion, it wiſhed to overturn that which exiſted, without any fixed plan for eſtabliſhing another in its place.

Another

Another reason for thinking so, is, that the convention, eager to decree liberty and equality, and to establish licence, has shewn no sort of impatience to establish any sort of law or government, and therefore the death of the king was not a measure of so pressing a nature as to require haste. It must either have been meant to gratify vanity, as we have said, to defy the powers of Europe, or to render the whole nation unanimous in defending the republic.

It would be to suppose, that men have two different opinions on this subject, wich is not the case, to enter into any arguments relative to the cruelty and injustice of the sentence. The whole human race, though not by the organ of the representative citizen Clootz, has testified its detestation of the convention, and its admiration of the calm firmness and moderate virtue of the king.

The reign of Robespierre seems to have displayed the ultimatum of human depravity and folly under a republican form, and to have exalted royalty, by displaying in a dethroned king an unexampled degree of human moderation and virtue. Humanity has suffered much, but posterity may gain a great deal. France has been a melancholy example, and it is to be hoped, that all mankind will profit by it, to the exclusion of those principles which only tend to make men criminal and miserable.

“ If plagues and earthquakes break not Heaven's design,
“ Why then a Borgia or a Cataline?

The

The progrefs of mind in individuals, and in mankind at large, is the fame; and it was natural, that as knowledge increafed men fhould arrive at that dangerous point where experience is abandoned and defpifed, and where they give themfelves up to theory. This happens to moft young men who have got a liberal education, when firft they throw off the trammels of the college or the fchool; but time and experience, (and often adverfity) bring them back to reafon. France had attained this point of knowledge; and perhaps the violence of the malady, by fhortening its duration, will in the end be a blefling to mankind. The impetuofity of the French will ferve equally as a means of exhaufting themfelves, and of difcouraging their cotemporaries or pofterity from ever abandoning themfelves entirely to theory.

It was during the latter months of 1792 that the efforts of the revolutionary emiffaries were the moft ftrenuous in London, and in the other great cities of England. Government had been fo completely overturned in France, and the poffeffion of power and property had been fo completely attained by the revolutionary banditti, that their courage and audacity were beyond all bounds. Every country* contains men who wifh for changes, and who expect to gain by revolutions;

---

* In proportion as the general run of the inhabitants of a country are dabblers in learning and metaphyfics, the Jacobin principles have been admired—in Scotland more than in England, at Berlin more than at Vienna. It was long the wifh of the Jacobins to perfuade the people, that men of learning and genious admired the revolution. The famous Abbe Raynal

volutions; such naturally united their efforts to the French emissaries through inclination; but the French emissaries had money at command; and it is as certain as any thing that has not actually taken place can be, that a revolution was on the point of breaking out in England. The French *organization* was begun, men had their different posts assigned to them, and

the

was said to be an ardent admirer of it, and a curious enough scene took place in consequence of this. Raynal arrived in Paris by accident in the year 1791, and sent a letter to the assembly; the president of which, either through negligence, or with a design to play the assembly a trick, announced the letter without having previously examined it. The constituent philosophers, expecting congratulations on their wisdom, called out with one voice to have it read. The president began, but what were the mortification and surprise of the lawgivers, when they found it contained one of the most bitter and well-founded criticisms on their conduct that ever was written. A great disturbance took place; the president was interrupted and abused;* he was accused of aristocracy and knavery. A long debate ensued, but the insult being public already, it was determined to hear the letter out, and to treat the writer as a dotard who had lost his senses. The letter itself was a proof that the old philosopher had neither lost that justness of idea nor elegance of expression for which he has been so deservedly famous; but Gorsas, and all the scribblers of the Jacobin society, set upon him, and endeavoured to prove, that he was not only a fool but even a thief, and every thing that was bad. Raynal, not trusting much to their humanity, wisely set off next morning, concealing the route which he took.

Amongst the patents of French citizenship, such as were sent to Dr. Priestly, Thomas Paine, Mr. Wilberforce, and some others, the assembly sent one to the German poet Klopstock, famous for his philanthropy. His answer is thus:

---

* It was a secretary, in fact, that was reading.

the fignal only was wanting to make rebellion break forth.

Happily for England, the minifters were not
in the fame lethargy that thofe of Louis XVI. had
been in the year 1789. We fhould have foon
found

THE POET KLOPSTOCK TO THE NATIONAL ASSEMBLY OF
FRANCE.

" Moderators of the French empire!

" I fend back to you with horror thofe titles of which I was
" fo proud, while I could think that they united me to a fo-
" ciety of brothers and friends to humanity. Alas! the de-
" ception is but too foon vanifhed away, and moft afflicting
" reality is come, to put an end to a delufive dream. Alas!
" I had vainly imagined, that from the diftant borders of the
" Seine that light fhould come, which would one day give an
" eclat to the happy reign of liberty amongft European
" nations.

" Why have you deceived me? *Your rights of man were*
" *only a fnare laid to make Frenchmen fall, that they might be*
" *the more eafily affaffinated.* Learn, then, that the excefs of
" your barbarifm and of your crimes has placed an eternal
" barrier between you and the poets of happy Germany.
" When they are told thofe tragical adventures which dif-
" grace your fanguinary hiftory, they are affrighted and fly
" away. There is no connection now between us, you have
" broken for ever the laft of the bands which connected us
" together.

" I pity thofe who call themfelves citizens, and who fhed
" torrents of the blood of citizens. O crime! when they
" have fhed blood they dance around their victim; they con-
" template with a dry eye the laft convulfion; they approach
" nearer to indulge their ears with the laft groan.

" Frenchmen, I turn away with affright from that impious
" troop which is guilty of affaffination, by looking on the
" peaceable witneffes of murder. I fly far off from the cries
" of that execrable tribunal which murders, not only the
" victim, but which murders alfo the mercy of the people."
Such

found plenty of leaders ftart up, but there was no friend in the king's cabinet. The chancellor of the exchequer was not a vain, difgufted foreigner like M. Necker, and we were faved. The malcontents in this country had one circumftance in their favour, which thofe in France had not when they began ; they had a powerful nation to fupport them with men and with money, and who knew the method of employing agents, who were eternally repeating their favourite maxim of *ce n'eft que le premier pas que coute*, and they expected to overturn the throne of England, as eafily as they had taken the Baftile.

It is true, that all this has been treated as a fiction by thofe who felt mortified at its want of fuccefs ; but how could we expect them to treat it otherwife, when we fee their mafters at Paris treat as a fiction what had happened in the next ftreet, and maintain as a truth what had never happened at all ?

There were at this time only two methods left for England to purfue, the one was to act as fhe has done, and the other to let French emiffaries and French affignats rob us of every thing. The queftion of the juftice and neceffity of the war has been often difcuffed ; it is fufficient, however, to obferve, that as the Jacobin principle decidedly is, that " thofe that are not for us are againft us," there was no medium (as thofe who are ene-

Such is the energetic letter of the old and virtuous Klopftock ; he had not attained the pitch of Condorcet and his companions, and they very probably confidered him as a fool and a dotard. This is not quite fo confoling as the addrefs of the Englifh deputies with the 2000 pair of fhoes.

mics

mies of the war pretend) as they plainly shewed by the example of Spain, which offered them peace; but as she did not propose fraternity, by establishing Jacobin clubs and revolutionary tribunals, war was proclaimed against her without any sort of ceremony.

Amongst the daring attempts of the revolutionists to attack the peace of other nations, one of the most blameable was the sending an army against the republic of Geneva, and we have only our own numbers and the British channel to thank for our not having been treated in the same manner.

It is a very singular thing, that men who pass over all these circumstances with as great silence as if they had never happened, have the effrontery to consider France as a persecuted and attacked nation. Do they think, that they are sitting at the mayor's house in Paris, and writing to all the municipalities of France, to tell them, that the palace of the Thuilleries had laid a plan to murder all the patriots in the kingdom? or, what do they think? Is it possible to believe that France, which in an open or in an underhand measure was attacking the government of every nation in Europe, and endeavouring to introduce the Septemberizing system and the revolutionary government, where peace and order had hitherto reigned, could itself expect to meet with no resistance? No, it is impossible: and to be convinced that it did not, we have but to read what Brissot says on that subject, in his publication in the month of May following. Brissot was one of the great deplomatic conductors

conductors at the time of which we are now
speaking, and his testimony may be taken; he
knew the truth and he had no motive for concealing it; at least could have none for writing
as he did.

Brissot was accused of being one of the causes
of the war with England; and he did not refute
the charge; far less did he pretend to say, that
England had declared war upon France without provocation. He has been on many occasions sufficiently lavish of his abuse both of England and of English ministers. It is, therefore, something singular, that we find amongst
ourselves people who will affirm what this daring
leader of the party never ventured to do, or,
which he thought it would be necessary to attempt doing.

In proportion as the victorious French army
advanced in Austrian Flanders and Brabant, Jacobin clubs* were established; the generals and
French commissaries were the patrons, and the
presidents and the soldiers mixed with the members. The armies were accompanied by Jacobin
orators, and followed by printing presses. The
proprietors of Belgium were robbed by the introduction of French assignats; but they were
terrified and remained silent, because those who

---

* The King of Prussia's army having been once repulsed,
there was no single body of troops capable of making any resistance, which is a proof that the Emperor, so far from having exceeded the number of troops which by treaty he was
intitled to have upon that frontier, had not availed himself of
his rights in this respect. This motive alledged for the war
declared against him, therefore, falls to the ground.

had

had nothing, the virtuous fans culottes, were advocates of the French fyftem, becaufe they were determined to eftablifh clubs and principles of equality.*

To the revolution of the 10th of Auguft, the maffacres of September, and the fucceffes of the French arms in repulfing the Auftrians and Pruffians, fucceeded a few months of lefs active operation.

The winter months were employed in endeavouring to amafs all the gold and filver in the kingdom in the treafury of the convention; in organizing the fale of the lands of emigrants, to infure the value of affignats, and in bringing to the fcaffold the unfortunate king.

As long as the world remains, or, at leaft, fo long as men read the hiftory of what has happened, the convention will be feverely reproached for the injuftice, the inhumanity, and the impolicy of putting to death their king. None of the charges that, for the fake of form, were brought againft him, had any foundation either in law or in fact. The king had acted as he had a right to do previous to the acceptation of the conftitution; and after that, he was the only man in the king-

---

* Briffot, who was one of the French leaders at the time, and for feveral months after, tells us that affignats were advanced at par there, (they were 50 per cent. below par at Paris) that the Belgians confidered it but as a double robbery, but that the convention diftributed large fums amongft the vagabonds of Bruffels to make them drunk, and to buy profelytes; and that the dregs of the people, flattered with the hopes of equality with their fuperiors, and affembled in clubs, reduced them to filence, to inactivity.

dom

dom who had remained faithful to it.*   Thofe
who tried Louis for treafon were themfelves traitors ; they had betrayed the nation : they accufed
him of tyranny and defpotifm, when they and
their co-adjutors alone were the tyrants and defpots of the nation : they accufed him of fhedding
innocent blood, when in one half-hour they immolated to their own ambition and revenge more
victims, than there had fallen criminals under the
feverity of the law, during the whole reign of the
king.

* It was not only a circumftance fit to infpire us with admiration of the French king, but it is a phenomenon which
muft excite aftonifhment, that, amongft a vaft number of
his fervants, fome of his former friends, and thoufands of
people who had accefs to know his conduct from his earlieft
youth, none could produce any one arbitrary act or accufation againft him.   We did not fpeak of the Red Book, as it
was called, that is, the lift of penfions given by the court,
at the time that affair was difcuffed by the conftituent affembly, becaufe it had turned out not to contain half the wafte
of public money that had been afferted and apprehended by
the enemies of the court.   Louis XVI. was, in fact, a rigid
economift in principle, and it would appear that the wafte of
public money was never made with his confent, but that the
fame goodnefs which made him wifh to fpare his people had
led him into the unwarrantable and ruinous habitude of paying the debts of the princes, and of fome other perfons about
court.   We fay unwarrantable, becaufe it is worfe in its ul-
timate confequences than granting penfions upon the ftate ;
but, at the fame time, the feeling under which it is done,
exculpates the doer with refpect to his intentions.   What
would have been refufed to fupport extravagance, is granted
to pay needy creditors, and relieve from thraldom an extravagant, but often an amiable debtor ; and thus a new letter of
credit is given to that fame extravagance of which it feldom
fails to make ufe.   Had the other princes of the Houfe of
Bourbon been guided by the fame principles with their illuftrious chief, he would not have loft his life in a revolution
which their great expenfes had accelerated.

The

The hard treatment of the king, during his confinement, as well as the mock trial by which he was brought to the fcaffold, are well known. On that head there is but one opinion in all Europe, and amongft all ranks of people; but it is not fo well known by what methods his enemies contrived to lull all France, and particularly the inhabitants of Paris, into a fort of fleep, till it was too late to prevent the execution of this fanguinary project.

The ruling party in the affembly, in the club, and at the Hotel de Ville, had one thing ftill to fear. The great majority of France, it was known, was not only againft any violence being done to the king, but difapproved in reality of the 10th of Auguft, and all that had been done fince then. The affaffination of the king might therefore, ferve as a fignal for the majority to break forth, and by uniting in one fingle point, crufh their adverfaries.

To prevent fo dangerous a point of re-union, the affembly difcuffed the queftion in a way that made the generality of the people believe that imprifonment or banifhment would be the utmoft extent of their vengeance. The king was long fince a prifoner, and the formality of a mock trial, and condemnation to continue a prifoner, did not appear to be any great fubject for alarm; as for banifhment, it appeared to all as a fentence to be wifhed for. The trial of the king was fo conducted, as, by holding up thefe two forts of punifhment, the fentence of death was not much feared until the trial approached very near its end; and then the precipitate execution prevented the

the poffibility of any effort on the part of the departments of France.

The people of Paris were next to be lulled afleep; the Jacobin method is always to do this by giving hopes, and letting it be underftood by their emiffaries, that more is to be feared from oppofing them, than from letting them act quietly.*

It would be paying the cowardly people of Paris a compliment they do not deferve, to fay that they might probably have refcued their king, if they had been certain that his death was decided upon ; but, though thofe who were determined on bringing him to the block could not have any great reafon to apprehend refiftance from a city which had been perfectly paffive in the arrefts of Auguft and maffacres of September, and which was daily fubmitting to unheard-of oppreffion ; yet Petion, and the conductors of this tranfaction, wifhed once more to make affurance doubly fure ; and it was artfully circulated in Paris that the king was only meant to be carried to the place of punifhment for the fake of form, and in order to imprefs kings in general with a proper awe for the fovereignty of the peo-

* Orders were given in Paris on the day of execution, which followed immediately that of the condemnation, to fire upon the carriage where the king was, upon the leaft appearance of any movement amongft the people in his favour; it was, therefore, impoffible at that ftage of this melancholy bufinefs for any of his friends to fhew themfelves, even if they had been inclined. There are many people who boaft that they intended to make an effort ; but on that fide of the queftion there has been fo much boafting and fo little acting, that it is difficult to give any credit to thefe gentlemen.

ple

ple of France. This was circulated, and, by obtaining credit, prevented any attempt from being made towards a refcue, if any fuch thing was intended.* The cruel and ferocious con‑ ductors of this affair had given orders publicly, that on the leaft attempt in favour of fallen ma‑ jefty, the king fhould inftantly be facrificed ; fo that, under the abfolute certainty on one hand of the order given for this purpofe, and the hope infpired of pardon on the other, the people of Paris, who looked calmly on were not fo much to be blamed as they have been on many other occafions. But the cenfure, from which the re‑ finement of Jacobin cunning refcues them on this occafion, will not wipe away the eternal ftain of cowardice which their tame fubmiffion to his murderers after the deed, has brought upon them.

The Jacobins,† always decided in their own plans, are remarkable for the addrefs with which they prevent their enemies from uniting in

one

* So much were many people convinced that the king would not be executed, that many wagers were laid on the place where it was done, that, on the moment of his prepa‑ ration for the laft punifhment, his pardon would be demand‑ ed and proclaimed. It was, indeed, very filly in any one to believe fuch a report, but that does not alter the fact, it was believed. It is well known that the quicknefs of that mode of execution is fo great, that, if the error was perceived even before it took place, it would have been fo very fmall an interval between that difcovery and the execution, that there could be no poffibility of effecting a refcue.

† The method of dividing the nobility from the clergy, the high clergy from the low clergy, and the bankers and rich merchants from both, is a mafter-piece of cunning, and

one opinion and in one will, and, therefore, in one determined effort ; knowing where their own ftrength lays, they exert their utmoft fkill to deprive their opponents of the fame advantage. We fhall fee that, with regard to the coalefced powers, they have acted in the fame manner ; and that the coalefced powers have let themfelves be duped upon various occafions by the fame artifices that have perpetually enflaved the majority in France to a minority of turbulent republicans.

It has been afferted by many, and believed by fome, that an attempt was made to perfuade the king himfelf that he fhould *not* be put to death.* The thing is probable enough ; but, that he never

was admirably well executed. The intention was in the end to treat them all in the fame way, for war was meant againft all property, not againft any one kind of property in particular. Neverthelefs the proprietors and rich people fell into the fnare. Previous to their invafion of foreign territories, the French propofed to declare war againft caftles, but protection for cottages, and this on purpofe to feparate the two claffes of inhabitants, that they might equally opprefs both. It has only been the experience of their real intention that undeceived their neighbours with regard to the pretended one.

* It has been the conftant cuftom of the Jacobin party that ruled, to give hopes of pardon to their victims during the trial, and fo prevent them from fpeaking out things that it might not be convenient to hear. When judgment is once paffed, the promptitude of the execution is great ; befides it is a rule with thefe republicans not to pollute their ears with hearing what a condemned criminal has to fay. Where juftice is the object, people are eager to hear what the condemned man has to fay before he is launched into eternity ; but tyrants ftop their mouths ; and in this refpect, as well as in many others, the rulers of France have acted like other tyrants.

liftened

liftened to fuch a delufive hope one moment, is certain; for the firmnefs of his behaviour, his calmnefs and refignation, prove beyond reply that his mind was divided or acted upon by no oppofite paffions.

The death of the unfortunate Louis put the feal to the maffacre of the prifoners and the priefts; and fhewed in the moft plain and de-cided manner, that the ruling party in France had determined to ftop at nothing fhort of the total deftruction of all thofe who ftood in the way of what they call liberty and equality. This bloody deed was throwing down the gauntlet to all the governments of Europe, and to all good men; it was a plain declaration that juftice was laid afide, and that the deftruction of govern-ment and of order was fully determined upon. The people of France had been at great pains, as we have feen, to lead all the nations of Europe into the errors of which they themfelves boafted, but of which they were afhamed, and for the ul-timate confequences of which they trembled; but, by this one action, they deftroyed a great part of their own work. Employed during feve-ral years in deceiving Europe by filling their ears with falfities, they, by one fingle action opened the eyes of all who were not blinded by their own paffions and intereft.

The juftice of this action was out of the quef-tion, it was impoffible to deceive people by calling Louis a traitor and a tyrant.*   It was impoffible

to

---

* Even the party of Girondifts treat the king as a tyrant, although they throw his murder upon the party of Robef-pierre.

to shew, that there were any grounds for his condemnation ; it was impossible to prevent the whole world from perceiving the contrast between the virtuous resignation of an innocent victim, and the ferocious vengeance of his accusers and murderers.   This one action shewed, that kings could be virtuous and republicans unjust, and it was impossible to lay the crime upon the effervescence, the hurry of the moment, or the mistake of patriots ; it was therefore necessary plainly and fairly to avow it as their voluntary act, and as such, to give all Europe the measure of their iniquity.*

Ever since the revolution took a violent turn, the number of its admirers in other nations had been diminishing. All men, to the honour of the

pierre.   The former party accuses the latter of distributing more thousands of lettres de cachet than were distributed in the old times by all the inquisitors, and yet they call Louis the last of tyrants, and as such aided to dethrone and imprison him.   All these factions are to be considered only as opposite to each other in interest ; but by no means differing fundamentally in principle.

* All the crimes of the revolution have been so banded about from one party to another, and so palliated, and changed from their real nature by the propagation of falsities, that they have never been seen in their full horror.   The crimes of Caligula, Nero, Charles IX. and other despotic princes, cannot be explained away as the crimes of a people may, at least it would seem so, by the French revolution. It would be well, however, to consider, that what with the agents, the vindicators, and the spectators, few escape the accusation of guilt ; and if we take the old maxim for our guide, that he who shares the spoils with the thief is himself a thief, we shall find, that the whole of the French nation is nearly in the same predicament as to criminality or cowardice.

human

human race let it be recorded, wifhed the French fuccefs whilft they imagined that liberty was the real object of the revolution. They blamed, indeed, the exceffes of the populace, and trembled for the precipitate carreer of the affembly; but they fearched for excufes as long as they could find any, either in accident or in their ignorance of the affair of reformation which they had fet about. The general approbation diminifhed when it was perceived, that the people continued to be cruel and their reprefentatives unjuft; but ftill thofe who were already free, in other countries, or who wifhed to be fo, were inclined to palliate what they could not excufe, and to attribute to a miftaken enthufiafm what arofe from particular paffions. Even the 10th of Auguft infpired lefs horror than might have been expected, becaufe neceffity, or a fuppofed neceffity of the meafure, appeared to have acted upon the minds of the people. The meafures of September uncaufed by fear, and unwarranted by neceffity, found yet fome * excufe in the irregular manner in which they were perpetrated; but

* Thefe maffacres were thrown, as we have feen, all upon one party, but unluckily for the other party, Manuel and Petion were the conductors of the common council when the maffacres took place; and though Danton and fome of their affociates joined Robefpierre and Marat, and began to denounce Briffot and his Gafcons, yet it will be impoffible for any one to make a diftinction between their degrees of criminality. Briffot long after that faid, *that France was arrived at the laft bounds of liberty and equality, trampling all human fuperftition under foot*, and yet he exclaims againft the murders of September. He had afked, with anxious expectation, whether his antagonift Demorande, was not affaffinated, and yet he exclaims againft thefe murders! We muft again repeat it, that there is no diftinction to be made with refpect to the principles of thofe men.

this

this laſt act ſtood in all its atrocity; it was un-provoked murder, premeditated and avowed, and, of conſequence, mankind had but one opi-nion on the ſubject.

It was ſoon after this that war broke out be-tween England and France, and it is extraordi-nary, concerning ſo recent an event, how num-bers of people have been miſled.

The conduct of Britain towards France had been of the moſt generous ſort. The troubles of that country offered an occaſion, and held out, indeed, a temptation to the Engliſh miniſtry to be revenged of that nation for the American war; for the troubles which had broke out in Ireland at the end of that war, and which were encouraged by the French;* for the attempt made to change
the

* It is well known in this country, that in 1782, when there were diſturbances in Ireland, France interfered by emiſſaries, who ſwarmed in Dublin. The ſupport intended, and promiſed to the enemies of the ſtadtholder in Holland, is equally well known; and it was the general theme in France, at the time when Tippoo Saib ſent ambaſſadors there, that we ſhould ſoon loſe our poſſeſſions in the Eaſt In-dies. The French nation then (and that was in 1788,) was delighted with this idea, ſo that the patriots of England muſt not count any more upon the affection of the people of France towards this country, than they did upon the good-will of the court. With reſpect to this nation all parties had the ſame views, and what is more, always will have; it was, therefore, certainly great generoſity in England not to take advantage of the firſt diſorders of France, which, if it had been inclined to do, Lord Gower would not, probably, have been ſent to re-place the Duke of Dorſet as ambaſſa-dor, becauſe the former nobleman was in no degree poſſeſ-ſed of the intrigue neceſſary; it is even to be queſtioned, if he was well choſen for giving that information which ſo important

the government of Holland by chacing away the ftadtholder; and, laft of all, for the attack projected upon our fettlements in the Eaft Indies in conjunction with Tippoo Saib. The ruin of England feemed to have been the view of the French court, and the wifh of the whole nation, yet England faw the whole of the French army difbanded by mutiny, and all the officers of the navy chaced away, without making any effort to turn it to advantage. If minifters acted thus, the Englifh nation acted ftill more generoufly as individuals; all men wifhed them fuccefs, and thofe who were enemies to the revolution do not feem to have been fo from being enemies either of the French or of freedom, but, on the contrary, becaufe they faw that they were not taking the road either to be happy or free, and that the revolution was conducted by men either unwilling or incapable of eftablifhing a free and firm government.

The war is one of thofe events of which the direct caufe is a matter of doubt with many, becaufe it is violently contefted by a few. An opinion has gone abroad in England, that though we did not declare war, the haughty conduct of minifters towards the emiffary Chauvelin, formerly ambaffador, occafioned the declaration on the part of the French.

portant a moment required. The fecond year of the revolution was that in which England might have been expected to act if fhe wifhed to do France any harm; but no traces of fuch a project are to be found, although all the French, both democrats at home and many emigrant ariftocrats, fay, that Mr. Pitt excited troubles in the interior of France Accufation without proof or probability requires no refutation.

The

This matter, however, does not admit of much difpute, if we will examine it without any regard to the feelings of either of the two parties in this country, who differ with regard to its juf-tice and neceffity.

Inftead of always calling it juft and neceffary, we fhould do better in faying, that it was inevita-ble, for fuch is the fact. There was no avoid-ing war, unlefs we meant to curb ourfelves be-neath the yoke of the proud republicans, and fee the crown of England fall before the red bonnet of France. If we can eftablifh this, there will, perhaps, be little doubt of the truth of the affer-tion, that war was inevitable; for fuch a humi-liating and miferable alternative cannot be confi-dered by Englifhmen as being any alternative at all.

The French divided into two diftinct parties, after the murder of their king and the war with England, and thofe two parties reproached one another mutually with having excited the war. Briffot's party* was condemned after having

been

---

* Briffot's party is ftill confidered in France as having been the caufe of the war; and it is certain, that Briffot, Kerfaint, and Condorcet, were the great projectors of conquefts. It was that party that endangered Europe the moft, yet from all that it does not abfolutely follow, that the other party did not contribute full as much, or more, to the declaration of hof-tilities. It is certain, that the party of Robefpierre dom-neered in the convention at the time, and it was the conven-tion that declared war firft on Spain and then on England; and it feems rather to be the faireft to fuppofe, that Robefpierre and his friends were moft active in declaring war, but that it was done in a moment of fuccefs, and when a reverfe came,

they

been accufed of bringing about the war with England, and after having retorted that accufation with vehemence and probability of truth. Both parties agree then, in two things, that the war with England was a misfortune, and that one or other of them had been the occafion of bringing it on ; this does not look as if it could have been thrown upon England.

If Chauvelin, who could neither be confidered as an ambaffador from the tenor of his conduct, which was unlike one, nor from his credentials, which were expired, was treated in a haughty ftile, it muft be recollected, that he began by being very infolent ; that he made no fecret of his attachment to the revolutionary principles of the Jacobins, and that he left no ftone unturned to encourage the malcontents of England to put themfelves in a ftate of infurrection, and folicit the protection offered in the decree of the 19th November, to all people who wifhed to throw off the fhackles of regular government. Would it have been proper for Englifh minifters, acting for a nation where kingly government is eftablifhed and cherifhed, to have fubmitted to republican infolence ? and would it not have been highly criminal to have permitted the enemies of Eng-

they wifhed to throw the blame on their enemies. It is to be obferved, however, that Briffot's party managed diplomatic affairs when a general invitation to infurrection was given to all the nations of Europe. Chauvelin and the Propagande emiffaries were all originally of that party. Since the war took a better turn for the French, the fuppofed inftigators of it are not inquired after ; and if that party had not fallen under twenty-two ftrokes of Robefpierre's guillotine, we might perhaps have feen its leaders *claiming the honour* of bringing on the war with England.

land to form plots in the middle of the capital, to overturn our government and undermine our profperity?

Will the enemies of the war pretend to fay, that Chauvelin did not play the part of a Jacobin emiffary, that his houfe was not a point of re-union for all fuch, and that he openly profeffed fuch principles; availing himfelf of the inviola-bility of ambaffadors, in which quality he had acted, and of that refpect which yet was fhewn him on account of the mafter who had fent him?

This fame Chauvelin was difgraced on his re-turn to France, and accufed of having aided the party that excited the war; it is therefore as clear as it is poffible to be, that the French attribute to themfelves this war, about the juftice of which we difpute fo much.

But the French may be miftaken, it may be faid, that it is certainly poffible, though they fel-dom make the miftake of accufing themfelves of what others are guilty of; however, if it even were fo, it does not follow that the war could be avoided.

We have already mentioned the manœuvres of Claviere to pump guineas off the Change of England, by means of bills upon Paris, which was in fact circulating affignats in England, and neither more nor lefs;* this thing alone would
have

---

* Affignats had actually began to circulate in certain quarters, that is to fay, juft as much as ever French Louis d'ors did; they did not ferve to pay a bill at a tavern, but
they

have been fufficient to warrant minifters in ftopping all commerce with France, and forbidding the intercourfe of bills of exchange which would have been a hoftile meafure, though of a negative nature ; the treaty of commerce, and all other treaties would have been broke by fuch a proceeding, which neverthelefs was rendered quite neceffary by the mode adopted of paying all bills on France in a fpecies of money that had no intrinfic value, and which the confufed ftate of the country would not permit ftrangers to convert into any intrinfic value.* Unlefs the

they could be converted iuto gold at pleafure. It was at this time that a man appeared upon the Change of London, and offered to deliver bank of England notes at a difcount, at the end of three months. This was fpeaking pretty plain, but the enemies of the war forget all this.

* The circulation of affignats might have been ftopt in England, without the violation of any treaty ; but the circulation of bills upon France could not becaufe an intercourfe of payments is the neceffary confequence of an intercourfe of fales, fo that when we were obliged to forbid the one, we were forbidding the other. Quibblers may fay that individuals will always take care of their own intereft, and that the price at which they fold their goods would be proportioned to the difcredit of affignats ; but that will not do, we have feen that the French had methods of raifing and lowering the change at pleafure, and that it was at the rifk of one's life that money or bullion could be brought out of France, fo that it would not do to truft entirely to the individual. Do not all governments make laws for the protection of trade againft fwindlers ? and yet what are fwindlers ? they do not take the property of the individual by force, nor againft his will, but by deceiving him with refpect to his real intereft. This was juft precifely what the national convention and their agents did when they decreed that bills negociated in London fhould be paid in Paris in affignats, and when they forbid the exchange of affignats for fpecie, or the carrying of fpecie out of the kingdom. There could not be a more manifeft impofition and dupery.

Englifh

Englifh nation was determined to fubmit to beg-
gary and bankruptcy, it was neceffary to fhut up
this ruinous intercourfe, and therefore war was
inevitable, for nobody will for a moment fuppofe
that the convention would have tamely fubmitted
to fuch a meafure.

The Jacobin manœuvres in this country rendered the alien bill, as it is called, neceffary;
this alfo was an infringement on the rights of
nations, which could only be vindicated by neceffity. When individuals violate the laws of
hofpitality, every government is juftified in acting as its own peace and fafety requires. It was
difputed at the time by thofe who oppofed the
war, that the manœuvres in queftion were of fuch
a nature as not to warrant a bill fo fevere in its
nature; but it muft be confeffed, that this is un-
fupported by any proof or any probability, or
the words and actions of numbers of individuals
have plainly fhewn what their intentions towards
this government were,*

The attack upon Holland was another caufe
for war with France; but though in the ordi-

* Briffot accufes Cambon for not having given the executive minifters a fufficient credit upon the national treafury, to
enable them to fill the coffers of France by ftock-jobbing with
foreign gold.—This proves the existence of the plan. He
accufes the other party of having excited jealoufies in Ireland, Scotland, and fermentation in England; that by ne-
glecting this, thofe plans were ftified which would have
enabled France to triumph over her enemies abroad, *and
eſtabliſh her liberty every where.* Ireland, whofe movements
towards liberty, fays he, we were bound to encourage.—
And yet we have people in England who pretend to doubt
about their intentions.

nary

nary diplomatic line, it may operate as a ftrong one, we muft confefs it deferves but little to be mentioned, when our commercial wealth, our profperity, our government, and our peace at home, were concerned.

In pointing out the reafons for which the war feems to have been inevitable, it is by no means to be inferred, that minifters conducted them-felves in the moft becoming or the moft prudent manner. Perfectly right in the main point, of maintaining Englifh independence and dignity at all events, it might have been done in a lefs haughty manner, and even with more firmnefs than it was done ; the cafe might have been ren-dered lefs intricate, and the whole nation would then have been of one mind. It is one of the greateft evils of circuitous negociations, that the real rights of the cafe are loft, or at leaft diffi-cult to be difcovered ; a plain, fimple declara-tion of the ftate of facts would, in this cafe, have been the proper way of treating with a na-tion which feduces ftrangers by its apparently open mode of acting.

Had England declared to France that fhe would neither have affignats nor emiffaries, that the one ruined her commerce and the other her peace, and that of courfe until France paid bills drawn, with money that had a real value, and until fhe renounced all interference, either by emiffaries or decrees, in the internal government of England, every fort of intercourfe muft ceafe between the two countries. If it had been added to this, that a treaty with Holland obliged Eng-land to interfere in cafe fhe was attacked, and

that

that England was determined, as a free and an independent people, to preferve her commerce, her internal peace and government, and to keep her word with her allies.

Such a declaration would either have prevented a war, or have made us more unanimous in fupporting it than we have been. The meafures adopted by minifters were good, but the manner of adopting them was by no means unexceptionable.

In cafes of great importance, people fhould be clear, diftinct, and laconic; nothing that is unimportant, foreign to the matter in hand, or merely relative to form and ceremony, fhould be mixed with what is weighty and important; it enfeebles our friends, and gives room for the chicane of our enemies.

It is not upon all occafions that ftatefmen can fpeak plain, but the habit of not doing fo ought not to be let grow upon them to fuch a degree, as not to do it when they may, for certainly it is in fome cafes a very great advantage, particularly when a mifunderftanding is likely to produce a wafte of blood and treafure.

Amongft the many faults of the Jacobins, and along with all their duplicity, they have the advantage of always appearing to fpeak plain, and they let flip no opportunity of doing fo *when they can.* It is excellent policy, and their enemies would neither lofe any thing of their dignity nor of their fuccefs, if they were to adopt the

fame

fame mode. The direct language of the Jacobins has made them underftand each other, and co-operate over all the countries of Europe, while a few crowned heads have miftaken each other's intentions on almoft every occafion ; and by their miftakes and the misfortunes which have followed, brought the fafety of all regular go-vernments into danger.

The evils of war, it is faid, are certain, its advantages hypothetical ; this is true, when war is made to obtain advantages, but when it is made in felf-defence, it is not fo ; and for fuch a pur-pofe was the prefent moft certainly begun. It is the beginning only that is a matter of inquiry here, the conducting of it is another matter, as is alfo the views which have arifen during its con-tinuance. If the combined powers have fhewn a defire of conqueft, France has fhewn it alfo, and therefore with refpect to that, there are no re-proaches to make on either fide.

The decree of the French convention had en-couraged the fomenters of anarchy here, to fo great a pitch, that a convention of felf-elected deputies met at Edinburgh, and began to imitate the French convention. Affiliation of clubs was alfo begun, and it was difficult to fay to what exceffes they might not have been carried, or fpurred on by the people, had not the civil power interfered in time, and delivered over fome of the ring-leaders to the law of the land.

As many obfervations have been made with refpect to the treatment of fome of the ringlea-ders, it may be proper, in a few words, to wipe
off

off from the judges and jury thofe reproaches
with which they have unjuftly been loaded.

As a matter of eftablifhed law, and of natural
juftice, the jury and judges deferve praife for
what they did, although the fame punifhment
could not have been inflicted in England for the
fame offence.

With refpect to the intentions of men who
imitated the leaders of the maffacres of September, there could be little doubt, and that doubt
it remained in the breafts of the jury to clear up
to themfelves; and as to the law being more fevere in Scotland than in England, it arifes from
this, that in Scotland, before the Union, treafon
and fedition were more common than in England, and therefore the law is more explicit on
that head; for in every country where any fpecies
of a crime is rare the laws refpecting its punifhment are lefs fevere.   An Englifh jury might
have been equally convinced of the bad intention, but the judges could not have been able
to pafs the fame fentence.   As to the neceffity
of rigour againft fuch men, the prefent hiftory is
the beft argument;   the men who committed the
maffacres of September, and thofe who had murdered their king, did not commence their career
of blood by demanding blood, they commenced
it by demanding liberty and bread, and the
members of the pretended convention in Scotland gloried in imitating them; the minds of
any reafonable jury could not be in much per-
plexity in fo evident a cafe.

In

In paying the proper attention to punishing the agitators of revolution, the judges and jury merit the thanks of all men who love liberty ; until such time as the French shall give us the example of a nation establishing real liberty, freedom, and happiness, greater than we enjoy in Britain, those who wish to hold her up as a model to copy from, are certainly deserving of the severest punishment the laws can inflict, for ignorance cannot now be alledged as an excuse.

When the unfortunate French Monarch was no more [*Note* O.] and the convention had seen its enemies repulsed, the divisions between Robespierre's party and the Girondists augmented every day. France was now only ruled by murderers, there were no more victims to be pointed out amongst the privileged orders, nor enemies to the public tranquility by bad conduct in the government; the savages now occupied the forest alone, and therefore were obliged to turn upon and tear each other.

The miseries of the people continued to augment in the midst of victory, and under the dominion of republicans. The same mode was still practised that had been employed before, to make the sovereign people have patience. The parties accused each other, and quarrelled about their power; they united, however, in proscribing and putting to death the rich proprietors of those attached to the old system, who remained ; they united their efforts to flatter the people, and to give them hopes by a sort of constitution which they made, by shutting up the churches, by persecuting those who shewed any attachment to religion, and by finally attacking the monied men.*

When this laft clafs of proprietors found themfelves likely to be attacked, they determined to gain over one of the parties in the affembly, and it was to the Girondifts that they applied. It was, in fact, a matter of little importance which of the two parties took up the protection of this fort of property, becaufe from the moment that any fet of men in France became attached to order, and the prefervation of property, they became themfelves a prey to the fans culottes, to the men who had nothing, whofe hunger for gold was never fatisfied, and whofe thirft for blood was never affuaged.

We have yet feen nothing equal to this combat; it was not that of the wild animal againft the tame, it was that of the tyger againft the tyger, and which ever party fell, it was now no longer a fubject for pity or regret.

The Girondift party thought proper to diftinguifh their opponents by the title of ANARCHISTS, and it was not at all wonderful, if their newborn attachment to order fhould be attributed to felfifh plans, or fome fudden motives; for it was but with a bad grace, that men who had headed

* When the convention affembled, moft part of the actors at the Hotel de Ville in Auguft and September were chofen. Robefpierre had left the commune to become a reprefentative; Talien, who was a fecretary, and Hebert, the judge of Madame de Lamballe, had done the fame; Danton had quitted the place of minifter of juftice, and thofe were the leaders of the Mountain, Briffot Condorcet, Thomas Paine, &c. &c. were of the Girondift party, and expected to continue their reign of laying the rich bankers under contribution, and then eftablifhing order.

insurrection

infurrection, and difleminated its principles from the very beginning of the revolution, now preached obedience to law, and regard for property; infurrection was a holy duty they ftill coul not deny, but it might, they faid, be *continued too long*.

The efforts of the Briffotins, affifted by thofe miniiters who had figned the death warrant of their* mafter, and by thofe who conducted him to the fcaffold, now preached order and humanity, and refpect to property and perfons. They then found themfelves in the fame fituation that the court had been in before the 10th of Auguft; the rabble was now no longer at their command, and their laft hour arrived.

* The minifters who figned the order for the king's execution, were

Roland—fince cut his own throat on the high road, his wife guillotined.

Servan—guillotined fince as a Briffotin.

Le Brun—guillotined.

Clavierre—cut his throat in prifon, and his wife took poifon.

Bournonville—a prifoner in Germany.

Pafhe—a prifoner in France.

Petion and Manuel, along with the above honorable gentlemen, now preached order, but the farce was too grofs even to be played in Paris, and accordingly the people of Paris never fhewed fo much pleafure as when thofe of them who were caught, were carried to the guillotine. Even the mob of Paris had yet fome refpect for virtue, and contempt for vice; none of the royalifts were infulted in the manner that the Duke of Orleans, Briffot, Hebert, Danton, and Robefpierre himfelf, were, when they were carried to punifhment. When confcience cannot fpeak loud, it whifpers, and it would appear every fentiment of juftice is never extinguifhed in the minds of men,   The

The Briſſotins had, as we have already ſaid, been accuſed by the other party of cauſing the war with England, and they had defended themſelves but in a feeble manner. A circumſtance which now happened, facilitated the triumph of their enemies; Dumourier was found to have ambitious views, which did not correſpond with liberty and equality; he had been defeated by the enemy, and the anger of the people was excited againſt the Briſſotins, as being Dumourier's friends, and the cauſe of ſo unfortunate a war. The ſtorm was now ready to burſt upon their heads, and their enemies haſtened it, by contriving to call them fœderaliſts (implying that they wiſhed to divide France into provinces, as the American republic is divided). The *unity and indiviſibility* of the republic was then put upon a par with the liberty and equality of its inhabitants; and to plot againſt the one was as great a crime as againſt the other. It was for this imaginary crime that the new apoſtles of order were attacked; and after having twenty times eſcaped merited puniſhment for their attack upon law and order, they were now going to be ſacrificed for daring to defend it.*

When the Girond party found themſelves ready to be attacked, they began with attacking the anarchiſts in a pamphlet. This pamphlet, writ-

---

* Dumourier, as far as the politics of ſo inconceiveable a man can be known, was attached to the Girondiſt party; and at all events, as this was ſuppoſed, that party ſhared a little in his diſgrace. It is certain that the plans of conqueſt, as propoſed by Briſſot, Condorcet, and Kerſaint, were ſuch as Dumourier approved of the moſt; and it will be recollected, he had been miniſter with Roland, Claviere, &c. during the king's life.

ten in the name of an Address from Briffot to his Conftituents, is, when taken all in all, one of the moft curious pieces of compofition that ever was produced.*   It is alfo one of the moft valu-able, if we confider it as the criticifm of a leader of revolutions, upon the principles of revolution, it unveils all the plans of the parties, and de-claims againft the evils of anarchy in as ftrong terms as any royalift could do. [*Note* **P.**]

This publication was a ftep very fimilar to that taken by La Fayette the year before, when he left his army to come to give a leffon to the affembly. La Fayette, after fhewing the example of rebel-lion, had the infolence to fet his face againft it; and now Petion and Briffot, juft as proud of the 10th of Auguft as La Fayette was of taking the Baftile, had the infolence, in their turn, to write a pamphlet againft anarchy.

* This pamphlet is the moft fevere criticifm or fatyr, con-fidering from whom it came, that could poffibly be written upon French liberty and equality; in it Briffot evidently fpeaks from conviction and experience, that the ftate into which the anarchifts had thrown France, was the moft deplor-able to which any country could be reduced; that the repre-fentatives enjoyed no liberty, and that the laws were totally without force, perfons without fecurity, and property with-out protection; yet he breaks out from time to time into ex-clamations in favour of glorious liberty and facred equality, fuch as it was in France.   There is fomething in that con-tradiction that it is difficult to explain. Vanity, it might appear, hindered him from renouncing his favorite fyftem (for repub-licans are the vaineft people in the world) and truth forced from him an avowal of the real exifting miferies.   One is tempted to think, that on this fubject of liberty and equality, his ideas had run fo much, that he had loft the faculty of rea-foning; for it is quite clear, that it was the very theory which he approved that led to thofe very miferies of which he com-plained, fo that without admitting fome derangement of ideas, it is difficult to account for his conduct and his writings.

The

The anarchifts now meted out to the Girondifts the fame meafure which they had meafured out to their king, and this pamphlet ferved as the fignal to begin.*

A committee had been formed by the convention to inquire into the illegal arrefts and confifcations carried on by the municipal officers, and other conftituted authorities. This was a meafure adopted at the requeft and by the power of the Briffotin faction, in order to keep their word with men of property. The addrefs of Briffot againft the anarchift had been publifhed on the 25th of May, and on the 27th a crowd furrounded the affembly, demanding the diffolution of this committee. This mob was headed by what were called *revolutionary committees*,† and as an armed mob

* Ever fince the month of September a fort of divifion had exifted between Robefpierre's, Marat's, and the Gironde party, becaufe Briffot had not fpoken favourably of the maffacres, and becaufe reftrictions had been laid upon the newfpaper printers, of whom he was one. As there is a vindictive fpirit of the moft implacable fort in all thofe chiefs of parties, this breach was naturally widening, but the protection of monied men, which was a profitable job in perfpective, brought matters to a conclufion fooner than they would otherwife have been.

† The meafures adopted now were all *revolutionary* ; this was the name invented by the violent party in the Jacobin club, to excufe their exceffes. The conflitutionalifts had given a leffon to their enemies of the folly of thinking to truft to laws and regulations for preferving an ufurped power. The government of Morocco may be called revolutionary, and by that means the emperors can make fome fort of refiftance when they are attacked, but Louis XVI. and thofe who adhered to the conftitution, could make none. It was neceffary for the king to have the order of the mayor of Paris, before

mob is an eloquent orator, the affembly decreed the deftruction of their committee by the ufual method of ftanding up. Next day, however, when the mob was not affembled at the gate, this decree was fufpended uutil the committee fhould have made its report; and on the 30th the *revolutionary* council came to intimate to the affembly, that it would be *neceffary to obey the order* given by the populace, and thus, in the midft of armed petitioners, and the cries and imprecations of the people in the galleries, the fuppreffion was again determined upon and decreed.

On the 31ft, the anarchifts, convinced that they had only yet the appearance of victory, but not the reality, fummoned to their poft the men of the 10th of Auguft.* The tocfin was founded, and the cannon of alarm fired, and Henriot the commandant ordered the guards to march and furround the affembly. A petition was then prefented, demanding a decree of arreft againft thirty-five members of the Girondift party. The

---

fore he could *legally* defend his own life, whilft thofe who revolted, fettered by no law, could attack him when or where, or in what manner they pleafed. Inftead of now having the conftituted authorities, they had revolutionary authorities, who having the faculty of acting as they thought proper, were upon a par with the populace, and could, upon occafion, make head againft them.

* When it was faid in the profpectus of the prefent work, that it would plainly appear, that the firft principles laid down by the conftituent affembly, in their rights of man, led on to the laft exceffes, it was by no means a miftake. This is now the third revolution upon the fame plan, and they are a as like each other as the fteps of the fame ladder; the materials and the diftance from the point of fetting out are different, but every thing elfe is the fame.

affembly,

affembly, in order to get rid of the armed force, demanded three days to examine this petition *.

Since the 30th of May the barriers had been fhut, and the ufual forms of infurrection were in full activity. The directors of the poft-office† were changed, and all letters were examined.

On the 2d of June, the revolutionary commit-tee appeared again at the bar, *and for the laft time demanded* the accufation of the members.

The ‡ affembly thought proper to pafs to the order of the day, upon which the petitioners made a fign to the fpectators to go out and take arms, that they might by force obtain what they wanted. At mid-day the tocfin founds again, and the cannon of alarm is fired, the citizens

---

* It is ftrange to fee how Petion and his friends had loft their intriguing energy of the 10th of Auguft; it is difficult to conceive, how the fame men, who were fo active and fo artful at difarming royalty, and attacking the king, fhould be fo inactive and carelefs, when for feveral days running the fame manœuvres were preparing againft themfelves.

† The directors of the poft had all been changed imme-diately after the maffacres of September, but had been fuc-ceeded by Girondifts; fo that the party now getting into power was determined not to leave this fuperiority in the hands of their enemies.

‡ The affembly did not now meet in a riding fchool as it had formerly done; the royal palace was converted into a national palace; and it was here that the attack was con-ducted againft the convention.

are

are called to take arms and obey their commander.*

The affembly was furrounded as the palace had been the year before, but with an apparatus ftill more formidable; more than an hundred cannon were pointed againft the houfe of affembly, furnaces for red-hot balls were prepared, and an order was given to let no one depart, but to fire on the firft of the reprefentatives of the nation who dared fo much as to look through the iron rails. Marat and the chiefs of the Mountain were very active on this occafion, and it is more than probable, that thefe formidable preparations were intended only to intimidate, for it would not have anfwered the purpofe of the anarchifts to fire upon the convention.

The promoters of the difturbance were many of them in the hall, and thofe did not certainly wifh to be fcorched with red-hot balls, neither could it be fuppofed, that if the convention were maffacred, Paris could continue to reign over France, by defiring them to fend more reprefentatives to fuch a city.

The ceremony of preparing grates for heating cannon balls was, therefore, probably only intended by thefe hardy fons of infurrection as a

---

* Santerre, named commander on the 10th of Auguft, was not now revolutionary enough for the party of Robefpierre; befides, he had been attached to the Duke of Orleans: to get rid of him he had been named general of an army to go againft the Vendee, and one Henriot, a commis des barriers, commanded in his place.

leffon to their mafters, feveral of whom were beaten and had their cloaths torn.*

Several battalions, which fhould have marched againft the royalifts in the Vendee before that day, arrived fuddenly, and took poffeffion of all the paffages and apartments adjoining to the hall, where they were bribed with affignats and wine, in order to induce them to be faithful and with-ftand the eloquence of the deputies.

The befiegers were well armed, and the na-tional palace (fay the deputies) became a prifon, where the reprefentatives of the people were menaced, infulted, and degraded. It was pre-cifely what had happened in the royal palace the year before, and the parties that then degraded royalty were the fame who complained of being themfelves degraded now.

Barrere was called upon to make the report of the committee on the accufed members. Barrere, floating in the uncertainty of which party might prevail, propofed, in the name of the committee, that thofe members who were accufed, but againft whom no proofs had been produced, fhould be *invited* to fufpend their functions. Some of the accufed members accepted of this *invitation*.† This
facrifice

---

* The reader will remember, that precifely the fame things took place previous to the 10th of Auguft, when the decree againft La Fayette was wanted from the affembly by the furrounding mob. The perfecutors then were the perfecuted now, that was all the difference.

† Barrere, who followed Robefpierre in all his exceffes, was a man never decided in opinion, but when he was either
obliged

facrifice being made to the people, the convention became more bold, and ordered the commandant of the troops to the bar. The order
was laughed at; feveral deputies were infulted,
the convention ordered thofe who infulted them
to be brought to the bar; this order was refifted
by force. It was then determined to adjourn, and
to fhut the TEMPLE OF THE LAW. This was attempted by all the members in a body, with the
prefident at their head. The prefident ordered
the centinels to retire, and the troop of lawgivers
got to the middle of the court, when Henriot the
commandant ordered them to turn back. The
convention, faid the prefident, will receive orders
from no perfon; poffeffed of powers received
from the French nation, the French nation alone
can give orders to the convention. *

The commandant on this drew his fabre, put
his cavalry in battle array, and ordered the artillery men to point their guns. The prefident and
all the members vied with each other in their
hafte to return to the hall, and decree, that the
accufed fhould be arrefted. Briffot, Petion, and

obliged to be fo, or knew that he was certain of fupport.
The appearance of moderation, in the prefent cafe, was, becaufe the real ftrength of parties had not been tried; Barrere
and the committee who made the report, and faid, that nothing had been proved againft the accufed, might, in time of
need, have made a merit of it with the accufed. When
things were decided, this fame Barrere joined with others in
fending the accufed to the fcaffold.

* The fimilarity of this fpeech and that of Mirabeau at
Verfailles is great. M. de Brezé was a courtier, Henriot
was a clerk at a toll-bar or turnpike. We fee which of the
two knew beft how to reduce the deputies to obedience.

their companions * were ordered to be confined
in their own houfes, and in going there they
ought to have remembered that their king was
not treated with fuch lenity. His houfe was robbed and plundered, and he was fent to a miferable prifon, and all thofe fufpected of attachment
to his perfon or family were maffacred, imprifoned,
or driven into exile.

Let us hear what the arrefted deputies themfelves fay on this occafion, in an addrefs to their
conftituents.

" Frenchmen, you who wifh to be freemen
" and republicans, behold fuch facts as cannot
" be denied; we only offer you the outline, and
" we fupprefs details of facts ftill more atrocious.
" The national reprefentation, imprifoned, de-
" graded, and deliberating under the poniards of
" the affaffins of an audacious faction, exifts no
" more. Let not your rights be any longer
" ufurped ; leave not the exercife of national fo-
" vereignty in fuch hands; fave liberty, facred
" equality, the unity, and indivifibility of the re-
" public: without thefe, France is loft. Repel
" with horror all propofitions tending to foeder-
" alifm. Rally, affemble, you may yet fave the
" republic: the republic is France itfelf, and does
" not refide within the walls of Paris. There
" your reprefentatives, prifoners, dare no longer
" fpeak;

* Briffot, Petion, Guadet, Genfoné, Gorfas, Vergreaud,
Silles, Barbaroux, Chambon, Buzot, Biroteau, Ledon, Ra-
baut de St. Etienne, Lafource, Languinais, Grangeneuve, Le
Hardy, Le Sage, Kervelegan, Gardier, Boileau, Bertrand,
Viger, Mollovaut, Govamaire, la Reviere, and Bergoin.

" fpeak; but, no matter, they well know how to
" die worthy of you, worthy of themfelves, too
" happy, if after that their country can be
" faved. When the moment of national ven-
" geance fhall be arrived, Frenchmen, do not
" forget that Paris itfelf is innocent; that the ci-
" tizens of Paris were ignorant of the plots of
" which they became the blind inftruments.   It
" is not upon Paris that the terrible and all-
" powerful hand of the nation fhould ftrike, but
" upon that horde of miferable wretches and
" robbers who have taken poffeffion of Paris and
" of France, who cannot live but by crimes, and
" who have no hope but in the continuation of
" crimes.   Adieu."

*Paris, 7th June, 2d year of
the French republic.*

Such were the complaints of the inftigators of
revolt, when it was turned againft themfelves.
They now made a very fevere criticifm on the refults of their own principles, and are an eternal
example for thofe who think to rule infurrection,
and turn it always to their own advantage.

This addrefs produced a confiderable effect. It
was not now one of thofe clear cafes of fufpected
ariftocrats and royal defpots; it was reprefentatives againft reprefentatives, and the infurgents of
Auguft 1792, againft thofe of May 1793. The
fame truths which the royalifts had never ceafed
to repeat from the beginning of the revolution
without any effect, now produced a fchifm and
divifion amongft the different provinces.

The

The Lyonefe, the people of Marfeilles, Bourdeaux, and the adjacent country, as well as part of
Normandy, took part with the arrefted deputies.
It was partly in confequence of this fame affair
that the port and city of Toulon were delivered
up to the Englifh and Spanifh fleets; and it was
this divifion in the interior of France that occafioned the inactivity of the French army during
the fummer, when Condé and Valenciennes were
taken by the allied armies.

Had the royalift party and the combined
powers feized this occafion to pufh matters, it is
probable that things might have gone much better for them than they have done. But the errors
of that campaign and of the cabinets of Europe,
were inexcufable, and are only to be equalled by
the long train of misfortunes which they occafioned.

The combined powers attributed their firft defeats to the want of fupport from the malcontents
in the nation---fupport which they had been promifed; and now, when France was a fcene of
open revolt and complete civil war, what did the
combined armies of Auftria and England do?
They wafted a whole fummer, fpent millions of
money, and fpoiled their beft pieces of ordnance,
in taking Valenciennes, to abandon it the year
after without firing a fhot.*

---

* Valenciennes was not abfolutely abandoned without firing
a fhot, but it was nearly the fame thing; the garrifon capi-
tulated without either a regular defence or a regular attack.

Lyons,

Lyons, which from its pofition, its riches, the vaft number of its inhabitants, * and, above all, their difpofition, was worth millions to the allied powers, was left to fink under the armies of the convention, without an attempt being made to give it affiftance, which would have been fo eafily done. Lyons fought for liberty and property againft anarchy and pillage; and, though it did not abfolutely fight for the Houfe of Bourbon, it fought for the caufe which interefts men much more, and which, had it triumphed, would have ultimately ferved the caufe of royalty.

But, if a royal caufe alone could excite the efforts of the cabinets of Europe, they had an opportunity to fupport it by affifting the royalifts in Britany; in that part of France where the fpirit of irreligion and innovation had not taken root, and which is called the Vendee. Arms, money, and a leader, were all they wanted, and the combined powers had all thefe at their difpofition. The Count d'Artois, brave by nature, and now rendered wifer by misfortune, offered himfelf as the leader † of the royalifts, and as a leader who

* Lyons was an immenfe town, not much lefs than half the fize of Paris; a very induftrious people, and might have been very eafily affifted from Savoy, or even from Alface.

† The Count d'Artois had been at Peterfburgh, which place he left with the expectation of going directly to the Vendee. The floop of war in which he was lay off Holland for feveral weeks. Government here, for reafons beft known to itfelf, would not confent to his landing in the Vendee. In military affairs as nothing is certain, it is poffible that this ftep was wife; but it is very certain that the fteps taken, of raifing troops and threatening an invafion were very foolith ; it was exactly exciting the republicans to the flaughter of the royalifts.

would

would have carried along with him all thofe emi-grant gentlemen who have been idle and unem-ployed, becaufe they did never know for what caufe, nor under what ftandard, they were to ferve. *

What did England do on this occafion ? Why, during the precious months that France was on the brink of a decided civil war, and when many parts of that republic had actually revolted, a fort of an army was collected in England under the command of an excellent and a brave man, with the profeffed defign of aiding the royalifts in Brittany, but without ever really attempting to do fo.† This expedition, which ought to have been

* The emigrants have been treated with a mixture of cruelty and good-nature by the Englifh government, for which it is very difficult to account, unlefs by fuppofing that they infpired pity, but not confidence, or that the minifter had no fixed plan of operations. Be that as it may, the emigrants might have ferved the ca fe of the coalefced powers very ef-fectually. They fhould have been confidered as a feparate body, and treated with upon a certain bafis, as independent powers treat. The reafon of this is, that their interett would then have led them to put every means to work, and ftrain every nerve to fucceed; at prefent they know not what is their interest.

† This affair, it will be faid, like moft others, has two ways of being viewed. The people of the Vendee were to have fecured fome fea port for our arms and troops to be landed at, and in that cafe we fhould have affifted them ; but it is a fact, that our preparations were fo publicly made, and fo long in making, that the forces of the convention came down in fuch numbers as to render it impeffible. Befides, it was never troops that were wanted, ftrangers would have only ferved to hinder the republicans from joining the royal-ifts ; money, ftores, and arms, were what fhould have been fent.

execut-

executed, but never made public, was made notorioufly public, and never executed. The confequence was, as might be expected, that the royalifts were foon after attacked with all the vigour that the convention could difplay; and what might have reftored royalty to France was only productive of carnage and bloodfhed to the almoft entire extinction of the unfortunate men who had trufted to promifes of affiftance from England.

Time and opportunity were loft, and if experience can inftruct, when it is attended with misfortune, there is not a doubt but that long ago the different leaders of the cabinets of Europe are convinced of their error.

Thofe who at the beginning of the war expected fuccefs would attend the combined arms, counted chiefly upon the diforders and divifions of France. Thefe diforders and divifions took place, but the combined powers did not turn them to advantage; fo that the miferable people who had revolted were obliged to fubmit to their cruel tyrants, and, if now not more unanimous than before with refpect to their own government, they are perfectly unanimous in refolving never again to depend upon the allies for fupport.

Thofe who look upon the defpotifm of Robefpierre and the guillotine, as being the caufe of the violent exertions of the French nation, furely then miftake the cafe. The unanimity of the French nation proceeded from the defpair to which thofe were reduced who had feen Lyons unaffifted, Toulon evacuated, and the Vendee ruined and laid waste, becaufe the Englifh had eftablifhed a camp of parade, and menaced an invafion from Jerfey, Guernfey, and the Ifle of Wight. The example of thofe unfortunate places which had been fubdued, were the caufe of men in France unanimoufly fubmitting to Robefpierre, and the cruelty which he exercifed was the confequence of his triumph, from which refulted the implicit obedience given to his orders, and the violent efforts of the next campaign.

The party of Robefpierre grew ftronger every day during the fummer, becaufe anarchy found fupporters, and thofe who wifhed for order found none. Some of the arrefted members found means to efcape, and the trial of thofe who remained in cuftody, and who were after fome time, transferred from their own houfes to a prifon, was commenced, but it went flowly on.

In proportion as Robefpierre's party gained ftrength, vigorous meafures were taken againft their enemies, and a revolutionary tribunal was inftituted, where a packed jury, paid witneffes, and judges who were totally at the command of the ruling party, daily put to death numbers without any crime proved, and frequently without any particular reafon affigned.

CHAP.

CHAP. III.

Robespierre's party acquires solidity—Massacres at Lyons—Trial of the queen—Her character justified from the scandalous imputations spread over all Europe on her account—Her expenses an example both to princes and people—Unfair trial and execution of the Brissotines—Robespierre reigns without controul—Marat assassinated—Great number of prisoners in the different jails of France—Danger of being a proprietor—D'Orleans, Barnave, Manuel, and Bailly, executed—Fête of Reason—Hebert's party starts up in opposition to Robespierre—System of terror completely established—Hebert's party falls—Danton's party falls—Robespierre's power again re-established without controul.

THE reduction of Lyons was the first thing that gave a solid foundation to the power of the ruling party. The national commissaries, who were sent there, exceeded in their cruel vengeance every thing that history relates. When an unruly soldiery enters into a conquered city, the desire of plunder and the thirst of revenge may, as it has on many occasions, lead to excesses which make nature shudder, but then they have been excesses which all men condemn, and which even

their

their perpetrators do not prefume or attempt excufing.   The maffacres at Lyons were done by
men in cold blood as matters of juftice and
right ;* they boafted of them to the convention,
and the letters of the commiffaries were filled
with execrations againft the inhabitants of the
devoted city, and profeffions of their own loyalty
to the nation, to liberty and equality.

Two hundred citizens, traitors, fay they, have
fuffered death this day, and to-morrow there will
fall double that number; the prifons are full,
and in the lower cells are barrels of gunpowder,
on the fmalleft fignal of evafion they will be all
blown in the air.†

When the rulers of France began to conceive
a hope of remaining mafters, the deputies who
had efcaped were declared out-laws and deferving
death, wherever they fhould be found.   Gorfas
was the firft who was caught, and he was guillotined in twenty-four hours after: this was
what they called the initiative of the decapitation
of deputies, and prepared the way for the trials
of the others.

---

* It was before Lyons was taken, and indeed before it revolted openly, that the commiffaries againft whom Briffot
complains infulted the people of Lyons by their cruelties and
exceffes.   After they had put in prifon the fathers of families, they obliged their wives and children, who came to implore pity and pardon, to dance, to drink, and to fing.
The commiffioners, after its reduction, were ftill worfe.

† The only reafon affigned for not blowing up all the prifoners in Lyons at once, was the danger to the executioners
themfelves.   Grape fhot, mufket fhot, and the guillotine,
were all employed, but the commiffaries were continually la-
menting the flownefs of the juftice.

To

To prepare the people for the judgment of the detained reprefentatives, and to divert them from the lofs of Valenciennes, the convention thought proper to gratify their thirft of blood and its own vengeance, by bringing to the laft punifhment the unfortunate queen.

Vengeance and favage ferocity were, however, on this occafion, completely humiliated, by the calm, mild, and dignified behaviour of an injured and infulted princefs. Never has the world been witnefs to a fcene where more modeft and becoming dignity was difplayed by the accufed, nor where lefs regard was paid to decency, truth, humanity, and juftice, by the accufers.

All Europe had been filled with libels, and afperfions againft the queen of France, even in the days of her power and profperity, and what the attachment of her friends could never accomplifh, the infamous accufations of her enemies effected in a moment. Calumny was filenced, and not a doubt left with refpect to purity of a reputation fo often and fo unjuftly attacked.

Neither offers of reward, nor threats of vengeance, had been able to procure one fingle proof of criminality or vice againft the widow of the unfortunate king, whom, in order to find guilty, though a ftranger, unprotected and alone, her enemies faw themfelves reduced to the neceffity of employing the moft difgraceful, abominable, and abfurd, of all expedients; her infant fon was intoxicated, and at the fuggeftion of that mifcreant Hebert, whofe name alone brings to mind every thing that is vicious or wicked, the

affectionate

affectionate careffes of a mother to a child of nine years of age were conftrued by thofe monfters into a crime, the committing of which would be unnatural, if it were not impoffible.*

The queen of France had long fuffered every infult and humiliation which it was poffible for her enemies to invent, and certainly if Frenchmen had retained any of that humanity and feeling which they pretended to poffefs, the depart-

* Hebert publifhed a paper, called the *Pere du Chefne,* in which oaths, blafphemies, and obfcenities, filled up two-thirds, at leaft, of every fentence; it would be neceffary to have feen a fpecimen of that precious morfel, in order to form an idea of the talents of its author, and the refined tafte of the Parifian fans culottes. Well, this fame Hebert propofed to bring the young prince into court and queftion him, after having him in a ftate of intoxication; not that even then he could be brought to accufe his mother, but queftions were to be afked in fuch a way, that the anfwers might be conftrued unfavourably for the mother. This artifice was fo glaring, that even the judges of the revolutionary tribunal objected to it; the fpectators, they faid, would fee through it: an examination was then fabricated by Hebert and fome of his companions. Even the fatellites of the tribunal found this accufation too abominable and abfurd, to which the queen very properly refufed to anfwer, but by an appeal to the hearts and feelings of *all mothers.*

Hebert was the projector of the worfhip of reafon; his miftrefs perfonated the goddefs of reafon; but Robefpierre's feaft, in honour of the Supreme Being, did away all this, the defpot having previoufly fent both the oracle and the goddefs to the guillotine. Paris was never difpofed to be more gay than when the Pere du Chefne mounted the fcaffold, even the executioner mocked and infulted him, to the great delight of the fpectators. Such circumftances lead to a hope, that all fentiment of juftice is not yet banifhed from the minds even of the Parifians, and that the day may yet come, when all the companions of his crimes will all be treated in the fame manner.

ments

ments and the whole of France would have joined in demanding for her that refpect which is due
to misfortune, and that juftice which is due to a
defencelefs ftranger. Such a ftep would have
been highly honourable. There was no reafon
for not doing fo, as it could have been attended
neither with tumult nor danger. But the French
nation has fhewn, that with a fuperabundant vanity, and pretenfions to every virtue, it poffeffes
none ; and that it would be better for defencelefs
innocence to be in a cavern of robbers in a foreft,
than to be before the revolutionary tribunal of
Paris.

As the character, the rank, and the accom-
plifhments of this unfortunate queen, have infpired her advocates with a warmth of expreffion
that is very natural and excufable, though ill-
fitted to convince the malicious, it may not be
improper to prove, as far as probable evidence
can go, that the queen of France was totally irreproachable on the fubject of fidelity to the marriage bed. This digreffion, it is hoped, will be
excufed, when it is remembered, that many of
thofe who once flourifhed in the fun-fhine of her
favour, contributed by their own levity of conduct, as well as by their filence to fupport calumnies which it would have been their duty and
their intereft to contradict; and when we have
the example of whole volumes being written to vindicate the characters of queens, who,
though perhaps more beautiful, were certainly
not more accomplifhed, were lefs unfortunate,
and much more liable to reproach, than the
daughter of Maria Terefa. It will be a relief to
us, after contemplating the horrors and villanies

of

of men, to dwell for a moment on the virtues of an amiable woman.

We ought, in the firft place, to confider, that innocence, unlefs when the charges are direct, can never be proved by pofitive evidence; we muft be contented with probable evidence, as the nature of things does not admit of any other.

The court of France was in a very corrupted and diforderly ftate when the late queen arrived and was married to the Dauphin. The example of a king, who in his latter days, had given a loofe to debauchery, was followed with eagernefs amongft a nobility naturally given to the fame fort of vice.

At that time Madame du Barry,* raifed from being upon the town, in a very inferior ftile, to be miftrefs of the king, difpenfed the royal favour amongft the courtiers, and of confequence, the young German princefs made her entry in the midft of cabals, intrigues, and enemies. Open, amiable, and generous, fhe foon had friends, but innocent and unfufpecting fhe expofed herfelf to the flander of her enemies, from which thofe friends could not protect her.

When, after the death of his grandfather, Louis XVI. began to reign, his fimple manner of life, his want of tafte for the pleafures and diffipations of the court, contrafted with the love

* Madame du Barry conducted herfelf, however, on moft occafions, with a moderation and prudence that did her great honour, the old king was not fo prudent as his young miftrefs, and often not fo juft.

of

of fplendor carried too far, and of gaiety which the queen did not attempt to conceal, gave room for the courtiers at Verfailles and the people of Paris, fo much addicted to fcandal, to fufpicion, and fo much accuftomed to find fcandal and fufpicion, juftified by the loofenefs of their own conduct, to raife thofe reports, which fpreading all over Europe, tarnifhed her character.*

The French always judge of others by themfelves, it is the failing of their nation, and they did not confider, that a princefs defcended from one of the moft illuftrious and the proudeft families in Europe, and who was accufed by themfelves of having too much Auftrian pride, would have been irreparably humiliated and ruined, had fhe put herfelf for a moment in the power of any perfon upon this delicate fubject.

But levity and the national character of the French did not alone contribute to fpread and circulate thefe reports, the Duke of Orleans, and all his adherents and affociates exerted themfelves to give plaufibility and probability to defamation ; and particular cicumftances which malignity had contrived, were circulated by unfufpicious credulity.

The levellers, who began to wifh for that fyftem which they have fince feen realized, feized upon this occafion to degrade royalty ; the king of France was laughed at and turned into ridi-

---

* The turn of the French for this fort of fcandal was fo great that by becoming univerfal, it feemed to have rendered their manner of fpreading it an affair of courfe.

cule, and before the revolution began no two perfons in the kingdom were fo much mifunder-ftood as to their real characters as the king and queen.

A myfterious affair of a trick played upon the Cardinal de Rohan, about a diamond necklace,* by fome of thofe fortune-hunters, male and fe-male, who fwarmed in Paris, in which the queen had been perfonated by a Mamoifelle Oliva, who refembled her confiderably in features and perfon, made a noife all over Europe, and as this affair was never properly fearched to the bottom and explained, many people believed the queen was actually one of the adventurers who duped the cardinal.

In France, as the firft impreflion is generally yielded to, things are feldom much examined and compared, otherwife the queen fhould either have been acquitted of this, or, if not, acquitted of the accufation of lavifhing away millions every week; for if fhe had fuch fums at her command, how could any one fuppofe that a lady who never fhowed that fhe would ftoop to play a mean part,

* This affair of the necklace was merely a trick practifed on the cardinal, who had been ambaffador at Vienna when the fcheme of the marriage of Louis XVI. firft took place.— He had tried rather to prevent the union, and as he did not fucceed was not in the good graces of the parties after it had taken place. The cardinal had always been furrounded with adventurers, who pretended to have difcovered the art of making gold, and other valuable fecrets in chemiftry; a plan was formed by fome of thefe adventurers to dupe him out of a great fum of money, upon the idea that the queen wifhed to be poffeffed of this necklace, and that if he could procure it, he would get into favour at court.

fhould,

fhould, for the fake of fo fmall a fum, put herfelf into the hands of her enemies, and in fhort, become the afociate of half a dozen miferables, who would probably finifh by dividing the fpoils among themfelves? this was ridiculous. The ftory of the necklace* would have been barely probable if the queen had been a mean fpirited woman, who had not any means of procuring money to defray her extravagancies.

Such were the caufes that operated principally in making injurious reports be fpread, and the queen, who though preferving dignity, through which a confiderable fhare of pride could be feen, was good-natured in the extreme, was unfufpecting, familiar, and generous; fhe had banifhed from her private focieties the ftiff etiquette of a court, which feemed the more ftrange in a princefs who came from a country where court etiquette is carried to an extreme; this gave a fort of probability to the accufations which were brought againft her.

The facts, however, were quite different; the queen was generous and loved power, but fhe

---

* The value of the necklace was only 1,400,000 livres, or 60,000l. fterling, and could not fell for half that fum; it was ridiculous for thofe fame perfons, who accufed the queen of giving fuch large fums to her favourites, to fuppofe fhe would go fhares with fix or feven fwindlers, for fuch a fum as this; befides, fuch a charge required fome proof, and none was ever produced.

Another report was, that fhe did this to be revenged of the cardinal; this is, if poffible, ftill more inconceivable, and requires no anfwer, after the difpofition to pardon her enemies which the queen had on fo many occafions, both before and during the revolution manifefted. *To remember, but not to retaliate,* was known to be her maxim with refpect to enemies.

had

had no other means of gratifying thofe, which were her ruling paffions, than by preferving the affection and confidence of her hufband; and it may be afferted, without danger of being contradicted by thofe who approached thefe two perfonages the neareft, that the king was literally in love with the queen *(amoureux d'elle)* during the whole of their union, and that though her turn for expenfe vexed him to the heart, in other refpects, fhe enjoyed his full confidence and efteem, and it is certain that the queen made no other ufe of this afcendancy fo obtained over her hufband, than to make her friends and thofe around her happy.

Thofe who imagine, that the king of France would have fubmitted peaceably to any thing that looked like a ferious indignity offered, knew nothing of his character.* Like moft good-natured, plain, honeft, men, the king was quite ungovernable when he found people were unjuft or treated him ill; he then became unmanageable and obftinate to a violent degree, and if the queen had once committed an *irreparable* fault, he certainly would not have pardoned her, and from that inftant fhe would have loft her power over him.

Thofe again, who think that the queen could have been guilty of infidelity without the king knowing any thing of the matter, are ftill more

* Since the revolution, if the king did not fhew this difpofition, he only acted like other prifoners, who know that ill-humour only doubles the evil, but when things ufed to vex him from wilful extravagance or mifmanagement, few people were more difficult to keep within bounds. This is often the cafe with well-meaning men.

miftaken.

miftaken. We have obferved, that fhe commenced her career at Verfailles in the midft of enemies, and that fhe never was without fuch, the flanders which we are refuting is a proof; thofe enemies never loft fight of her motions, and if the fmalleft ground had been given for ferious fufpicions, it would immediately have been turned by them to their advantage.

Thofe who * were friends to the queen, and who depended upon her bounty, or, at leaft, who profitted of her bounty, were as much interefted in watching her conduct, to *prevent* any thing that might deftroy her influence and blaft their hopes, as her enemies were to watch *for* fuch an event ; fo that on all hands the queen was furrounded with fpies, and the fharpeft of all fpies, thofe who were looking after their own intereft.

Nothing, therefore, would have been fo foolifh or unnatural in a princefs who had ambition, who knew her dignity and fupported it well, though not by ftiffnefs and etiquette, as to have rifked all, and run fo headlong into a fcene of difgrace and humiliation, as nothing could be more impoffible than to efcape difcovery and the fatal confequences,

Scandal, fupported by envy and felf-intereft, firft robbed the queen of France of her reputation, and they were facilitated in their enterprife by the levity of the age, and by the high rank

---

* It is a great reproach to many gentlemen who were protected by this amiable queen, to have permitted fufpicions to be whifpered that difgraced fo generous a friend.

and profperity of their victim. ' A cruel reverfe and the unexampled fortitude, temper, and patience with which fhe bore it, have however proved, that fhe was an affectionate wife, a tender mother, and a princefs who knew, on all occafions, how to fupport her own dignity better than how to punifh her enemies.*

In aiding to defend a character which has been fo unwarrantably traduced, it would be injuftice to herfelf and the world not to add, that though blamelefs as to the things of which fhe was accufed, fhe was not fo with regard to her expenfes ; they were great and without arrangement ; fhe was generous often without judgement, and her conduct was by no means a model to be held out for princes, whofe real glory is in alleviating the burdens of their people, in rendering nations rich and eafy, and not in taking upon themfelves to diftinguifh individuals, and enrich them at the expenfe of the whole.†

This

---

* To all thefe ought to be added, that if there had been any guilt, her enemies would have found the means of bringing it home on the trial ; they had the inclination, and they could not want the means ; but this is fo evident a vindication arifing from the trial itfelf, that it is not neceffary to infift upon it : that the queen was innocent is clear—the above vindication is meant to fhew *how fhe was fuppofed to be guilty.*

† There is here a ftriking refemblance between the conduct of princes and of democratic leaders, although they are in their effects diamatrically oppofite. Princes take upon themfelves to *fufpect* certain people of having more merit than others, they make favourites of them, and tax the nation to enrich them. Democrats take upon themfelves to fufpect certain perfons of crimes, and of turning their punifhment to the advantage of the nation, confifcate their property,

This unfortunate queen is a terrible example to princes, who feeling themſelves generouſly diſpoſed, turn the feelings of a good heart from their country and exert them upon individuals. Ingratitude from many individuals, and vengeance from her ſubjects, were the conſequences of this conduct; let it therefore, be a leſſon to princes, and let it alſo be a leſſon to people; let princes form wiſe rules for their conduct, and let people without either anger or ill-humour fix rules for princes; let there be grandeur of conduct on both ſides, let them be great in their generoſity, but let it have fixed bounds which it cannot paſs.

There are many things that might be ſaid to excuſe the queen of France for thoſe errors and expenſes into which ſhe run; her youth, her inexperience, her being a *ſtranger*, and not knowing the conſequences of what ſhe was about; but, above all, the intrigues and extravagancies with which, at her firſt arrival, ſhe found herſelf ſurrounded, are the principal circumſtances that tend to diminiſh the fault, but nothing can take it entirely away. She was too expenſive, and thoſe expenſes haſtened the cruel revolution which awaited herſelf, her family, and her kingdom.

property. In the one caſe, part of the property of the nation is *confiſcated* to enrich an individual, choſen by caprice for the purpoſe; in the other, individual property is confiſcated to enrich the nation. The one is wrong, the other is abominable; and in each caſe it is the ruler gratifying his own feelings at the expenſe of juſtice. Surely thoſe Jacobins who cry out againſt princes will be ſatisfied with this note.—— This hiſtory is not written to flatter any party, but with a deſign to ſhew things as they are.

When

When the people had been for the second
time gratified with the fight of expiring royalty;
they were confidered by Robefpiere and his
friends as being prepared for the exhibition intended of the Briffotines. The accufations
brought againft this party were juft as void of
foundation as thofe brought againft the queen,
but as the philofophers fell a facrifice to their
own principles, and to their own practices, they
do not require our pity; they perfifted juft as
obftinately in the principles that brought themfelves to the guillotine as their enemies did, but
then they did not intend that they fhould have
had fuch confequences with refpect to themfelves.*

The trial of Briffot, and twenty-one of his
companions, could not have ended in condemnation to death, according to the laws of the men
who judged them, but the method practifed every
day againft the innocent perfons who were
brought to be fummarily judged by this tribunal
were employed againft them † alfo.

The

* Certainly, according to republican principles, and even
according to thofe of liberty and equality, Briffot's party did
not merit death ; as, however, by all other principles they
had merited it an hundred times, their death was a victory
to thofe who wifh to fee order eftablifhed in France ; it was
the firft great ftep towards the purging their miferable
country of thofe men who had ruined it.

† By way of ridicule, Briffot was placed on an elevated
feat during the trial, with all his partifans around him ; he
appeared pretty collected and tranquil. The prefident of the
tribunal, in order to fecond the clubifts who petitioned the
convention to fhorten the proceedings, wrote, that nothing
could equal the loquacity of the accufed, that the trial had
lafted

The firſt ſtep was for the violent Jacobins and members of the club of the Cordeliers to extort from the convention a decree, which abridged, as they termed it, thoſe forms *which enchained the conſciences of jurymen and ſtifled conviction.* It was decreed, that the jury might ſhorten the proceedings and refuſe to hear witneſſes, by declaring to the judges " that their opinion is formed." By this means, ſay they, you may for the future elude the queſtion of forms.

When this decree for eluding forms was paſſed, the mob carried it to the tribunal, and the obe‑ dient jury declared the proceſs was at an end, and condemned to death Briſſot, Vergniaud, Genſonè, Duprat, Valazé,* Lehardy, Ducos, Boyer Fonfrede, Boileau, Gardien, Duchatel, Sillery, Fouchet,† Duperry, La Source, Carra, Beauvais, Mainvielle,

laſted five days, and that only nine witneſſes had been heard ; that there was no reaſon why there might not be 400 witneſ‑ ſes brought forward, and that therefore there was little hopes of finiſhing.

Engliſhmen, contraſt this conduct with that of your judges and juries in criminal caſes, and you will at leaſt ſuſpend experiments of reform, till you ſee how a nation, once in the convulſions that a revolution brings on, may get rid of them. If civil cauſes in England were tried with as much regard to juſtice as criminal cauſes are, we ſhould then indeed be a happy people. This merits inveſtigation, and demands it.

* Valaze cut his throat in priſon ; he had been an officer in the regiment of French guards, and aided the revolt at the beginning of the revolution.

† Fouchet was an abbé before the revolution and became a biſhop ; he opened *a ball for political lectures* in the beginning of the revolution ; and to excite the people againſt ariſtocrats, he ſaid, that it was the ariſtocracy of the Jews that

Mainvielle, Antiboul, Vigée, and Lacafe, as authors and accomplices of a confpiracy which exifted againft the unity and indivifibility of the republic, againft the liberty and fafety of the French people. Their property to be confifcated to the republic, and the execution to take place, &c.

The day after, the 31ft of October, the execution took place, with the unufual ceremony of the difcharge of artillery.* The people, who ufually attend fuch ceremonies, were uncommonly gay and pleafed when they faw fo many of the reprefentatives mount the fcaffold; and in this, if they fhewed no humanity, they fhewed at leaft that fome idea of juftice ftill remained.

condemned Jefus Chrift. Clootz turned the tables againft him at laft, and faid, that Jefus Chrift was an ariftocrat, for he ordered to render unto Cæfar what was Cæfar's, and fpoke of lords and mafters; this, faid the Pruffian philofopher, is againft liberty and equality.

* The condemned deputies cried *Vive la republique!* when they were on the fcaffold. Briffot preferved his ufual *fang froid*, and remained filent; he was guillotined laft of all.— Thirty-feven minutes were only neceffary for the execution.

The ruling party in France has uniformly purfued one method with accufed perfons; they are always encouraged with hopes of life till the moment fentence is going to be paffed, and after that they are never allowed to fpeak. This rule was never more ufeful than on the prefent occafion; otherwife, the loquacity of the condemned might have produced fome difcoveries not much to the advantage of their accufers.

When Danton and his party were guillotined in their turn the year after, they were condemned at three o'clock in the after noon, and at fix the fame evening mounted the fcaffold. From ancient companions this treatment was a little hard.

It

It was during the detention of thofe deputies that Marat was affaflinated by a moft extraordinary woman, who appears to have imagined, that that Monfter was the only one in the convention. Charlotte Cordé will ever be efteemed for her heroifm and fortitude, but it will always be lamented, that a woman of fuch courage and good intention, fhould be led to commit affaflination; and that by the eternal harangues made in favour of Brutus,* and particularly by the man whom fhe affaflinated.

The fall of Briffot's party difconcerted the Jacobins in all other countries. A fimilarity of views had connected feveral of thofe leaders with *the patriots* of other nations, fome of whom boafted of a perfonal acquaintance with Briffot, and all of whom confidered him as a model for a revolutionary leader. So cruel a fate excited great uneafinefs among them. The revolution now began to devour its own children; it had long ago put to flight its fathers, and from the national convention to the fartheft corners of Europe, revolutionifts inquired with eagernefs *when this butchery of the deputies would end?*† In France they butchered thofe who afked the quef-

---

* Mirabeau was the firft who was called the French Brutus; fince his time many Brutus's have appeared. We have feen fathers demanding the condemnation of their fons for finging royalift fongs, by way of imitating the Romans. This cannot be attributed to any thing but that derangement of intellects called fanaticifm.

† A plot was contrived in confequence of this queftion having been afked, and feveral deputies, Merlin, Chabot, and Bazire, amongft others, were guillotined for this childifh but anti-civic anxiety.

tion, and who explained themfelves, that it was
not from any anxiety about the deputies, but becaufe it would be an amufement to the ariftocrats,
that they wifhed the butchering to ceafe. The
amufement of the ariftocrats, however, was a
lame excufe, for every day faw them mount by
dozens the fcaffold, and they had ftill more reafon to weep for the lofs of friends, than to laugh
at the deftruction of their enemies.

About this time there were above fix thoufand
prifoners in the prifons of Paris, and the other jails
of the kingdom were proportionably full. The
total number of perfons confined in France was
eftimated at above two hundred thoufand, of
which number were the richeft bankers, merchants, and manufacturers.

Equality was the end propofed, but an agrarian
law could not fuit a corrupted people; it was
thought much better to attack fortunes individually, by accufing the poffeffors, and confifca-
ting the property; this was done in all the great
towns in the kingdom. But as the acts of injuftice and cruelty became fo multiplied over the
whole face of the country, it is impoffible to
give any fort of form or order to the detail of
what was going on; the reader is therefore re-
ferred to note of detached facts at the end
[*Note* Q.] of the work, where it will be feen in
what a fummary manner people were arrefted,
judged, and executed.

The life of a man was now no longer confidered as of any importance, and therefore guilt
or innocence was fcarcely inquired into. All
                                         thofe

thofe who had no protectors in the Jacobins clubs were liable to fall, and thofe who had any enemies in them were certain of their fate.

Moft part of the people who had any property, had fome good-natured friends amongft the Jaco-bins, who wifhed to eafe them of it; and as all confifcated property was put up to fale, and fold upon very eafy terms, the way to become a man's heir was to accufe him, and have him guillotined. The only limit fet to this practice was, the fear of *becoming a proprietor*, which could not fail to bring on the fame fate fooner or later, fo that the danger of poffeffing property was now the only thing that afforded any protection to the proprietor.*

With refpect to the cultivators of land in France, they were forced to work, but they were alfo forced to give up the fruits of their labour at a fixed price paid in affignats, and then they were put upon an allowance of fo much bread for each perfon every decade (or ten days). The flaves in the Weft India colonies enjoy more liberty than thofe poor peafants, who were obliged to call out *vive la liberté*, in the midft of their mifery, and a murmer againft their rulers was fufficient to have them dragged from their families, and thrown into prifon, and probably led to the guillotine.

To add to all thefe misfortunes, bread and nourifhment were almoft wanting. Paris was the beft fupplied, ond there were but one hun-

---

* It is difficult to conceive this *maximum* of wretchednefs; proprietors, in France, were fituated like a dog with a filver collar in one of the bye ftreets of St. Giles's.

dred

dred and fifty cattle flaughtered every week. There were almoft as many men flaughtered as there were oxen ! !

The Jacobin club continued to dictate to the affembly, and the affembly continued to fpread terror and defolation through France.   That terrible period was now arrived when the hiftory of the republic offered nothing but a daily repetition of robbery and murder, and when robbery and murder were fcarcely any longer objects of hatred or of terror. The fpectators had long been dead to the feelings of humanity on thofe occafions ; they were now dead to every other feeling, and to every emotion.   Not a day paffed that the bloody tribunal did not fend victims to the fcaffold, and the populace went to look on as an affair of habitude, and as a method of paffing time.   Even the unfortunate fufferers feemed to have loft their feelings, and a few excepted, neither fear nor grief was to be perceived on their countenances.

Not an hour paft that injuftices were not committed, that would raife general indignation in any other country in Europe, and afford matter bf difcuffion for months, and perhaps for years. The names of the moft part of the victims in France were forgotten in lefs than half an hour, and their crimes were never inquired into at all.

A few exceptions, however, are to be made to this general uniformity. The Duke of Orleans, long fo active and fo powerful, was brought to Paris from Marfeilles, where he had been imprifoned in confequence of a decree for imprifoning
all

all the princes of the houfe of Bourbon. Neither
the name of Egalité, by which, at his own requeft, Manuel had chriftened him, nor his for-
mal declaration, that he was the fon of a coach-
man, and therefore not of the royal blood; not
even his voting for the death of the king could
fkreen him from the vengeance of Hebert and
Danton. He was accufed of being the accomplice of Briffot's party; this was fufficient to
condemn him before the revolutionary tribunal,
he was guillotined the fame day, and died with
more fortitude than thofe who knew his cowardice on many different occafions expected.* The
leffon which the fate of this prince gives to men,
who, in a high rank of life, difturb the peace of
their country from motives of ambition or of vengeance, is written in fuch legible characters, that
it requires no commentary. In his fhort paffage
from the prifon to the fcaffold, he was infulted by
the fame fcoundrels whom he had formerly paid;
and the general contempt into which he had

* The Duke of Orleans was a coward from calculation,
rather than from nature. When there was any mode of
efcaping, or when he had an alternative, he never rifked
himfelf. The fecrets of which he was mafter, induced his
enemies to keep him in hopes till the laft. When he arrived
in Paris from Marfeilles, he was actually perfuaded that he
was to be again re-inftated in his palace. As foon as the
fentence was paffed, the execution was haftened, and the
firft prince of the blood went thither in a cart, accompanied
by a ftock-broker, an under delegate of a department, and
a journeyman flater ! ! This was at leaft that equality which
he had fo long pretended to feek after ! !

Among the crowd was one of the duke's agents, well
known in the firft two years of the revolution, St. Huruge.
This fellow was, it is faid, particularly vociferous in infulting
the duke.

fallen,

fallen, was evident in the countenances of all the
fpectators.

To the Duke of Orleans fucceeded M. Bailly,
the former mayor of Paris, and Manuel and Barnave. The rulers of the prefent time, feemed determined to deftroy all thofe who had ever enjoyed any degree of popular favour. The deaths
of Manuel and Barnave could be regretted by
none; that of M. Bailly was different, he had
been the caufe of much evil, but he was ignorant of the great extent of the evil of which he
had laid the foundation.*   A good deal is to be
attri-

* M. Bailly, of whom much has already been faid, becaufe he was of the firft who protected infurrection, and
brought it into vogue, was efteemed before the revolution
for feveral publications, particularly his *Lettres fur l'Atlantide
et l' Hiftoire de l'Aftronomie.* The fudden elevation of Bailly
to the place of prefident of the affembly, and after that to
the mayoralty, had a great effect upon literary men, not only in France, but all over Europe. A revolution feemed to
be the triumph of genius, and above all of literary merit.
His punifhment operated likewife upon the minds of the people in different countries; if the virtue, the good fortune,
and the talents of Bailly, could not fave him from the fcaffold, faid they, it would have been better for him to have
continued to live quietly on his penfion of ten thoufand livres
a year, and not revolt againft the king who gave it him,   It
would, indeed, have been better. M. Bailly was dragged
to punifhment with particular marks of infamy, becaufe he
was condemned for having affaffinated the people in the
Champ de Mars. It would feem that fome particular infatuation prevented fuch men from quitting France, where
their fyftem of government was juft as much out of date as
that of Louis the Fourteenth. The fate of M. de Cler-
monte Tonnerre on the 10th of Auguft, and of all the con-
ftitutionalifts, whom their enemies could lay hold of, might
have ferved as a warning to him, that nothing was to be expected but death, if he remained; the Jacobin fyftem had
perpetually

attributed to his vanity and ambition, but more to his ignorance. Though a man of learning and of fcience, he was totally unfkilled in the art of leading men to happinefs ; he had fallen into all the miftakes to which the declaration of rights leads, and his errors might have been forgiven, had he not been felfifh and ungrateful.

On the fame day that this ancient magiftrate, aftronomer, and member of the academy, was fuffering for his having become a politician, a fête was celebrated in the cathedral of Paris, to the honour of reafon, virtue, and philofophy. At this fête Hebert prefided, and the bifhop of Paris officiated to the fans culottes at Paris, in the midft of a fcene of licentioufnefs and ridicule.* The intention was to banifh religion from France

perpetually been to turn with implacable vengeance againft thofe who had once been popular, but were not ready to follow them in all their extremes. This plan had been regularly followed from the beginning, and his not having feen that, fhews that M. Bailly was by no means, in political affairs, a man of profound knowledge ; on the contrary, he feems not to have at all conceived the progreffive motion from bad to worfe, and from the Capitol to the Tarpeian rock.

* At Lyons, the *feaft of the afs* merits notice for its fingularity, all the conftituted authorities, the revolutionary tribunal, and the guards, affembled at the Hotel de Ville with an afs. Commiffaries were fent to feize the plate in all the churches ; the poor animal was then dreffed in a bifhop's robes, with a mitre on his head, and a bible attached to its tail ; the facred vafes, &c. were put on its back, and followed by a proceffion of the club, the municipality, &c. it was then marched to the Place de Bellecour, where it was burnt, along with the bibles, prayer books, robes, &c. with this infcription, remains of fuperftition ; the whole attendants calling out, *vive les fans culottes.*

entirely; as that had been very nearly accomplished already, the subftitution of what they called reafon was thought neceffary, that on the decades people might have fomething to do, and not fall back through idlenefs into their ancient errors.

Amongft the fufferers by the guillotine, the generals of the republic made a very confpicuous figure. Even Houchard, who commanded at Dunkirk, when the Englifh under the Duke of York were repulfed, was obliged to lay his head upon the block. As to thofe who had not been fuccefsful, it was perfectly natural that they fhould be executed, and accordingly very few of them efcaped.

Robefpierre did not, however, yet reign alone, and what is more, was not the moft fanguinary of thofe who did reign. Hebert, and fome of his companions were worfe ftill, and Robefpierre was frequently obliged to interfere to prevent their crueltics from going too far.* Robefpierre was the moft methodically and unfeelingly cruel, but

* Hebert had repeatedly demanded the death of the remains of the unfortunate royal family, and declared himfelf incapable of containing his rage when he faw the fifter of Louis Capet (the virtuous Madame Elizabeth) in exiftence, after fo many crimes. Her features, faid he, are a picture of her atrocious heart. Robefpierre had treated Hebert as a fool; but a man who was capable of fuch IMPRUDENT denunciation, was not fit for an affociate, and he was dangerous as a rival. Robefpierre could fcarcely expect that his own phyfiognomy would be fafe from the attacks of this inconceivable difciple of Lavater, and accordingly, as foon as he found himfelf attacked by him, his vengeance was prompt and fevere. Hebert had been the principle caufe of the death of Bailly, and the other friends of the conftitution.

                                                    he

he does not feem to have been cruel from enjoyment in the flaughter of his fellow men, but from
fyftem.* Hebert, Petion, Manuel, and many
others, feem to have enjoyed cruel actions, and
committed many merely for the fake of the pleafure, which their diabolical minds received; but †
Robefpierre did never give any figns of fuch a
difpofition; cool, interefted cruelties feem to
have been what he excelled in; he would have
facrificed three-fourths of the human race to
have reigned over thofe who remained, but it
would not have given him any pleafure to affift
at their execution.

The cool, calculating murderer is, however,
the moft terrible of all,‡ when he has it in his
power,

* In the back ground all this time was the Abbé Seyes,
he was one ftep beyond Robefpierre in cold, fyftematic cruelty, and one ftep farther removed than him from the other
party in perfonal vengeance, and cruelty in detail. One
might be apt to attribute to principle, and not to felfifh motives, this *abftract fort of cruelty* of the Abbé Seyes, were it
not that the man who has always lent his aid in council to
the ufurper of the day, muft be very felfifh, and equally
void of all principle.

† The manner in which Petion and Manuel tormented the
king, when that unfortunate monarch was prifoner in the
temple, is a proof of their cruelty in detail. The manner in
which the whole of the royal prifoners were treated, was
only equalled by the particular inftances of cruel mortification, which when either of thofe two went to the prifon, the
king and queen were certain to experience. Charles the
Firft never experienced any thing harfh or hard, in comparifon to what Louis the Sixteenth fuffered.

‡ It was by this cool method of propofing affaffination,
that Robefpierre was enabled to follow out his cruel plans
with order and method. The others went without order,
and fometimes ceafed their crimes for a moment, but Robefpierre

power, and finds it his intereft to be cruel; for as he does not even take the pains to think what it cofts humanity to gratify his views, he does upon the great fcale what others do on the fmall. It was the organization of the fyftem of terror by Robefpierre, that gave Collot d'Herbois the means of maffacreing the inhabitants of Lyons with grape fhot;* that gave le Bon, the national commiffary,

pierre brought it to that pitch, that *every day innocent blood was fhed as certainly as the fun rofe.* There was no method of eluding perfecution and death under the reign of a man who had vowed the deftruction of all his enemies, of all his rivals, and of all thofe whofe reputation or property gave them any fhare of importance. This man had thoufands of agents, and the tribunals were always ready to execute what he ordered. This has been fully proved fince, for as each faction falls to the ground, its crimes are brought to light.

Although the revolutionary tribunal did not acquire all its activity in Paris till the time Robefpierre reigned *alone in Paris;* yet it is to be confidered, that as the other towns in the kingdom had not the fame means of refifting oppreffion that the capital had, an inferior degree of power was fufficient for oppreffing them; befides, Robefpierre and the Jacobin club acted together, fo that any refiftance from the departments was impoffible to be attended with fuccefs. In Paris, on the contrary, the Jacobin club had fome rivals in the other focieties, and of confequence its power was not abfolutely without limit. It is here neceffary to obferve once for all, that though thofe fraternal focieties or clubs differed in their names from the Jacobins, as each had its orators and favourites, yet the whole of them were nearly the fame as to revolutionary and fanguinary principles. With refpect to the world at large, they were all Jacobins alike; with refpect to their favourites alone were they different, and this difference was only perceivable to the people in Paris.

* Collot d'Herbois, and d'Orfiil, two indifferent comedians, who had the management of the affairs at Lyons, put to death three thoufand prifoners with grape fhot. They were all put into one large fquare, all the avenues were fhut up, and then the cannons began to play upon the miferable victims. Many
were

commiffary, the means of exercifing unheard-of cruelties in the north of France, and Talien at Bourdeaux. It was to the fyftematic cruelty of Robefpierre that the exceffes of Carrier, the execrable Carrier, at Nantes were owing, when men, women, and children were drowned in boats without refpect to age or fex, or guilt or innocence.

The fyftem of terror was fupported by fwarms of commiffaries and agents, with unlimited powers, who went through the whole of France ;*
their

were only wounded, becaufe when once they fell from any fevere wound, they feldom were again ftruck by the fhot ; thefe were, after languifhing, put to death by pikes and the bayonet. Many were thrown into the Rhone half dead, and carried off by that river.

An affectionate wife who implored mercy for her hufband, was chained to the guillotine while he was executed.

Le Bon has been, fince he was commiffary in the north, and fince the death of Robefpierre, denounced for numerous acts of wanton cruelty. As for thofe of Carrier, at Nantes, they were fo enormous, and proved in fo diftinct and fatis-factory a manner, that they merit particular notice, and are to be found in the tranfactions after the death of Robefpierre, when the change of men and meafures led to their difcovery.

* Befides the clubs which were fo numerous, and which were centers of re-union every where for the robbers, there were eftimated to have been above fifty thoufand agents of one fort or another, going about like roaring lions, feeking whom they might devour. Barrere complained in the convention, that befides thefe regular and good agents, there were men in red bonnets, with pantaloons and long fabres, who collected the taxes, and put the money received in their pockets. He fuppofed thefe tax gatherers to be Hebertifts ; but let them be of what fect they might, it is pretty clear, that the frogs and locufts were not near fo terrible, and they could not be much more numerous than the patriotic banditti
who

their great bufinefs was, to find out the fufpe&ed perfons and the ariftocrats ; to find out where any treafure was concealed ; to bring accufations againft people who were rich ; to enforce the law that fixed the price of provifions ; and to pro-cure recruits for the army, horfes, carriages, and grain.

The revolutionary army,* clothed in black, faced with red, was intended to enforce obedi-ence if it was wanted ; but fo great was the dif-may which thofe rigorous meafures had occa-fioned, that force was not neceffary, a few fol-diers, who were at the command of the commiffa-ries, were fufficient to exact the moft abfolute obedience in the hardeft of cafes.

If grain was wanted, and the farmer refufed to deliver it, he was fhot at his own door.† Were
the

who defolated France. Thefe latter filled every place, the frogs and locufts could do no more, and they could neither burn, ravifh, nor affaffinate.

* Robefpierre difbanded the revolutionary army as foon as he got fairly the victory over Hebert, but his real motive for doing fo does not appear very evident. It feems to have been through fome fecret fear of his enemies having more inter-eft with the gene rals of that army than he had himfelf, otherwife it was an excellent inftitution for the fupport of the revolu-tionary government. Had Robefpierre kept this army at his command, and in his intereft, it would have been more dif-ficult for his enemies to get the better of him than it after-wards was ; but Robefpierre probably confidered that this army received his orders from the committee of public fafety, and that as he was not certain of always reigning there, it would be better to truft to the Jacobin club alone for power and protection.

† An agrarian law would not have been half fo unjuft as this mode of taking the grain. The one only divides the foil,
the

the fons demanded for the army, and the affectionate father hefitated, the whole family was dragged away or maffacred, without form of procefs or delay, and the neighbours durft not venture even to look on, much lefs to fhew figns of grief.

The miferies of the people were not a little augmented by numbers of falfe commiffaries, who committed the fame exceffes as the true; and as nobody dared afk a commiffary to fhew his powers, thofe vexations went on almoft always without either difcovery or punifhment; it was only when the true commiffaries and the falfe

the other divides its produce, and of confequence robs the labourer of what arifes from the fweat of his brows. The mode of punifhment was, they allowed, rather fevere, but it was *neceffary, it was revolutionary* (they fhould have faid revolting).

Thefe expeditions to compel the peafants to give up their grain and their children, were always attended with pillage, and whenever it fuited them, with ravifhment and murder. Imagine a detachment of this army arriving in a village, and placing a centinel at the door of the houfe they were employed in fearching, with a bloody flag flying. Imagine all the neighbours fhutting their doors, and trembling till their turn fhould arrive, while the father, mother, and children were fuffering thofe cruel vexations of which we have fpoken, without daring either to refift or cry out, which even if they did, it was to no purpofe, and was certain to finifh with the maffacre of the whole. Blind fubmiffion alone fkreened the inhabitants from the laft of the exceffes, for wherever there was the leaft hefitation or murmur, all pity and refpect was at an end.

By this time there was no poffibility of putting a ftop to oppreffion, it arofe from fo many different caufes, and its agents were fo numerous, fo defperate, and fo impoffible to be traced out, that there was nothing to be done but to wait for fome of thofe movements in the capital, which, whatever its nature might be, would regulate the whole of the republic.

met

met on the fame fpot, that either took place, for
the inhabitants trembled at the name, and durft
never make an inquiry.

The cries of liberty and equality never abated
in the midft of all this mifery, where it might
truly be faid, that there was not a man in France
who did not rife in the morning under the painful fenfation of vengeance to fear, or vengeance
to gratify, and frequently of both.*

Robefpierre, during this progrefs towards the
maximum of human woe, fell ill, and Hebert,
who was the orator and oracle of the club of the
Cordeliers, took advantage of his abfence from
the Jacobin club and the national convention ;
a new revolution was threatened, and at firft the
advantage feemed to be in favour of Hebert, but
it only feemed to be fo, for though the club of
the Cordeliers was more violent than that of the
Jacobins, and even furpaffed it in atrocity and
extravagance, yet it did not pofefs the great
authority which the affiliations gave the latter
all over France.† The club of the Cordeliers
was

* Since the fall of Robefpierre, thofe perfons who acted
with him, or under him, have thought proper to throw upon
him and his party all the odium of thefe meafures, and to attribute to him all the mifery which followed; but it is to be
hoped, that nobody will give them credit for one moment for
fuch an affertion.

† We have already obferved, that the club of the Cordeliers
had propofed to have a legion of twelve hundred king-killers
regularly trained, and bound by an oath to extirpate the race
of monarchs. This plan only wanted one thing, like Collot's
project for blowing up the prifoners in Lyons---it wanted bold
executioners. As to the fimilarity of ftile and fentiment with
the

was very well for Paris, but the Jacobin club was for the whole of France, and Robefpierre was triumphant.

The battle of favage beafts in the Arena is interefting only becaufe it is a difplay of fury and force. That of Hebert and Robefpierre is not fo on any other account; the fate of both muft be indifferent, yet curiofity is excited when two fuch enemies of the human race give a little repofe to mankind by turning their efforts againft each other.

Hebert was procureur of the municipality,* and as fuch could reckon upon its fupport.— Robefpierre was the chief of the committee of public fafety, in which feveral members feemed to favour the Cordeliers. This gave Hebert courage, and on the fecond of March he began his attack by denouncing Robefpierre.

the Jacobins, we may cite the fpeech fo much applauded in that latter fociety made by Robefpierre's brother. "I am "not," faid he, "a lover of human flefh, yet I would willingly "eat a pye made of all the kings in Europe." It was a wonder that he did not prove by that fpecies of logic, fo much in vogue, that kings were monfters, and not men, and that therefore this would not be eating human flefh. The boafted conftitution was founded on arguments little better than this, and it is certain the French people would have adopted the idea with admiration and enthufiafm.

* The municipality had undergone many revolutions fince the 10th of Auguft; one fet of vagabonds had made place for another. But in all thefe there was only a renewal of crimes, accufations and vengeances; fo that they have been paft over. Befides, it is now become impoffible, as well as ufelefs, to attempt following out the confufion of men and things that was in Paris; the main outline only can be drawn, and even that but imperfectly.

The committee of public safety had arrested a favourite member of the club of the Cordeliers. It was determined to demand his liberty: a black crape was thrown over the bust of Marat, as a sign that the *friends of the people deplored the fate of the people.* Carrier mounted the tribune of the club and said, " Cordeliers, you want to com-
" pose a *Journal Maratist* (after the manner of
" Marat) I applaud your design, but that will be
" only a feeble defence against those who wish
" to kill the republic; *insurrection, holy insurrec-*
" *tion, that is what you ought to oppose to wicked*
" *people.*"†   La Fayette the father of insurrec-
tion, could not have spoken more to the purpose, nor with more effect, for Hebert followed, and with general approbation, repeated the demand for *a holy insurrection.* These changes, but still more the enthusiasm they occasioned, made the committee of public safety, and even the Jacobin club, stagger for a moment; but the victory was not of long duration ; and as soon as the party of Robespierre saw their superiority, a report was made in the name of the committee of public safety, the conclusion of which was, that Hebert and his accomplices ought to be arrested; it was done accordingly on the 14th of the month.

This was the most remarkable and the most vigorous combat that had yet taken place between two clubs. This was a proof that CLUBS AND
INSURRECTION

---

† It is very surprising that Carrier should have outlived the fall of Hebert after such a speech; and it is equally surprising that the advocates of the French constitution should cry out against the anarchists, considering *the purity of their principles and their attachment to the main article of the rights of man.*

INSURRECTION were juft as neceflary for fupporting defpotifm, as they were for refifting government. This is precifely what we have found the revolution proving all along; and upon this inflance we find it confirmed in the moft decided and unequivocal manner.

The different popular focieties, or clubs, of Paris had come to join that of the Cordeliers, on the day that the members had been arrefted. This formidable junction prevented the conftituted authorities of Paris from taking any decided part by congratulating the affembly, as was their ufual practice when vigorous meafures were taken, and when thofe vigorous meafures ended in victory. Cuthon, the intimate affociate of Robefpierre, and who afterwards mounted the fcaffold with him, made on the 18th a fpeech to the convention, in which he declared his aftonifhment that the municipality and the revolutionary army, fo ready on other occafions to congratulate the affembly, now remained filent. * A decree was then paffed empowering the committees of public fafety and of general fecurity to examine the conduct of the conftituted authorities in Paris, amongft whom were many traitors. This

* The victory of Robefpierre on this occafion feems to have been occafioned by this fpeech of Cuthon, which, by putting his enemies in fear, made them come over to his fide. It was the neglect of following the advice of this fame Cuthon, that brought Robefpierre's party to the gullotine in their turn a few months after. All this fhews that rigour and activity (and no half meafures) are the means to difconcert thofe who want to rebel. Rebels are often cowards, and factious men always are; fo that their occafional courage is exactly meafured by the idea they have of their force.

had

had the defired effect; and the next day the municipality of Paris fent to felicitate the affembly on
its courage, and make excufes for having been fo
flow in its congratulations. The committee of
public fafety immediately named Cellier and Le-
grand, two of its partifans, to fill the places of
Hebert and Chaumet at the municipality. This
bound the members of the municipality to the
fide of Robefpierre, and his triumph was now
certain. So true is it that, in cafes of revolt,
ftrength finifhes by being on the fide where it is
fuppofed to lay. The municipality no fooner
thought by the boldnefs of Cuthon, that it was
on the weaker fide, than it actually, by transferring its power to the other party, decided the
victory.

Boldnefs and promptitude, it would feem, are
the chief qualifications neceffary to a leader of revolutions; we fhall fee this exemplified ftill more
in the triumph of the enemies of Robefpierre a
few months afterwards, when that fame municipality, that now joined him through a conviction
that he was ftronger than his enemies, by endeavouring to fupport him on the fame idea,
drew down a very heavy vengeance on itfelf.

During this interval, the convention, or rather
the ruling party, fhewed its power, and gratified
the people by putting to death a number of perfons, amongft whom were feveral of its own
members.

Whilft the conftituted authorities congratulat-
ed the affembly for the victory of Robefpierre,
the revolutionary army, which Cuthon had likewife

wife accufed, fent a deputation to congratulate the Jacobin club. It was propofed by a member of the club that the revolutionary army fhould take an oath never to obey any other but the committee of public fafety and the national affembly. This was done with enthufiafm and unanimity; and Robefpierre declared from the tribune of the club a moment after, that the conduct of the revolutionary army was above all praife. *

To this fucceeded a plan for an addrefs to all the clubs in the kingdom on the new confpiracy, which had been difcovered and ftifled; but Collot d'Herbois, who now joined Robefpierre with warmth, though he had kept aloof till the victory was declared, objected to the addrefs as not being fufficiently vigorous; accordingly he wrote another, and prefented it, which other was adopted.

The next operation was, to purge the club and the miniftry of the friends and adherents of Hebert. But the triumph did not end here; the conquered club of the Cordeliers came by deputation to congratulate the Jacobin club on the victory it had obtained over themfelves, alledging that they had been mifled. The Jacobin club, in

* The orator of the revolutionary army addreffed the club thus : " Citizens, you fee before you brave republicans, fin" cere friends of their country, and who will always be wor" thy of the name they bear. You fee before you thofe whom " calumny had pointed out as your executioners, but never " fhould we have confented to fuch a crime. Thofe who " could have had the bafenefs to propofe to us fuch a crime, " would themfelves have fallen under our indignation."

the pride of victory, refused to admit this deputation, or to have any connection with the Cordeliers, until they were purified, by striking off from the lift of members all thofe who were of the party of Hebert. This humiliating condition was complied with, and the enemies of Robefpierre were profcribed every where. From this time the club of King-Killers, which had been prefided by the patriot Marat in its better days, and which had always been the moft violent in its patriotifm, funk into infignificance.

The accufation againft the party of Hebert was now brought regularly forward; it included many of the perfonal enemies of Robefpierre, and is a very curious relict of Jacobin defpotifm. * Had Hebert triumphed, the fame charges would have been brought againft Robefpierre, and the public would have applauded in the fame manner as it did in the prefent cafe.

The accufation was to this purpofe, that the accufed were the agents of the coalefced enemies of France; that they had endeavoured to ftarve the nation, and to degrade the convention; that they had endeavoured to re-eftablifh monarchy ;† and that the moment for feizing all
power,

---

* Hebert, Clootz, and Kok a Dutch banker, with feventeen other perfons, one of whom was a woman, were comprehended in the fame accufation ; but, as they were only known for their fanguinary projects, and thofe were now become fo common as fcarcely to attract the attention of the people on the fpot for more than a few hours, it is not worth while to repeat them.

† It feems a little fingular that Hebert, who had diftinguifhed himfelf on all occafions againft the royal family, who
had

power, and employing it in this atrocious manner, was nearly arrived, when luckily it had
been difcovered.

With refpect to the proceedings of the tribunal, they deferve no particular notice ; to be accufed and condemned was all the fame thing.

The whole of thefe violent enemies of government and of religion were conducted to the
fcaffold on the 29th of the month, amidft the hif-
fes, the reproaches, and evident marks of joy
from the people. *

Hebert was infulted more than the others, and
all the grofs witticifms with which he ufed to load
his enemies, or with which he generally infulted
the unfortunate, were applied to himfelf. This
monfter, one of the greateft which the revolution
had produced, ended his career like a coward
along with nineteen perfons, all of them deferving of death, but certainly, not all accomplices in
the

had fabricated the infamous accufation againft the queen, and
who was prefident of the club which, above all others, had
railed violently againft kings, fhould be charged with being
the agent of the coalefced powers. This fhews, that now
either very little attention was paid to the opinion of the people, or experience had taught their leaders to think that they
were fo confufed, or fo credulous, that any thing would be
believed. Hebert, it will be recollected, was judge at the
Hotel de la Force, and delivered over Madame de Lamballe,
and the other prifoners, to the affaffins.

* Anarcharfis Clootz, who had figured fo often as the
orator of the hu

the fame project, as fome of them were at that time enemies.

This is a fecond victory gained over the enemies of the human race, in that miferable country where crimes and punifhments were multiplied to a degree of which there never has been, and, it is to be hoped, never will again be an example.

The revolution had now accelerated its courfe, like a comet when it approaches the fun, and events fucceeded each other with an amazing rapidity.   The execrable party of Hebert was executed only on the 29th, after a ftruggle of a few weeks, and Danton, Camille de Moulins, la Croix, and Philipeux, were arrefted early on the morning of the 31ft, as accufed of having confpired with d'Orleans, Dumourier, and Fabre d'Eglantine, in order to re-eftablifh royalty, and deftroy the republic.*   In this charge were included many more perfons, and in the punifhment, more ftill---Herault, Bazire, Fabre d'Eglantine, a Spanifh banker named Gufman, the Abbe d'Efpagnac, General Wefterman, Chabot, and his two brothers.†   This

---

* When Camille de Moulins was interrogated as to his age, he anfwered, " The fame at which the fans culotte Jefus " died, thirty-three years."   Danton, when queftioned as to his abode, anfwered, " My refidence is a non-entity, and my " name will no longer exift but in the pantheon of hiftory." Danton treated the judges with great contempt, and threw balls of bread at the face of the prefident.   The criminals, judges, jury, and fpectators feemed rather to be acting a farce than any thing elfe; all was uproar, and a fort of favage merriment during the time the prifoners were at the bar.

 † We fpeak in England of a *batch of peers*. This feems not to be much amifs as a batch of fcoundrels. But it is very difficult

This party did not make the ufual fort of ſtruggle for victory; others, as we have ſeen, reſiſted
before their arreſtation, but not after. Danton,
and his companions were taken ſuddenly and
unexpectedly, they therefore could not reſiſt;
but when before the tribunal, they were as loqua-
cious as Briſſot's party, and much more reſo-
lute.

To get rid of the arguments which they produced, and which puzzled the judges, and of the
inſults which offended them, a decree was folicited from the convention, declaring the accuſed
refractory, and ordering that refractory people
ſhould be condemned without being heard.
While the decree was getting ready, Danton and
his companions were perſuaded to retire for re-
freſhment into an adjoining room, and they were
not allowed to re-enter the court, till the decree
was arrived. This finiſhed the buſineſs; they
were condemned without any more form or ceremony,* dragging along with them a number of
perſons detained in the priſons, who were fufpected, as it was pretended, of intending to refcue the criminals.

During this violent conflict amongſt the leaders, France looked on peaceably, and the army

ficult to conceive how they could be all jumbled together in
one accuſation.

* Even with ſuch men as Danton, this mockery of judgment is revolting. The ſudden arreſtation of Danton was
thought to be owing to a declaration made by Hebert, not
of any intentions of Danton's party againſt Robefpierre, but

was quite paffive.   As foon, however, as victory
was declared, all the conftituted authorities, the
clubs, the municipalities, the departments, and
the commanders in the kingdom, joined in addreffes of congratulation, and in enthufiaftic expreffions of approbation.

Robefpierre, at the head of the committee of
public fafety, of the Jacobin club, and of the
municipality of Paris, was now a defpot fingle
and alone.   Thofe who faw him only from a
diftance, conceived that he was one of thofe
great men who can controul events, and domineer over fortune: thofe who approached him
nearer, knew well that his fuccefs was owing to
circumftances, more than to his own abilities;
but all joined in fearing, detefting, and in granting a fervile obedience to his defpotic will.

C H A P.

CHAP. IV.

General view of the situation of France with regard to its enemies—Assignats—Conduct of the coalesced powers—New method of attacking by masses of undisciplined troops—Energy of the Jacobins, and their efforts in England and America—Retreat of the combined forces—Robespierre reigns alone—Bloody decrees and perpetual massacres—Madame Elizabeth, all the farmers general, and ancient judges condemned—Jacobin despotism come to its last pitch of horror—Robespierre begins to decline—His enemies venture to accuse him—The tyrant loses himself; he hesitates and delays—His fall, and that of the violent party.

DURING the different contests amongst the parties at Paris, the revolutionary measures for recruiting the army had produced an immense crowd of soldiers. It had been decreed that the nation was to rise in a mass. This decree at first seemed ridiculous, but its effects were frightful. The method of repulsing their enemies from the lines of Wissembourg, which had perfectly succeeded, inspired the committee that conducted

The lines of Wiffembourg, defended by excellent foldiers, might be attacked, but could not be forced by any multitude of raw men, whatever their number might be, until the veterans were worn out with fatigue.   Orders were received from Paris to attack thefe lines day after day, and new levies were made to fupply the place of thofe who were killed on the French fide.   What was propofed fucceeded; the lines were abandoned after a defence renewed every day with great vigour and bravery, during three weeks; frefh enemies were always oppofed, and the fecret of the method of making numbers triumph over difcipline was difcovered.

It is to this difcovery on the fide of the French, and the want of any meafures to counteract its confequences on the part of the allies, that the misfortunes that fo foon after took place, are to be principally attributed.

The retreat from before Dunkirk, with a great lofs to the army commanded by the Duke of York, had given courage to the French army in the north, which had been much difcouraged by the precipitate retreat made by Dumourier, the battle of Famars, and the taking of Valenciennes. The republican armies in the fouth had retaken Toulon, and kept Spain at bay. The great numbers of troops fent againft the royalifts in the Vendee, in confequence of the imprudent conduct of England, had effectually checked that alarming revolt. In Italy and in Savoy head had been made againft the combined efforts; fo that, before the winter had fairly fet in, the convention

faw

faw its armies triumphant in fome parts, and in all out of immediate danger.

The great difcovery made at the lines of Wif-fembourg was, however, the moft important victory. It gave a hint for a plan which the ftate of France and its defpotic government, as well as its pofition, and the nature of the people, rendered very practicable.

The defpotifm of government furnifhed the convention with the means of forcing the peafantry to the army, and their own mifery inclined many to prefer arms and bread to oppreffion and ftarvation. The law of the maximum, the affignats, and the guillotine, furnifhed horfes and provifions for the army, and means of paying the foldiers. The decay of all trade and commerce left plenty of people idle to make arms and accoutrements; fo that, though France could not find either good foldiers, nor good equipage, fhe could raife them quickly, and in great numbers. This was precifely what was wanting to put in practice the new mode of attack determined upon.

The revolutionary government and the law of the maximum had deranged every calculation that had been made at the beginning of the war, with refpect to the force and refources of France; and it is not to be wondered at if nobody was able to forefee the effects of two meafures, which were totally new in their nature, the like of which never had been feen, and the poffibility of which had never been thought of.*

Without

Without thefe two meafures the army could neither have been recruited nor fupplied, but with them, the laft man in the country able to fight, and the laft fack of corn to eat, was at the command of the convention.

The coalefced powers, during this time, made no attempts to rival the convention in ingenuity, though the horror of its crimes ought not to have infpired them with any contempt for their genius, and for the refources which were at their command.

The convention had organifed maffacre, but it had gone further to encourage difcovery in fuch arts as it had ufe for, than any government that ever exifted.   Men of merit were not guillotined, they were flattered and rewarded, and every new hint, every new idea, was received with thanks; moft of them were put to the trial, and whatever was found deferving was adopted.

France, during the ancient government, was a nurfery for fcience, and above all for military fcience.   There were vaft numbers of men of merit, who had formerly been neglected, who now ftarted forth to notice; not as the political fire-

government, by putting people's lives in queftion on all occafions, put difputes about the value of property out of the queftion.

The error of thofe who counted upon the ruin of affignats, from the great increafe of their quantity, and the weaknefs that would foon follow in the French government, was only, therefore, occafioned by the unforefeen event of a new fpecies of tyranny.   This is farther proved by the rapid depreciation of affignats fince the government became lefs violent.

brands

brands ftarted up in the clubs, but as men of knowledge and genius always will when left at liberty, and when they meet with encouragement.

A man who would have been obliged to dance attendance half his life-time after the minifter of war, or of the marine, only to receive the honour of an audience, where he was more likely to be treated with contempt, than to be encouraged, could now make himfelf certain of a candid hearing, and a fair trial, and the vices of a government which produced fuch advantages he very naturally overlooked and became zealous in the caufe.

Hiftory ought not to be written with an intention to lead men into errors, but to *teach them by example ;* therefore, from the fame principle that we blame the conduct of thofe who have covered a miferable country with blood, we muft praife the means which they took to defend themfelves and their caufe againft their enemies; we moft decidedly blame them and their caufe, but when that is done, we muft not refufe them thofe qualities of another fort, with which their blameable actions were accompanied.

On the fide of the allies we have feen no exertion, except according to the common routine of making war; millions of money, and thoufands of lives have been facrificed to no purpofe, becaufe they would not condefcend to look at their enemies, and fee with what fort of arms they fought.

An indifferent spectator, if such an one, there can be in the present contest, would think that, when the greatest nations in Europe joined to protect themselves from a species of anarchy that menaced them all with ruin, they would have laid aside every consideration but that of self-preservation; and that when they condescended to fight with the armies of the convention, they might have condescended to study the means by which they might be the most easily resisted.

It would have been very natural for the combined powers, after experiencing the unfortunate end of the campaign of 1793, to have studied, though late, the best way of re-commencing the operations in the spring with a probability of success; and, in order to begin, they should have considered the new method of attack, which the French had with success adopted.

The French had called their government republican, and European statesmen calculated upon the want of energy that republics display; but when France had transformed itself into the most despotic of governments, that calculation could no longer hold good, and should have been abandoned.

The convention did not let its interior divisions derange the military operations. The committee which directed the plans of the campaign was directed by old experienced military men, who had nothing to do with the different parties, and who were protected by all of them. Those men spared neither pains nor expense to ensure their undertakings success, and intrigue was added to

military

military fkill. Commiffaries were difpatched in
a myfterious manner to Mayence and Frankfort,
in order to give fome appearances of a treaty
being on foot with the King of Pruffia. This
puzzled and perplexed the different cabinets, and
augmented that miftruft, which is generally the
ruin of armed coalitions. The king likewife,
who on his part wanted to be well paid for his fervices by the other powers, acted as myfterioufly
as the commiffaries, and England and Holland
were induced to give him a large fum, on condition of his keeping up the army which he had on
the banks of the Rhine. The uncertainty of the
event of this negotiation, till the campaign was
ready to open, prevented thofe plans of operations from being laid, that were fo neceffary.

Meafures were taken and means were employed
on the fide of the French, for a vigorous and
offenfive campaign ; and, on the fide of the allies,
meafures were not thought of, and means were
wanting.

A fpirit of difcontent reigned amongft the officers of the allied armies. The greater number
of the Auftrian officers had not tafted repofe fince
the beginning of the war with the Turks in 1788.*
The Englifh officers who had come over only for
glory, not finding that glory fo likely to be acquired fince the affair of Dunkirk, and defpifing
the Dutch troops with whom they had come to
act, were difcontented, and wifhed to return to

---

* Nations feem to get tired of war in about feven years.

England.   Though this never hindered the Englifh and Auftrians from behaving bravely in the field of battle, it damped the operations, and prevented that cordiality, that alacrity, and exertion, which were fo neceffary.

The ftates of Brabant, too, had many pretended grievances againft the houfe of Auftria; the wounds received during the laft revolt were not yet healed, and though they faw the plundering difpofition of the enemy they had to deal with, no cordial fupport was given to the Emperor; and certainly if the reign of liberty, equality, and affignats, is eftablifhed amongft them, they may blame themfelves for it, and not the Emperor, who perfonally is as irreproachable as any of the coalefced powers.

The French began by paying fpies and informers at an immoderate rate, and the coalefced powers refufed to pay any thing that was worth while for the ingenuity and rifk of a fpy, neverthelefs the campaign opened very brilliantly for the combined powers in Flanders.   The fuperiority of difcipline and courage over maffes of peafants was never more confpicuous, but the military committee at Paris had expefted this, and was not difcouraged.

The fate of the lines of Wiffembourg put them perfeftly at their eafe, but as long as they afted on the defenfive, that plan could not be adopted.

The order therefore arrived for General Pichegrue to penetrate into Weft Flanders, and leave the victorious army of the Emperor to the right;
                                                    this

this fucceeded, and the allied armies were obliged to feparate, to prevent the French from getting poffeffion of that rich country, and all their ftores, which were at Oftend, Ghent, and Tournay, as well as to prevent them from falling upon their rear, which might happen, if no efforts were made to drive them back.

Menin and Courtray were taken, and Lifle ferved as a fupport for the French army. Great courage was difplayed by the Auftrians and the Englifh, and it is only doing juftice to the Emperor and the Duke of York to fay, that no two commanders ever fhewed greater courage; and in the unfortunate affair between Courtray and Lifle, few generals ever conducted themfelves better than his Royal Highnefs; but the race was not now for the fwift, nor the battle for the ftrong, the inceffant and unremitting efforts of a mafs that augmented every day, proved victorious.

General Clairfayt behaved with equal conduct and bravery, and with a very fmall army difputed the poffeffion of Weft Flanders, inch by inch for fifteen days running; but the fate of General Wurmfer, at the lines of Wiffembourg attended him, and it was found in vain to remain, a good retreat was all that remained for him to attempt, and this he certainly accomplifhed.

It was well enough known before the campaign opened, that the finances of the Emperor were exhaufted; the payments made to thofe wl)

pofed in England, but why it was not then adopted, it is difficult to conceive; or if it was for good
reafons refufed then, why it fhould be adopted
now, is ftill more difficult to conjecture.   The
difappointment of this affiftance in money, added
to an invidious kind of an idea circulated by
French emiffaries amongft the Auftrian officers,
that England, which had got the Weft India
iflands, was alone likely to profit by the war, and
Auftria alone likely to fuffer, completed a mifunderftanding already begun.*   The fate of the
campaign was now determined, the allies had
nothing for it fince they had feparated, but retreat, and accordingly each army began in its
own way to march off.

But though the places of Weft Flanders were
falling into the hands of the French every day,
Charleroi, which is on the direct road from the
French frontier to Bruffels, oppofed a vigorous
refiftance.   General Beaulieu, on the banks of
the Sambre, had repulfed the enemy repeatedly,
but the fate of Wurmfer attended him alfo.
Charleroi was repeatedly relieved, once by the
Emperor in perfon, and the Hereditary Prince of
Orange difplayed before it equal conduct and
bravery; but all this fignified nothing, the
French mafs flying from famine and the guillo-
tine, came on, and Charleroi, after being nearly

* The decree of the convention, ordering no quarter to be
given to Englifh and Hanoverian foldiers, increafed the dif-
like of the foldiers of the Auftrian and Britifh armies; it was
confidered by the former as a token of efteem and regard, and
by the latter it was thought to denote an unfair intention of
leaving them in the lurch.

demolifhed,

demolished, was obliged to surrender.* Bruffels then fell a second time into the hands of the French, and the combined armies formed a chain of posts from Maestricht and Aix-la-Chapelle to the borders of Holland.

The Duke of York made an appearance of a stand at Antwerp, where he had taken a position behind the river Scheldt, but the certainty of being attacked day after day, till his army should be fatigued and diminished, made it prudent to retire without being attacked at all.

Thus was the single discovery of a new plan of attack, productive of the most complete train of victory ever witnessed, and where numbers triumphed over bravery, and the discipline and tactics of war, such as they have been practised in Europe since the invention of fire-arms.

* The armies having once separated and abandoned the frontier towns, it was not possible to make any stand, until they had traversed the country, and come to another chain of fortifications; but though any serious stand was impossible, there does not appear to have been any occasion for their precipitancy, the confusion, and the want of order with which the retreat was made. It was a retreat of regular and well-disciplined troops, with generals regularly bred, who fled before a mass of peasants, without discipline, and headed by men of yesterday; yet the order and regularity was all on the side of the undisciplined peasants, for the regular troops were in great confusion. The reason was certainly that the former followed a plan, and the latter were guided by no plan, and neither had resolution to make a stand, nor prudence to send off their magazines and stores before them; sometimes they had the appearance of intending to retreat no farther, and every thing remained for a few days stationary, then all

With regard to the manner of the retreat, and some of the miftakes committed in it, we fhall fpeak hereafter.

As the French armies advanced in one of the moft fertile countries in the world, they exchanged their affignats for every fort of neceffaries, and the whole of the money fpent during thirteen months by the allied armies, with a great part of their ftores remaining on hand, fell into the poffeffion of the conquerors.

One of the moft furprifing things in all this was, to fee old experienced generals, when reduced to the neceffity of abandoning that country, do it without taking any of the precautions that are fo neceffary. There was no plan, no fyftem in their retreat, while the army of Sans Culottes turned every thing to their profit, with as much fyftem and regularity as if they had been accuftomed to conqueft during a century.

Had the French armies been obliged to abandon Flanders and Brabant, they would ftill have been immenfe gainers by the conqueft and momentary poffeffion of it, for every thing was immediately and regularly put in requifition for affignats, a part was fent to France immediately, and the reft was all ready to be fent upon the fhorteft notice.*

Whilft

* Perhaps activity, energy, and combination of invaders, never gained a greater victory over the oppofite qualities in thofe who abandoned a country, than on this occafion. The tarifs of merchandizes of all kinds, at the price of the maximum, were circulated and proclaimed every where; foldiers were fupplied with affignats to purchafe what they wanted,

but

Whilſt theſe things were going on upon the continent, the factious democrats of England* having got the better of the fear which the puniſhment of ſome of the members of the pretended Scotch convention had inſpired, began again to arrange their plans of attack upon the Engliſh conſtitution.

The correſponding ſocieties, or affiliated clubs, redoubled their activity, and things were going on ſo as to have procured, in time, all the advantages of liberty and equality, ſuch as we have ſeen eſtabliſhed in France. Luckily, however, miniſters were ſtill upon their guard, and the plans in agitation were diſcovered before they were quite ready to be executed. The miniſtry, by a laudable ſtretch of power, arreſted a number of perſons concerned, and obtained a ſuspenſion of the habeas corpus act, which is the guardian of the rights of citizens in ordinary times, but the ſuſpenſion of which is neceſſary for the ſafety of the nation in times of public danger.

but robbery and pillage were puniſhed with death, without the leaſt mercy. By this the ſoldiers were ſupplied with every thing at no expenſe ; the army might be ſaid to exiſt by pillage and robbery, yet the ſmalleſt act of theft was puniſhed with death. Our armies, on their retreat, paid for every thing they wanted in hard caſh, and at a high price, and yet on account of a few irregularities, were accuſed of pillage, while the invaders were praiſed for their diſcipline. This requires and deſerves a longer inveſtigation than we can with propriety give it here.

* This name may appear hard, but we muſt confeſs, after following French democrats, firſt through their reforms, and then through their maſſacres, it is not ſafe

The freedom of a nation is to a certain degree, the enemy of its safety; but as it is absolutely neceffary to give to every body politic a means of protecting itself,* the Englifh patriots of the laft century, with much lefs metaphyfical whim than the conftituent affembly in France, but with more attention to the real welfare of the nation, were not afraid of entrufting pofterity with a power of preferving the conftitution in cafes of danger, by making it lawful for the three powers of, king, lords, and commons, to fufpend a law, which, while it is a fecurity for the good citizen, is alfo a protection for the bad. Where men are governed by written law, it is always poffible to ftir up difcontent without incurring any pains or penalties, becaufe the letter of the law is obliged to attach itfelf to open acts. Now open acts, of a feditious nature, are not always neceffary to excite difcontent, and bring on infurrection. The advocates of the democratic fide fay, why do not minifters wait for open acts? They might as well afk, why does not the traveller wait till the robber has difcharged his piftol.

The fufpenfion of this act was evidently neceffary, for though the individuals apprehended had not committed any actions that feemed to a jury to come under the defcription of *treafon*, for which they were indicted; yet their trial proved evidently that affiliated clubs were eftablifhed for the purpofe of effecting a reform, which affiliation being a new invention, there did not exift any law for punifhing it.

* For a fair and plain examination of this, fee an anonymous publication, *Scylla more dangerous than Charibdis*, publifhed by Mr. Stockdale, a few months before the act was fufpended.

The

The acquittal of the men who were tried, juft depended upon this circumftance of the law not having forefeen the fpecies of tranfactions of which they were guilty, and of confequence not having determined the punifhment which they were to draw down.

The fuccefs of the French arms, as we have feen, was owing to the difcovery of a new mode of conquering good and regularly difciplined armies, by attacking them day after day without intermiffion, by bodies of frefh troops: the combined armies were defeated becaufe they had not difcovered a method of refifting this fort of attack. The conftitution of England was in danger, and ftill is in danger, of finking under the CO-OPERATIONS OF AFFILIATED CLUBS, and that danger will not ceafe until laws are made to prevent fuch co-operations.*

Confederates, affiliated, have ruled over France, and we fee to what they have reduced it: and until the laws of England have extended their dominion to this new fpecies of attack upon the peace of men, there will be no fecurity. Confederates will affemble for purpofes that feem to

* A work is in forwardnefs upon this fubject, recommending to the legiflature of England, to pafs an act, making it a crime for felf-elected focieties to enter into combinations upon political reforms. The bafis of which work is, that fuch combinations give a fmall minority of perfons fo connected, an undue influence in the nation, and that a great majority, *unaffiliated*, may be domineered over by an inconfiderable number of *affiliated confederates*; and that therefore, though the object in view may itfelf be lawful, and even meritorious, this mode of attaining it is d...

be praise-worthy, and when once properly eftab-lifhed, they will do what they pleafe.

Fable was invented, in order to convince men by a fhorter mode than argument, and by a mode that made a deeper impreffion upon the mind. Hiftory has, however, a double advantage, when attended to, it leads us to unerring conclufions, without having recourfe to long arguments ; and it is impoffible in the prefent cafe not to fee that the affiliated clubs, or correfponding focieties, were the firft caufes, as well as the fupporters of the unexampled crimes and miferies of France.

Weapons of offence have always been invented before weapons of defence. Swords and fpears were known before fhields and helmets. Gunpowder was invented before Demoivre and Vauban altered and perfectioned the art of fortification ; but it muft be allowed, that during thefe intervals, there muft have been confiderable danger to the human race. Revolutions muft at fuch times have been very eafy, if the method of attack had been brought to any confiderable degree of perfection, before the mode of defending was known.

The Jacobins met with no phyfical difficulties, fuch as the inventors of cannon had to ftruggle with, the phyfical difficulties were all overcome by the invention of printing and poft roads, fo that the affiliation of clubs was realized almoft in an inftant. The danger that mankind runs from this invention is great, till a remedy is found out ; and as a proof, we refer to the hiftory of the revolution of France.

The

The Englifh government, whilft it acted with becoming feverity towards thofe who wifhed to ftir up diffenfion, has by no means acted wifely with refpect to the principles which thofe men profeffed. We have already obferved, that perfecution, in cafes of opinion, produces obftinacy, and not conviction; and it is very certain, that if affiliations continue to be permitted, they will end in being victorious; they will end in making the people think themfelves oppreffed ; minifters fhould employ the powers now in their hands, not to refift wife reforms, but to prevent men frcm demanding wife reforms, in a manner inimical to the conftitution, and to the intereft of the majority. It would be as well to fee the Houfe of Commons reformed by a regiment of mutinous foldiers, with arms in their hands, as to fee it reformed by an affiliated minority of the nation.

The juftice of the reform, and the manner of attempting it ought not to be confounded ; but as minifters have gone to work, they are confounded together, and will continue to be fo; and if England fhould ever have the misfortune to have the confidence of their king given to minifters who approve of *affiliated confederacies*, a revolution will be operated immediately. The punifhment of a few individuals will not avert the danger, and it is below the rulers of a nation to employ that power in fearching to punifh a crime which might be employed to prevent it.

The United States of America have not been free from the fame attempts of affiliated clubs; rebellion actually broke out at their inftigation,*
and

and certainly it was not becaufe the Americans are not free that fuch a revolt took place, and fuch manœuvres, but it was becaufe the difturb-
ers

danger from clubs, and that a *free republic* is no more fecure againft their manœuvres than a free kingdom.

" On the fame principles with thofe in France are founded " the democratic focieties in this country; and fhould they " become numerous here, as they are there, they will infalli- " bly have a fimilar effect. Their pretence is, to watch " government—they mean the fœderal government. But " this, like each of the ftate governments, is chofen by the " nation at large ; and, of courfe, every man in his individual " capacity has an equal right and an equal intereft in watching " its meafures. What prefumption then is it, and what an " ufurpation of the rights of their brethren, for private affo- " ciations, unauthorifed by the laws, to arrogate this charge " to themfelves? Admitting the propriety of fetting a watch " upon congrefs and the prefident, are not the ftate legiflatures " fully competent to the bufinefs? Is not their intereft at " ftake, and their jealoufy always awake, ready to notice " any fault or error in the general government? What then " is there for thefe private affociations to do? Good they " cannot do; and if they do any thing, it muft be evil.

" Their meetings are fo many collections of combuftibles ; " and fhould they be generally extended, the whole country " will be in a flame. The members of thofe focieties, by vir- " tue of this relation, neceffarily become the mere tools and " dupes of their artful leaders, who have their own ends to " ferve by all their profeffions of patriotifm. ' The moment " a man is attached to a club, his mind is not free; he re- " ceives a bias from the opinions of the party : a queftion in- " different to *him*, is no longer indifferent, when it materially " affects a *brother* of the fociety. He is not left to act for " himfelf; he is bound in honour to take part with the focie- " ty—his pride and his prejudices, if at war with his opinion, " will commonly obtain the victory ; and rather than incur " the ridicule or cenfure of his affociates, he will countenance " their meafures, at all hazards; and thus an *independent free-* " *man* is converted into a mere walking machine, a conveni- " ent *engine of party leaders.*' In this way a few ambitious " individuals are enabled to extend their influence ; and as
" they

ers of public repose who composed those clubs having the power to create disturbance, never want the will, and that if there is not a Bastile to overturn, they set about overturning a General Washington.

When Robespierre had got quit of his open enemies in the interior, the first apparent change was in the greater method in the murders committed by the revolutionary tribunal, and, of course, greater expedition; the next thing was the disrepute into which the religion of reason, as instituted by Hebert, fell. Chaumet, and Gobet, the bishop of Paris, who had contributed to that fête, were condemned for wishing to introduce atheism into France, which it was declared

" they rise in power and consequence, to infringe upon the
" liberty of the public.

" Each individual member of the state should have an *equal*
" voice, in elections; but the individuals of a club have more than
" an equal voice, because they have the benefit of another influ-
" ence, that of extensive *private attachments*, which come in aid
" of each man's political opinion. And just in proportion as
" the members of a club have an undue share of influence in
" that proportion they abridge the rights of their fellow citi-
" zens. Every club, therefore, formed for political purposes,
" is an *aristocracy* established over their brethren. It has all
" the properties of an *aristocracy*, and all the effects of tyran-
" ny. It is a literal truth, that the *democratic clubs* in the
" United States, while running mad with the abhorrence of
" aristocratic influence, are attempting to establish precisely
" the same influence under a different name. And if any
" thing will rescue this country from the jaws of faction, it
" must be either the good sense of a great majority of Ame-
" ricans, which will discourage private political associations,
" and render them contemptible; or the controuling power
" of the laws of the country, which, in an early stage, shall
" demolish all such institutions and from

Pitt and Cobourg were at the bottom of, in order to animate other nations against the French.

The syftem of terror now came to its laft pitch of perfection: amongft a variety of rulers who differed in opinion, if there were a number of vengeances, there were alfo fome who were faved from punifhment by favour and protection; but Robefpierre and his terrible committee had all the fame enemies and the fame vengeances : accordingly St. Juft made a report from the committee fufficiently fevere to gratify them. This report contained twenty-fix different articles to the purpofe, that all people accufed of plotting againft the republic, in whatever part they were, fhould be brought to Paris to be tried by the revolutionary tribunal ; that their accomplices fhould be fought after and brought to Paris likewife. That no foreigners nor nobles of either fex fhould be allowed to remain in Paris, nor in any of the frontier or maritime cities of the kingdom, from which they were to be obliged, under pain of death, to depart in three days : that all perfons who fhall ever have been heard to fpeak againft the revolution, all perfons who had neither trade nor profeffion, unlefs they were infirm or lame, fhould be tranfported to French Guyanne : that all citizens who do not difcover thofe who hold incivic difcourfe, or are guilty of other crimes, are to be confidered as accomplices.

And, in addition to all, that the conftituted authorities fhould confine themfelves to doing their duty, and that they fhould be immediately under the controul of the committee of public fafety.

This

This was laying the foundation for denunciation and punishment, without any sort of bounds or restriction.

Although the number of persons put to death, and the obscurity of the greater number would render it tedious and disgusting to enter upon that detail, yet, as the three months of the reign of Robespierre and his committee are the only example of pure and uncontrouled republican tyranny, we cannot pass over it without taking notice of a number of the victims who from circumstances were the most remarkable.

On the 19th of April M. de la Borde, one of the richest bankers and merchants in France, and seventy years of age; M. de Guibeville, ancient president of the parliament of Paris, with his daughter and grandaughter; a director of the India Company, and counts, countesses, servants, and common workmen, about twenty more persons were put to death.

Next day six ancient presidents of the parliament of Paris, two presidents of *la cour des aides*, and fourteen members of the parliaments of Paris, Toulouse, and Dijon.

Each day saw the same scenes renewed; the virtuous M. de Malsherbes, who had defended his royal master, with all those of his family who remained in France; the famous and once popular M. Desprimesnil, who first resisted the court in 1787; the Duchess of Grammont, the Prin-

of the city of Verdun, accufed of favouring the Pruffians, were, in the courfe of a few days, fent to the guillotine.

The Duke de Villeroi, M. Nicolai, prefident of the grand council, M. de Crofne, the ancient lieutenant of the police of Paris, and M. Delany, civil lieutenant at the age of feventy-eight, with thirty-fix more perfons of different ranks and fex, and from eighteen to feventy years of age, fuffered the fame fate.

This was now the triumph of men who had always feared and difobeyed the laws over thofe who had refpected and executed them.

All thefe bloody fcenes were acting, whilft the combined powers were advancing in the month of April; it was at laft, however, impoffible for the committee of public fafety any longer to conceal their defeats, and accordingly Barrere mounted the tribune on the 30th of that month, and, after expatiating againft the ariftocrats, who exaggerated the misfortunes of the republic, he finifhed with reprefenting them as trifling, and with a wifh, that he had the lofs of fome important place to announce, which, faid he, would waken up the nation, and make it difplay that energy which was not to be found amongft republicans, but when they are actuated by fhame and revenge.*

The committee acted in the manner of the cruel minifter of fome Afiatic defpot ; the people

* Barrere, in this avowal, does not do great honour to the republican character.

were

were called the fovereign, and they were treated as fome fovereigns are; their paffions were flattered, and truth, when difagreeable, fuppreffed. Defertion was at this time fo frequent amongft the *mafs* of citizens, from the age of eighteen to twenty-five, particularly in the fouth of France, that by a proclamation of the commiffaries, Robefpierre the younger, and Salicetti, all fuch, together with thofe who gave them fhelter, were declared as traitors to the country: they, and their relations who gave them an afylum, were to be delivered over to the tribunals as royalifts, and the municipalities were ordered to make fearch after fuch. This meafure feemed fo excellent to the committee that ruled in Paris, that a decree was paffed, rendering it general for the whole kingdom.

Thus, after the fyftem of liberty and equality had profcribed nobles, clergymen, and rich proprietors; after it had made a number of laws, which, from their feverity and general fignification, put the life of moft of the inhabitants in danger; by one clear and pofitive law, it was made death for any young man, from the age of eighteen to twenty-five, to be feen in France except in the armies.

The occafion which Barrere had affected a few days before to feek foon arrived; on the 4th of May, he mounted the tribune, rather, however, as if he wifhed to avoid giving the news of the taking of a city belonging to the republic. " Citizens," faid he, " *victory has abfented it-*

" return. Landrecy is no longer ours." Before this news was certain to the committee, added he, it was announced with a melancholy voice and dejected countenance by many perfons who are ariftocrats in difguife, and who affect to be forry though they inwardly rejoice. The ariftocracy will never be corrected, it muft be annihilated ; every moment tumults are excited in the large towns by the ariftocrats on pretext of famine ; fometimes they are directed againft the butchers, fometimes they are directed againft the bakers, and when the mafters are not excited to infurrection, the workmen are excited againft them for an advance of wages. All thofe efforts are directed by traitors, againft whom we ought to employ every exertion. To this complaint followed a decree, which put in a ftate of requifition all thofe citizens who were employed in manufacturing, carrying, or felling objects of neceffity. A fecond decree followed that, ordering the public accufer to profecute, before the revolutionary tribunal, all thofe who fpread abroad bad news, or who feem to have laid a plan for frightening the people.

The day following a decree was paffed, which tended to fend the whole band of the farmers-general to the fcaffold. The whole were accufed of mal-practices under the old government, and as fuch delivered over to the revolutionary tribunal.

Whilft Barrere was thus exerted in averting the anger of the people from the committee, by pointing out new victims, forty-eight more of the number mounted the fcaffold, amongft whom were the two brothers Taffin the bankers,
a rich

a rich notary, a rich ftock broker, and many gentlemen, feveral of whom were above feventy years of age.

But the vengeance of the committee was not to be fatisfied with fuch victims, whilft there remained in the prifons of the Temple the virtuous Madame Elizabeth. This princefs, againft whom, except Hebert and his companions, no perfon had ever ventured to utter a complaint, not that there wanted plenty who had malevolence enough, but that it was impoffible to give any fort of probability to accufations brought againft a woman, who, to benevolence and virtue, added a degree of moderation and prudence, left no foundation for attack.

The fame day that twenty-eight farmers-general mounted the fcaffold, this princefs was fent for from the Temple, carried before the tribunal, and, without either defence or accufation, was condemned, and immediately fent to the place of execution.* With regard to an act of injuftice towards an individual, this is, perhaps, during the whole of the revolution, the moft flagrant, the moft unprovoked, and the moft ufelefs.

* The interrogation of this princefs was ftopped on her faying fhe was aunt to the king : *no other* crime was attempted to be brought to her charge, fhe was immediately fent to the place of execution, and even the fpectators feemed to be forry, fo that the committee loft rather than gained by this cruel act.

O Death ! made proud by pure and princely beauty,
The earth hath got no hole to hold this deed ! ! !

Fifty more victims of different defcriptions, amongft whom were many of the very loweft clafs of workmen and feveral ancient financiers and nobles, were led to execution next day, and the remainder of the farmers-general were carried off by one, two, or three at a time ; even the great age of M. Mercier, who was feventy-eight, and whofe mother had given fuck to Louis XV. could not fave him from the fate that attended his companions.

But along with the innocent fell alfo many per-fons who merited richly their fate ; Jourdan, fur-named the cut-throat, who had prefided at the maffacres of Avignon, now fuffered for his crimes. Robefpierre had new armies of cut-throats as good as this man, and his affected pre-eminence, by affuming to himfelf a title which belonged equally to all the minifters of the tyrant, was of itfelf a fufficient crime.

It would not have been at all furprifing, if fome enraged relation, or lover, or friend of one of the victims of Robefpierre, had really affaf-finated him, but there was but one Charlotte Cordy in France, unlefs fuch as exifted in Robe-fpierre's imagination. At this time, however, on the 23rd of May, one Cecilia Regnaut, daughter of a ftationer in Paris, who feems to have been deranged in her mind, but without having any fixed plan, came to the door of the houfe where he lodged ; her queftions made her fufpected to thofe who fufpected almoft every one, and fhe was conducted to prifon.

Whether

Whether this foolish girl really intended to attempt taking the life of Robespierre or not is of very little importance; but it served as an occasion, in conjunction with an attempt made at the same time to affassinate Collot d'Herbois, to prop the declining popularity of those violent patriots, and to renew the enthusiasm of the people. In the Jacobin club, Cuthon, who had overturned the Cordeliers, proposed, *that by a spontaneous movement* the club should solemnly declare, that the British government, the authors of those affassinations and crimes, committed against the representatives of the people, was guilty of *leze humanity*. All the members rose to approve of this. Robespierre in person was present, and next day Barrere made a report to the assembly on the subject of the affassinations, which concluded with accusing England of many crimes towards the republic and the neutral powers, and directed above all against the national representatives. It was upon this occasion that a decree was past, which forbid the soldiers of the French armies to give any quarter to English or Hanoverian prisoners.

Robespierre then began to speak :* " It will
" be a superb subject for the contemplation of
" posterity, it is already a sight worthy of heav-
" en and earth, to see the representatives of the
" French people placed upon an inexhaustible
" volcano of conspiracies, with one hand lay at
" the feet of the Eternal, the homage of a great
" people, and with the other lance thunder against
" the tyrants conspired against them ; lay the

" foundations of the firſt republic in the world,
" and call back amongſt mortals, exiled liberty,
" juſtice, and virtue.

" Surrounded with aſſaſſins, I have already
" placed myſelf in that new order of things where
" they wiſh to ſend me. I am no longer attach-
" ed to life but by the love of my country, and
" a thirſt after juſtice; I find myſelf more and
" more prepared to attack with energy thoſe
" wicked perſons who conſpire againſt my coun-
" try and the human race. The more they haſ-
" ten to ſend me hence, the more I will exert
" myſelf to be uſeful to my fellow creatures; I
" will leave them at leaſt a teſtament that it will
" frighten tyrants and their accomplices to read.

" The deſtiny of the republic is not yet made
" ſure, the vigilance of the repreſentatives of the
" French people is more neceſſary than ever.

" The republic does not depend upon riches,
" nor victory, nor dominion, nor momentary en-
" thuſiaſm; it depends on the wiſdom of its laws,
" but, above all, on public virtue; it is neceſſary
" to give ſtability to law, and to regenerate man-
" ners. If either of theſe fail, there will then
" only remain error, pride, paſſions, factions, am-
" bition, avarice; the republic, far from correct-
" ing ſuch vices, will give them free ſcope, and
" vice leads naturally to tyranny. Whoever is
" not maſter of himſelf, is made to be the ſlave of
" others.* Would you know who the ambi-

* The ſtrange mixture of good and bad in the diſcourſe of
democratic leaders, marks evidently a derangement of intellects.

" tious

" tious are ? Confider who thofe are who protect
" rogues; who encourage thofe who feek to de-
" ftroy the revolution----thofe who execute the
" crimes, who defpife virtue, and corrupt mo-
" rals.

" Some perverfe beings have contrived to
" throw the republic into a ftate of confufion;
" we muft extricate it, and create moral and po-
" litical harmony. The French people has two
" certain guarantees of that regeneration, in the
" principles of its reprefentatives and its own vir-
" tue. It is eafy to confolidate liberty, or eafy
" to deftroy it. If France were governed only
" for a few months by a corrupted, a miftaken
" affembly, liberty would be undone. Your
" unanimity and energy have aftonifhed and con-
" vinced Europe; if you know that as well as
" our enemies do, you would eafily triumph.

" I have mentioned the virtue of the people,
" and that virtue proved by the whole of the re-
" volution, is not fufficient alone to defend us
" againft factions. Why fo? becaufe there are
" *two peoples* in France; the one is the mafs of
" pure citizens, plain men, lovers of juftice and
" liberty.

" The *other people* is compofed of the factious
" intriguers; it is that babbling mountebank,
" artificial people, which fills every place, and
" abufes every thing; which fills the tribune,
" and often difcharges public functions. It is
" that people of rogues, ftrangers, and counter-
" revolutionary hypocrites,* who place them-

" felves between the French people and their re-
" prefentatives, to deceive the one and calumni-
" ate the other, and to counteract their opera-
" tions. As long as that impure race fhall exift,
" the republic will be unhappy, and its duration
" precarious ; it is your bufinefs to deliver it by
" an awful energy, and by a determined unanim-
" ity. Thofe who feek to divide us, and to ftop
" the progrefs of government, thofe who cry
" out every day againft it, and who form a dan-
" gerous coalition to oppofe government, are
" your enemies, and the enemies of your coun-
" try ; they are the agents of other nations, and
" the fucceffors of Briffot, Hebert, and Danton.

" In faying fuch things, perhaps I am fharpen-
" ing thofe poignards which are directed againft
" me, and it is therefore that I fay them. Per-
" fevere in your principles and in your triumph-
" ant career, you will then ftifle crimes and fave
" your country.----I have lived long enough——

" I have lived long enough, I have feen the
" French people rife from the meaneft flavery to
" the height of republican virtue and glory. I
" have yet feen a greater wonder ftill ; a prodigy
" which the corruption of monarchical govern-
" ment, and the inexperience of the firft period
" of our revolution, made us regard as impoffi-
" ble ; an affembly invefted with the power of
" the French nation, marching with a rapid and
" firm ftep towards public happinefs, devoted to
" the caufe of the people, and to the triumph of
" equality,

thieves were murdered by the people for ftealing filver fpoons.
The citizens of Paris were enraged at the mob, till they were
informed that they were ariftocratical thieves.

" equality, worthy of giving to the world the
" fignal of liberty, and the example of all the
" virtues.

" Finifh, citizens, finifh your fublime deftiny ;
" you have placed us in the front to fuftain the
" firft attack of the enemies of humanity----we
" merit that honour, and we will trace for you,
" with our blood, the road to immortality. May
" you always difplay that unalterable energy of
" which you ftand in need, to ftifle all the mon-
" fters of the univerfe combined againft you, and
" at laft enjoy the public benedictions due to
" your virtue."*

Such was the fpeech of Robefpierre, upon which
the only comment neceffary is, to contraft it
with his own actions, and with the actions of
thofe whom he celebrated as virtuous republicans.

During all thefe harangues about virtue and
juftice, and the purity of the people, and of their
reprefentatives, the executions of fufpected perfons went on ; from ten to fifteen were executed
every day, and a new degree of terror, and activity of punifhment was preparing.

Robefpierre had now reigned fome time alone ;
and what for himfelf was more dangerous, the
people faw that he reigned alone, and his colleagues felt it, fo that though all the fections of
Paris came to congratulate him and the affembly
on his efcape, his popularity was on the decline,
Bourdon de l'Oife and Talien were the firft wh-

ventured to shew their discontentment openly,
and from the moment they did so, it was looked
upon as certain that they muft fall, unlefs they
fhould be lucky enough to overcome the tyrant.

The fpeech of Robefpierre was certainly intended to give hopes to the people, and as a
threat held out to his enemies; but what were the
people, were they to be catched with profeffions
of virtue and juftice from the mouth of Robefpierre? or his enemies, could they be intimidated,
when it had fo long been known that the leaft
fufpicion was fufficient to carry his moft intimate
friend to the guillotine?

The tyrant had faid, his time was but fhort,
and he would employ it well, accordingly he fet
about a fête in honour of the Supreme Being,
which was juft as ridiculous as any of the other
fêtes of Hebert and his affociates.

Robefpierre acted as high prieft in this ceremony, which was intended to deftroy Atheifm ;*
and which the people thought was to re-inftate
the Supreme Being in his rights. But neither
farcical ceremonies, nor unmeaning phrafes, could

* This fête was celebrated in the garden of the Thuilleries ; Robefpierre, after preaching a fort of fermon, defcended from a balcony of the palace, with a lighted flam-
beau, and fet fire to a monument reprefenting Atheifm.
When this monument was reduced to afhes, a ftatue of Pal-
las, reprefenting Wifdom, ftarted up as by enchantment ;
from thence they went to the Champ de Mars, and the ceremony finifhed with applaufe beftowed on Robefpierre, who
had fo domineered over the people of Paris, that printed
papers were diftributed before the fête began, containing a
defcription of the whole, and marking the points of his
fpeech which they were to applaud.

long

long contain the people, who faw their armies triumphant in Flanders, who were therefore no longer afraid of invafion, but who ftill wanted bread and a change of mafters.

Two days after the fête of the Supreme Being had been given, Cuthon (on the 10th of June) came to the affembly, and propofed a decree on the new organization of the revolutionary tribunal, which may be confidered as the laft perfection given to the fyftem of terror, and the maximum of human ferocity and injuftice, and as fuch merits being preferved for an example to pofterity.

After three articles which regulate the form of the tribunal, a fourth article declares, that it is inftituted for punifhing the enemies of the people.

The enemies of the people are defined to be, all thofe who fearch to deftroy liberty by force or by fraud; thofe who feek to eftablifh royalty, or to deftroy the convention and the revolutionary and republican government, of which it is the center.

Thofe who, as commanders in the armies, or in any public office, or military office, have held correfpondence with the enemies of the republic: who have laboured to promote famine, or to prevent provifions from arriving at the armies or into Paris.

ing at the retreat or evafion of confpirators and
ariftocrats; thofe who perfecute or calumniate
patriots, who bribe members of the convention,
or who find fault with the principles of the revolution, or the laws or meafures of government,
by falfe and perfidious explanations.

Thofe who deceive the people are the enemies of
the people, to lead them into errors unfavourable
to liberty.

Thofe who difcourage the people, in order to
favour the tyrants coalefced againft France.

Thofe who have fpread falfe news, to divide
and trouble the people.

Thofe who have fought to lead the people into
wrong opinions, and to prevent their inftruction;
to deprave and corrupt their manners and the
public confcience; to change the energy and purity of revolutionary and republican principles,
or to ftop their progrefs, either by counter-revolutionary writings, or other infidious machinations.

*The punifhment for all crimes brought before the
revolutionary tribunal is death.*

The proof neceffary for pronouncing a ver-
dict, is every kind of document, whether material or moral (moral documents are a new invention); whether written or verbal, which carries naturally evidence with itfelf.

The rule of judgments is the confcience of the
jurymen; their view is to enfure the triumph of
liberty

liberty ; the means is such proceedings as good sense dictates, as being proper for determining the truth of facts.

Every citizen has a right to seize and carry before the magistrates all conspirators, and is bound to denounce all those he knows to be such.

The convention alone can deliver over the accused to the revolutionary tribunal, with the exception of the committees of public safety, and of general surety, and the members of the assembly sent out upon commission ; but the constituted authorities may do so if they have the permission of the two committees.

Examination privately is suppressed.*

If there exists proofs, either material or moral, independent of testimonial proofs, *it will not be necessary to hear or examine witnesses, unless when that* FORMALITY *is necessary to find out the accomplices.*

The law gives for defenders to patriots, who are accused, patriotic jurymen as voluntary advocates ;† *it allows none for conspirators.*

This criminal code would require no sort of

---

* Under such a criminal code, it would be possible to attack any person whom it might think convenient to condemn.

† *Defenseurs officieux*—persons, whether lawyers or not, who plead without hire, sometimes of their own accord,

commentary, were it not that it is only putting in writing what had been the practice during the greatest portion of the revolution, which an English orator declared was the most glorious fabric of integrity ever raised by man. Another English orator spoke of the distinction between *the true public and the false*. We see that Robespierre in his speech, after the attack meditated on his life, spoke also of the *true people and the false*; so that it appears that great statesmen in all countries stumble nearly upon the same ideas, and that Robespierre was not removed in theory so very widely from English patriots, as he happened to be by the circumstances of the times and his own situation.

In the time of the first assembly, Robespierre was suspected of having too much humanity; but we see how revolutions improve men, and develope their characters; by giving scope to the application of theory, we see how that camelion ambition, leads men to change their manner of acting.

> When Cataline by rapine swell'd his store,
> And Cæsar made a noble dame a whore;
> In this the lust, in that the avarice,
> Were means, not ends, ambition was the vice;
> For had that Cæsar liv'd in Scipio's days,
> He'd aim'd like him by chastity at praise;
> Lucullus, when frugality could charm,
> Had roasted turnips at the Sabine farm.

We must never trust much to the humanity of theorists, who are willing to let loose the people for the sake of an experiment. The alchymist is

avaricious

avaricious, but he is not economical.* A reformer, who will talk a week to save a seditious man from the gallows, would, perhaps, hazard the lives of a million of his fellow subjects in order to try an experiment, and when once in danger of losing his credit by his bad success, he would, when half his country was covered with massacres, and himself on the brink of destruction, invoke, even in the jaws of death, his favourite system.

In Briffot's time, the supreme court at Orleans was constructed nearly upon the same principle as the revolutionary tribunal, and Garan de Coulomb a famous philanthrope, and his intimate friend, was one of the leading members of that court. M. de Leffart; the minister; La Riviere, the justice of the peace, and the other forty-five victims, afterwards immolated to the patriotic fury of the people, were all sent to that court to be tried for nondescript crimes against the people; and this Briffot was the friend, and some suppose, the model of patriots in England. The distance between reformers in this country and in France, is not therefore so great in reality as it may appear to be.

It would only be a fair precaution for the nation to take, for its own safety, to have the French

* Is not there a great similitude between the *charlatan* who duped Balbinus of his gold, in order to make him rich, and the charlatans, who enslaved and ruined France, by way of making it free and happy? More gold, Balbinus, and more blood, Parisians; new experiments will ensure success; and in so talking, alchymists lose their gold

laws printed for the infpection of lawyers and jurymen, when the trial of perfons who are *active
amateurs* of French liberty, are to come on ; it
would form a glorious contraft for England, and
perhaps might convince the amateurs themfelves
of their miftake.

What would a learned counfellor here fay to
that article which fets afide evidence by witnefs
where there are *moral documents ?* or to that which
allows defenders to patriots, but none to confpirators ? Attention being duly paid to the circumftances, that it is not merely a matter of chance
that brings men before a tribunal, and that till a
defence is made, it is impoffible, to know whether the accufed is a patriot or a confpirator.

The worfhip of a Supreme Being had been decreed, and it would appear that Robefpierre,
when he united in himfelf the functions of Mofes
and Aaron, was determined that facrifices fhould
not be wanting. A new confpiracy was difcovered by his emiffaries, and befides the common
victims of the day, a number of nobles and princes
were fent to the guillotine as accomplices of the
girl who was fufpected of an intention to murder
the lawgiver and high prieft, Robefpierre.

The whole family of the foolifh girl, her father, brother, uncles, aunts, all were fent to the
place of execution ;* fo that as a fort of atone-
ment

---

* It has appeared fince by the declaration of Fouquier Tinville, who was public accufer at this time, that Robefpierre
wifhed more people to be executed upon this occafion, in order
to give the affair greater eclat, but that he had objected to it

ment for the deed intended, seventy-two victims mounted the scaffold, amongst whom were twenty-one ancient judges of the parliament of Thouloufe.

To this conspiracy succeeded one of another sort. An old devotee, who had acted the prophetess in the time of the constituent assembly, acted now the same sort of farces in France, that Mr. Brothers and his friends have been employed at in England. This old girl, Miss Theos, as Vadier declared in his accusation, is at the head of a counter-revolutionary assembly; she pretends to be inspired of God, and promises immortality to her followers, and many of those who have never done any thing for nor against the revolution are of the number. She sits in an armed chair, which she pretends is to be the throne of Louis XVII. The young prince has already been inaugurated in effigy. Dom. Gerle, a democrat in the beginning of the revolution, and member of the first assembly, applies the enigmas of the apocalypse to the events that are now passing, and swears, that the old girl is inspired, that she is a prophetess. In short, Vadier concludes with demanding, that the whole of that fanatical assembly should be delivered up to the guillotine, and orders be given to search out, arrest, and deliver over for trial the whole of their adherents and accomplices, most of whom, he had already said,

as being too ridiculous, that it would be seen through by the people. The victims on this occasion were treated with particular marks of infamy, each had on a red shirt in sign of assassination. Many of them had been in prison long before

were idle people, who had never done any thing for nor againſt the revolution.*

Day after day brought on its pretended conſpiracies and puniſhments; † the guillotine was removed to another quarter, for the ſake of the ſpectators, and orders were given to dig trenches out of the city, in order to prevent the number of the dead bodies from bringing on a diſeaſe by infecting the air.

As a ſpecimen of juſtice in civil matters which is fit to be hung up oppoſite to the decrees concerning revolutionary crimes, the following were adopted in the beginning of July, in order to prevent ariſtocratic farmers from miſapplying the grain of the republic.

1. The produce of the harveſt is put under the watch of the citizens, and confided to their care and their probity.

This firſt article is what they called the oil put upon the wedge to make it enter.

2. Grain of all ſorts is put in a ſtate of requiſition for the uſe of the armies.

* What muſt Mr. Halhed, M. P. think of treating thus an old propheteſs and her adherents?

† Amongſt the victims of this period were twenty-two young girls, from ſeventeen to twenty-five years of age. Babbling againſt the revolution was their crime:

Ils avent tenu des propos contre la revolution.

3. As

3. As soon as the harvest is over, an account will be made out of what it has produced.

4. Each farmer shall be obliged to give in a declaration of the quantity and quality of his productions, and to sign the declaration, which is afterwards to be verified, and what shall have been concealed shall be confiscated by a justice of the peace.

A number of other articles follow, which are only intended for assuring the execution of this decree.*

As tyrants are always deceived by their slaves, the convention, which had declared the people to be the sovereign, dared not to confess the defeat of the 1st of June by sea.† After delaying two weeks to give any account of that affair, Barrere began his report, by asking with what new mark of honour they should distinguish their conquering heroes, and finished by proving, that the English were beat; that the French had not only got

* It is to this decree that is to be attributed the great scarcity of corn in France since that time. It must be observed, at the same time, that though the decree was only passed now, it had been executed during the last twelve months by the ambulant commissaries.

† It was at this time that a conspiracy was discovered at Turin, which had been set on foot by French emissaries, and which had for its object, to put the royal family into the hands of the conspirators, and overturn the government during an insurrection which was to have been excited. A body of French troops was to have arrived at a signal given; the conspirators were to have massacred the royal family, and give the

their merchant fhips from America fafe home, but that the French fhips of war had been inferior in number and fuperior in battle to the Englifh ; that a captain, who was a traitor, had indeed let the Englifh admiral out the line, which was unfortunate, but that the traitor would be punifhed.

Flattery for the people in a mafs and cruelty in detail—fuch were the means of Robefpierre, and in that he imitated, in part, the conduct of Louis the Fourteenth, who firft difcovered, that if the French were flattered, and thought themfelves the greateft nation in Europe, they would confent to be the moft miferable ; not, indeed, that Louis the Fourteenth was cruel, but he was oppreffive, and he was as much attached to his own glory as the nation was to theirs, and both king and people thought, that to difturb their neighbours was the road to greatnefs.

Barrere knew that every thing is comparative, and to prop the falling credit of his chief, he did precifely what Englifh Jacobins do to make difcontents here : he wifhed to prove, that the French were free and Englifh flaves : (our patriots here fay the fame thing) he knew that the two nations are in a perpetual habit of drawing comparifons, and that neither is contented but in proportion as it furpaffes the other in happinefs, or liberty, or glory.

Formerly, the French were contented to be more polite, and to fee the fine arts flourifh more in Paris than in London, to have a more brilliant court, and to laugh at the ferocity, as they called it, of the Englifh : but they allowed they were

not

not so free as the English. Barrere, however, chuses that they shall have the joy of excelling their rivals in every thing; in giving his account of taking Ostend, where, he said, many ships and military stores had fallen into the hands of the republic, which was not quite true, because they did not get one single ship, and but few stores. He goes on with the following abuse.

It is now, says Barrere, to the great lords of parliament in England, and the disinterested orators of the commons, to vote an address of thanks to the paternal government of George, for the taking of Ypres and Ostend, Mons and Charleroi. Let them not forget the battle of Fleureus, which, like that of Jemappe, has given Belgia to the victorious French.

What does that treacherous and ferocious people want? Slave at home, despot on the continent, and pirate at sea! What can that people expect in return for so many crimes? Does it yet think to rule over the Seine and the Thames? The English monarchy, will it yet long provoke the republican indignation of France? No, you will be punished *London, self-fish and shopkeeping city*, thy lot is thrown, and thy destiny begins to be written on the harbour of Ostend.

No corresponding society in this country could speak more degradingly of England, nor in more lofty terms of the French republicans; but some of them have equalled Barrere; and yet the pride of Englishmen has not been overbowed

familiarity, and the Englifh for diftant pride; but the latter feem now to have abandoned all regard for the importance and reputation of their country, for it is now a mark of patriotifm to run it down, to fay that it is degraded, ruined, and enflaved. This is precifely what M. Barrere fays to animate his countrymen.*

But all thofe eloquent and flattering harangues were incapable of preventing the downfall of Robefpierre, and the fame Barrere who made them prepared now to follow fortune and abandon his mafter. Paris had long been in mifery, and in fear of an invading enemy; it was ftill in mifery, but no longer in fear, therefore the parties had liberty to act, and now prepared for Robefpierre the fame downfall which he had brought upon fo many of his rivals.

The committee of public fafety, which governed all, but which Robefpierre governed by means of the Jacobin club, was divided into two parties, but that of Robefpierre's was the ftrongeft. Neverthelefs, as the tyrant had of late frequently been attacked by Talien, Bourdon, and others, and as he had not been fo much applauded lately

---

* Several other pieces of Barrere's difcourfe are capital in the Jacobin way. Kings, fays Barrere, muft ceafe to exift before they ceafe to confpire againft liberty; they will ceafe to exift when they have no longer money, nor taxes, nor foldiers, nor authority; let us, then, make a war of extermination with them. Reckon that we have twelve millions of foldiers, and that they are all of one family; let us look with pity on thofe thoufands of flaves whom the emperor fends to the flaughter with ftrokes of canes, the king of Pruffia with flaps of fabres, and whom the Duke of York makes drunk with rum and with gin, &c.

in

in the club as ufual, his adherents began to calculate the poffibility of his fall; and in this, as
in all the other infurrections, we fhall fee, that
the party which thinks itfelf the ftrongeft, and is
thought to be fo, inftantly becomes fo.

Robefpierre feems either to have been in fome
degree deranged in his mind, or to have depended
folely on the Jacobin club for fupport againft his
enemies; for during the latter part of the month
of June, and the month of July, he feemed to
have totally abandoned all regard for his power
in the committee and his popularity in the affembly, and he was perpetually at the fittings of
the club, in wich, however, he did not meet
with the fame applaufe as formerly.

This abfence from the committee gave the
members more occafion to differ amongft themfelves, and thofe who were the enemies of Robefpierre more opportunity to cabal againft him.
The infurrection againft Robefpierre was moft
probably retarded by the fort of popularity which
his affaffination had given him, and in confequence
of the addreffes of congratulation which were every
day arriving from the clubs, now called popular
focieties, of the provinces; which, in imitation
of Barrere, threw all the blame of the meditated
affaffination on their two ftalking horfes, the execrable Pitt and that vile nation of flaves and
robbers the Englifh. The applaufes of thofe focieties were unanimous and violent in favour of
the decree, which ordered that all Englifh prifoners fhould be put to death.

The national convention, though Robefpierre did not now preponderate there as ufual, does not feem to have become more juft; for, under the pretext that thofe merchants, whofe partners had emigrated, received fums due to thofe emigrants, it was decreed, that the partners in all fuch houfes fhould, in twenty-four hours, give up their books to be examined and marked by the adminiftrators of diftricts, and that the property belonging to thofe who had emigrated fhould be delivered up *under pain of death.*

A decree was made at the fame time, which for its fingularity deferves mention: all directors of diligences and public carriages are ordered to give the preference for places to fuch perfons as are fent for to give witnefs at the revolutionary tribunal. A decree had been paffed fome time ago, which ordered thofe perfons confined in all parts of France to be brought to Paris. If Robefpierre excited the firft, his enemies facilitated its execution by this decree about the diligences.

Never were the French popular focieties, the municipalities, and the convention, more unanimous in their enthufiafm and approbation of the fyftem of terror; never did the guillotine labour more inceffantly to deftroy, and at no time could it be faid, that the French appeared to be filled with more republican energy.

Whether it was the falfe public or the true that applauded the fyftem of terror muft be left to connoiffeurs to determine. If it was the true public, other nations cannot much admire
the

the humanity and virtue of the French; and if it was the falfe public, the fyftem of liberty in France does not feem to have been completely eftablifhed; fo that the only alternative left to us is to moderate our admiration, for if the true public in France was free, it was not humane and virtuous, and if it was humane and virtuous, it was not free.

It will, perhaps, ftagger fome people a little, when they find, that in lefs than a month after, thofe fame popular focieties, the fame convention, and the fame committees, (about two hundred perfons excepted, who were guillotined), applauded the overthrow of the fyftem of terror, and the death of Robefpierre. So that, whether they compofed the falfe public or the true, they were, in all changes of government, the acting public, the talking public, and the reftlefs public.

We have already feen that it was the conftant practice of the party that triumphed, to throw all the odium of the horrors committed upon thofe who had fallen. But people in other nations fhould not be dupes, neither of the falfity nor the vanity of the republicans. The majority of the convention, and of all thofe who acted in France, were partifans of the fyftem of terror while it lafted. Each aided with energy to execute and applaud, though by their manner of reafoning fince, each individual appeared as if he had acted by force: it would be difficult for them to explain how the whole number of individuals lent fo willing a hand to force themfelves.

The enemies of Robefpierre were defperate be-caufe they knew that he fpared no man in his vengeance ; and they were, therefore, prepared on the firft fignal of attack to oppofe him with vigour.

Robefpierre in the Jacobin club, and Barrere in the convention, had been employed in ftirring up the public mind againft a new fect of *indul-gents*, by which name they thought proper to mark out their enemies.

On the 25th of July a deputation of the Ja-cobin club arrived at the bar of the affembly to denounce this new fect, paid by foreign nations to favour criminal indulgence and degrade im-partial juftice. Dubois de Crancé, perceiving that he was attacked, defended himfelf with vi-gour and retorted in half accufations complaints againft Robefpierre.

Next day, the 26th, the conteft was renewed with more vigour. Robefpierre appeared in per-fon in the tribune : after many praifes beftowed on his own character and virtue, he accufed the committees of public fafety and of general furety, as well as the committee of finance ; then he clofed his fpeech with a bitter complaint that the decree for putting Englifh prifoners to death had not been obeyed by the armies.

Bourdon de l'Oife, who had long been a victim marked out by Robefpierre, thought it was time to refift him, and, therefore, oppofed the print-ing of this difcourfe ; alledging, that though it might contain many truths, it might alfo contain

fome

fome falfities. Barrere voted for the impreffion, becaufe, in a free country no truth ought to be concealed. Cuthon propofed, that in place of refufing its being printed, it ought to be fent by the convention to each municipality in the kingdom.

Cambon, who belonged to the committee of finance, at the head of which he had all along been, mounted the tribune, and attacked Robefpierre. After defending the committee of finance, he had the courage to finifh with the declaration, that it was time to fay all the truth; that a fingle man paralyfed the will of the national convention; that man, faid he, is him who has now fpoke—It is Robefpierre; therefore judge.

A tyrant attacked becomes generally a coward, and Robefpierre, equally aftonifhed and afraid, began by excufing himfelf on the fubject of finance, in which he declared he never interfered, and that he had no inclination to attack the intentions of Cambon.

Billaud de Varennes, finding Cambon's attack had been fuccefsful, called Robefpierre a traitor and an impoftor, on account of falfities contained in his difcourfe; and finifhed by faying, that " if " liberty of opinion was no longer to be enjoyed, " he would rather that his dead body fhould ferve " as a throne for an ambitious man, than that he " fhould, by his filence, become the accomplice " of his crimes."

Panis, another member fuccceded, and

Jacobin club, and expelling whatever members he thought proper; that a lift of profcriptions was made out by Cuthon and Robefpierre, and that he was one of the profcribed. He demanded an explanation of this.

Robefpierre anfwered evafively: " I am," faid he, " an independent man in my opinions; " never will any one draw from me an involun- " tary retraction. In throwing down my fhield " I have left myfelf open to the attacks of my " enemies. I have flattered no one, I fear no " one, and have afperfed no one. They fpeak " to me of Fouché; I won't occupy myfelf with " him; at prefent I fet all this afide, I only liften " to my duty; I will neither receive the fupport " nor the friendfhip of any perfon; I don't feek " to form for myfelf any party. It is not, there- " fore, right to demand that I vindicate this or " that perfon; I have done my duty, let others " do the fame."

This violent conteft finifhed with Robefpierr's difcourfe not being ordered to be printed, many members of the convention obferving, that it was ridiculous for Robefpierre to think that he alone was right.

From the affembly, where the tyrant had been defeated, he went to the Jacobin club to prepare the means of crufhing his enemies. But the mo- ment of his fall was approaching; for, that fame night, in a council held in a room adjoining the Jacobin club, by Robefpierre, Cuthon, St. Juft, Le Bas, and Henriot the commandant of the Paris guards, it was determined to ftrike a bold

ftroke

ftroke by arrefting their enemies, but previoufly to make a fpeech in the convention, in order to confult public opinion, and fee how far it was in their favour.

This method of harranguing upon moments of crifis, when action is become neceffary, had ruined Briffot's party and Hebert's; but now Robefpierre fell into the fame error. Had he arrefted Barrere, Billaud de Varennes, and a few more of his enemies, that fame night, he might probably have triumphed; but it was determined to delay that meafure till the following night, after, as we have faid, having confulted the public opinion.

Robefpierre and his friends could depend upon fupport from the Jacobin club and the municipal officers, but their power in the committees and in the affembly were doubtful; and it was to try this, that they meant to make the experiment next day; St. Juft was to read a fpeech to the affembly that might ferve that purpofe.

When on the morning of the 27th St. Juft mounted the tribune to fpeak, the whole convention rofe in a mafs to prevent his being heard.

Talien then demanded to be heard, and Billaud de Varennes, Delmas, and others of the party in danger, haftened to inform the affembly that the Jacobin club had voted its deftruction; that Henriot, commandant of the national guards, was a traitor; that Robefpierre had protected

of public fafety.   That the men who were always talking of virtue and juftice in the Jacobin
clubs and in the convention, were thofe who
trampled both under their feet when it fuited
their intereft.   The applaufe with which this denunciation was received, fhewed Robefpierre
that his fatal experiment upon public opinion
was made; he endeavoured to be heard, but
was prevented by the repeated cries of *down with
the tyrant.*

Talien now attacked the man, whofe tyranny
had long been proclaimed all over Europe, except in the national convention, where it was
only newly difcovered; and finifhed his fpeech
by demanding the permanence of the affembly
till his partifans fhould be arrefted.

The convention being now ready to obey the
enemies of Robefpierre, and to decree whatever
was demanded; Barrere, who had but two days
before been the firft to fupport him in all his
oppreffion, mounted the tribune, and, in the
name of the committee of public fafety, denounced *Robefpierre's party, as being bought over by the
combined powers to make a difgraceful peace ;* that
an Auftrian officer had difclofed the fecret.

Amidft the cries of Robefpierre to obtain a
hearing, and of the accufations brought againft
him, the convention decreed, that the two Ro-
befpierres, Cuthon, St. Juft, and Le Bas, fhould
be arrefted, which was with difficulty accomplifhed.   The convention then broke all the officers
of the national guards fuperior to the comman-
dants of divifions; a proclamation which Barrere
                                                had

had prepared for the provinces followed, and the victory was reckoned as being complete.

The municipal officers, however, were in the interest of the accused, and instead of going to prison at the Luxembourg, as they were ordered, the criminals were carried to the Hotel de Ville, where, assisted by the municipality and part of the national guards, they prepared to attack the convention.

So certain had the triumphing party imagined itself of the victory being already gained, that the sitting of the assembly had been suspended, and it was only upon its being renewed in the evening, that the members found out that the greatest danger was yet to come; that the Jacobin club and the municipality had conspired together, and that Henriot had already attacked some of its members. It was then proposed by the deputies, that the members of the municipality and of the department should be ordered to the bar on purpose to be examined. The department obeyed; but the municipality, being at that time occupied in the holy duty of insurrection, could not come. Robespierre and its members were indeed preparing to come to the assembly; but not in consequence of orders received, they were coming with cannon and armed men.

Meanwhile, the committee of public safety, which was armed at all times with the power of arbitrary arrests, and had its messengers for the purpose, was very busy in arresting those who were known to be the principal agents of their

numerous, finifhed by declaring the accufed deputies and the commons of Paris outlaws, and,
as fuch, fubject to the pain of death, as foon as
they might be caught.

Amidft the various relations publifhed of what
paffed on this extraordinary occafion, it is only
poffible to perceive diftinctly, that the affembly
and its committees acted againft the municipality
and Jacobin club ; that the two latter, not having
expected the bufinefs would come on fo foon,
were not prepared to difplay their force as ufual ;
and that the great mafs of the people, uncertain
which fide to take, were divided between the two
parties, until they found that the convention
was likely to get the better, and then, according
to cuftom, the great number came over to its
fide immediately.

Revolutions were now become fo common in
Paris, and, certainly, very properly fo, as free
citizens could not be better employed than in
fulfilling the duties of infurrection, that the manner of conducting them was a matter well underftood : an addrefs to the people, and to all the
provinces ; congratulations from the people, apparent unanimity, and rejoicing the moment that
fuccefs declared for one party, was the routine
of a revolution ; fo that each ftep was taken in
its proper place, and was prepared for before it
was taken.   Barrere, fo long the chief organ of
the committees, drew up all the addreffes on this
occafion, juft in the fame ftile that he ufed to do
for Robefpierre.

The

The convention sent its members into all quarters of the city to bring the people over to its interest by reason, intreaty, and persuasion; but the fortune of the day was, in fact, decided by the want of previous arrangement on the side of Robespierre; no plan had been laid, and, of consequence, the measures pursued were partial and ill followed up.*

Between two and three in the morning, a party of armed men was dispatched under the command of some of the deputies to attack the Hotel de Ville. In some streets they met friends, who joined them, crying *vive la convention;* in others, they met enemies, who cried *vive les patriotes et la commune;* but none of them, however, were sufficiently determined to come to any open act of aggression. This force arrived at the Hotel de Ville, and, as it was the only party of armed men that was fairly determined, its sudden appearance decided every thing at once. Robespierre attempted to blow out his brains with a pistol, and mortally wounded himself; his brother broke his neck by jumping out of a window; Cuthon stabbed himself, and Le Bas crept under

* We have already seen that Robespierre did not intend to arrest his enemies till the night of the 27th, and, of consequence, all popular explosion would have been posterior to that, at all events, according to his calculation. But he probably expected to meet with no resistance, for experience had taught him that the people of Paris do not rise in insurrection to defend men who are imprisoned. It must have been owing to these reasonings, or some such like, that the Jacobins had neglected to raise the people sooner. Their emissaries were only at work to do so in the Fauxbourgs late in the evening of the 27th, and were counteracted by the

a pile of firewood to fave himfelf. The commandant of the guards, Henriot, was attacked
by Coffinhall, one of his affociates in the confpiracy, for having deceived the municipality by
faying that they might depend upon the fupport
of the national guards. Henriot was thrown
by him into a common fewer, from whence he
was with difficulty dragged out.*

The whole was over in lefs than an hour after
the firft attack; and before five o'clock in the
morning, fo quickly did the ftrongeft party meet
with obedience, that congratulations were arriving from all quarters, and continued to do fo as
faft as the news arrived, from the neareft fection
in Paris to the moft diftant municipality in Au-
vergne.

When Legendre, the butcher, was certain that
victory was decided, he went to the Jacobin club
armed with a piftol, at the head of a mob of patriots, and in order to fhoot the prefident, who
had had the wifdom to quit the chair. The club
was expelled, Legendre locked the door, and
brought the key to the affembly; thofe who were
then in the club, finding their party the weakeft,
being very much obliged to Legendre for giving
them an opportunity to retire from a poft which
was now become dangerous, and could not be
for the time productive of any advantage.

The wounded tyrant was brought on a litter to
the door of the convention, which declared, that

* As foon as the guards, headed by Leonard-Bourdon,
and fome other deputies, entered the Hotel de Ville, the
chiefs of the fubdued party began to put an end to themfelves,
and Robefpierre was the firft.

the

the presence of the man they had so long obeyed, and from whom every word which fell was received formerly with enthusiasm and applause, would defile that holy place, the temple of the laws; he was, therefore, ordered to prison till the preparations for his execution should be made, together with that of his adherents, who, having all been outlawed, the only form necessary was to certify their personal identity, and then conduct them to the scaffold.

Amongst the congratulations which arrived at the bar of the triumphant assembly, was one from its friends, the Jacobins, which is not a little remarkable, after the conduct of that society.

The orator of the Jacobins said, " Citizens,
" you see here the *true* Jacobins who have merit-
" ed the esteem of the French nation, and the
" hatred of tyrants ; you see here men who
" took arms to combat those perfidious magis-
" trates, who had usurped the national authority.
" True Jacobins, in the moment of alarm, have
" no particular place for assembling; they are
" wherever their presence is wanted, to combat
" with, or watch over conspirators.

" That monstrous assemblage of conspirators
" which defiled our hall, was composed of men
" who had no tickets, and who were at the direc-
" tion of their infamous chiefs ; but we, we were
" marching with our sections to overturn the new
" tyrant."

This discourse was received with applause,

energy and patriotifm of that celebrated fociety, which had rendered fignal fervices to the revolution, which will be immortalized in hiftory.

Perhaps nothing could be fo fevere a fatire on the Jacobin club, nor fo decided a proof of the danger of fuch a fociety to a government, as this fingular addrefs, when contrafted with the conduct of the club, and its having fo lately been fhut up by Legendre.

The friends of the Jacobins will no doubt maintain, that what its orator alledged was true, that they were not the *real Jacobins* who occupied the club at the time the confpiracy broke out. It muft, however, be remembered, that it was not only during one night that the Jacobins had fhewn their intentions to take part with Robefpierre; it had been their practice for fome time previous to the open acts of hoftility to prevent Collet d'Herbois, and thofe who had feparated from Robefpierre, from being heard. The fame prefident who had prefided before was there when Legendre fhut up the hall, but he had mixed with the members in the hall, in order to fave himfelf from the attack of the valiant boucher. It is likewife perfectly clear, that it was impoffible for the tyrant to have trufted to the Jacobin club, if its members had really been what they now pretended to be, his enemies ; it was impoffible for intruders to have ufurped the hall of that celebrated fociety, for feveral days together, without incurring the indignation of its true members ; and it may even be obferved, that if it had been fo, its true members could not have been more ufeful to the convention in

any

any place than in their own hall, driving away thofe falfe traitors who had occupied it.

Talien, the prefident, was not impofed upon, neither was any one prefent, but it was convenient to afford fo powerful a fociety a method of getting off and embracing the party of the conquerors; this was what was meant on both fides, but the poffibility of doing it in this manner, fhews how dangerous a thing it is to have a felf-created affembly that can deny its identity, and avoid punifhment by fo grofs a trick. Had Robefpierre been triumphant, it is certain beyond a doubt, that in place of the club appearing to make excufes to the convention, the members of the convention who efcaped maffacre, would have been going to the club to make their excufes, and to be admitted into its bofom. The club in that cafe would, perhaps, not have treated the members of the convention fo well as they were themfelves treated; and Talien, who now anfwered them fo favourably, would have certainly been one of their firft victims.

The executions of accufed perfons had gone on as ufual during the whole of this ftruggle; it was not till the 28th, when the party really fell, that the guillotine ceafed to work upon the ordinary victims,* in order to cut off the heads of

thofe

---

* As this is the laft moment of the violent reign of terror, it may not be improper to give the lift of executions for Paris only, during the month of July.

thofe fame men who had given it fo much eclat and activity.

On the 28th in the evening, fuch of the conquered party as were feized, were conducted to the guillotine. Robefpierre was nearly dead from the piftol fhot which he had given himfelf, and another which he had received from a fol-

Number of victims during the month of July.

		Clergy.		Nobles.		Com. people.		Total.
1ft July		1	.	0	.	13	.	14
2	.	3	.	5	.	22	.	30
4	.	1	.	4	.	21	.	26
5	.	3	.	7	.	18	.	28
6	.	5	.	40	.	23	.	68
7	(omis)	2	.	22	.	6	.	30
9	.	6	.	21	.	32	.	59
10	.	7	.	14	.	23	.	44
11	.	1	.	2	.	3	.	6
12	.	0	.	6	.	22	.	28
13	.	8	.	8	.	22	.	38
15	.	3	.	8	.	19	.	30
16	.	4	.	6	.	21	.	31
17	.	1	.	1	.	38	.	40
19	.	2	.	12	.	15	.	29
20	.	1	.	4	.	9	.	14
21	.	4	.	11	.	14	.	29
22	.	0	.	26	.	20	.	46
23	.	10	.	21	.	24	.	55
24	.	6	.	18	.	12	.	36
25	:	8	.	23	.	6	.	37
26	.	9	.	30	.	14	.	53
27	.	3	.	16	.	25	.	44
		88		305		422		815

dier

dier at the Hotel de Ville.* The other principal leaders were all either dead or wounded, fo that the people of Paris, who rejoiced in feeing their cruel mafters go to the fcaffold, gave a fcope to their merriment and their ridicule. No cavalcade, they faid, could be more grotefque, more ridiculous, nor a more fit object for rejoicing, than that of the mangled maffacrers of the nation going to expiate their crimes on the fame fcaffold where they had fent fo many innocent perfons.

Twenty-two perfons fuffered with Maximilian Robefpierre the firft day, feventy-one were guillotined the day after, and on the 30th of July, twelve more. The execution of the ufual vic-

* Maximilian Robefpierre, 35 years of age, born at Arras, deputy.

A. P. J. Robefpierre, aged 34, deputy.

A. St. Juft, born at Lifer, do.

G. Cuthon, aged 38, born at Orfay, do.

J. B. E. Lefcot Fleuriot, aged 39, mayor of Paris.

C. Payan, jury of the revolutionary tribunal, and national agent.

F. Henriot, aged 33, born at Nanterre, commis des barrieres, and commandant of the national guards of Paris.

L. C. F. Dumas, aged 37, lawyer and prefident of the revolutionary tribunal.

N. J. Vivier, aged 50, prefident of the Jacobin club during the night preceding, alfo judge of the criminal tribunal.

A. Simon, fhoemaker, tutor to the young king ; befides ten other municipal officers

tims was fufpended, and humanity began to breathe.   The men who had carried the Jacobin fyftem to its moft terrible extent, were now no more, and there feemed fome ground for a reafonable hope, that the revolution having got to the worft, might now take a better turn, and that mankind might fee with pleafure the diminution of thofe evils, the rapid and conftant increafe of which had filled them with horror and affright.

CHAP.

CHAP. V.

The system of terror not abandoned, but its rigour diminished after the fall of Robespierre—French vanity sadly mortified by being obliged to confess they had been slaves—No attempt made to establish a constitution, or regular government—The destruction of assignats, or the removal of the convention, are the only things that can restore order—New governors expose the cruelties of Robespierre's reign—Address of the ruling party in destroying the coalition of kings—Seconded by the heavy taxes in different countries, which produce discontent—Necessity for the English government acting with firmness, wisdom, and moderation, and making ameliorations, if it will avoid violent reforms and revolutions—General reflections and conclusion.

THE triumphant party, though composed of men who had signalized themselves on all occasions, by aiding, abetting, executing and defending the different cruelties during the reign of Robespierre, found nothing so politically wise as

it was not for the intereſt of its members to avow as their own, and the criminality of which afforded them ſo ample a field for diſcuſ-ſion and triumph. Nor is it at all to be doubt-ed, that Talien and others had diſapproved heart-ily of the ſyſtem of terror, ever ſince the time that they apprehended they were themſelves likely to become its victims.

All this was in favour of humanity, for in proteſting againſt the cruelties of Robeſpierre, it was an affair neceſſary, of courſe, to act differ-ently from what he had done, and accordingly the ſyſtem of terror diminiſhed amazingly; it was even propoſed to ſuſpend the revolutionary government, and to adopt fixed principles and laws for their future conduct. But this was over-ruled; the preſent maſters of France, though declared enemies to the crimes which the revolu-tionary government had given birth to, approved ſtill of the principles upon which the cruel party had acted, and thereby left open for themſelves a door for the perſecution of their own enemies, and for the firm eſtabliſhment of their own power.

The whole of the departments now combined in declaring, that they had, during the life of Robeſpierre, groaned under the moſt terrible ty-ranny ever known; but what is very remarkable, no attempt was made to prevent a repetition of the ſame deſpotiſm, by renouncing for ever thoſe falſe principles which had led to them; this was the more extraordinary, that the vanity of the nation ought to have been humbled: it had re-ceived a wound difficult to be healed, when it

was

was obliged, after boafting of the freedom and equality eftablifhed, to confefs the extent and rigour of its arbitrary government. The fhame of this, however, only led to denunciations againft Robefpierre, his accomplices, and his agents ; but no one thought of changing the declaration of rights, nor of reinftating the clergy, nor of annulling the decrees about the property of the emigrants, nor of doing away any of thofe things which had led to that great degree of mifery and flavery ; the vanity of fuch men is inconquerable, and they confoled themfelves for the affront they had received, by declaring that now they were again free, that they detefted the tyrant, and adhered more firmly than ever to liberty, equality, and their former principles.*

It will only be when the caufe is removed, that the effect will ceafe : and though it is true that the fituation of the French is lefs deplorable fince the deftruction of fhe violent party, there is not the leaft guarantee againft the repetition of thofe fame fort of crimes ; nor is it with any propriety or truth, that thofe who have fince ruled, cry out about their moderation, and the

* In this country, where it is a fixed principle that rulers fhould not be entrufted with arbitrary power, left they fhould make a bad ufe of it, the revolutionary government, which is the moft unlimited arbitrary government, fhould be confidered as the moft terrible infringement on the liberties of the fubject ; but this is not the cafe. The prefent government of France begins to be counted moderate, and ours begins to be called defpotic, becaufe it has yet too much energy to be deftroyed by the factious and difcontented. It is true, that it is only fuch as are of that defcription who complain of its defpotifm : it is a confolation which the

cruelty of the Jacobins, they have been, and still are Jacobins, to all intents and purpofes, juft as much as Hebert, Danton, and Robefpierre him-felf. With individual Jacobins, and Jacobin leaders they have differed, but with Jacobin prin-ciples they have been of accord.

The tranfactions in France fince that period are of little importance; no attempt has been made to eftablifh a regular government ; no at-tempt has been made to improve the adminiftra-tion, nor to procure order and happinefs, fo that the firft infurrection that takes place, may put things again in the pofition that they were in du-ring the time of Robefpierre ; or it may amelio-rate the ftate of the people, by producing fome-thing like order. There are only two things that are to be looked to for procuring for France fomething like law and government.

One great caufe of the want of order is the dominion exercifed over the convention by the Jacobin club, and the mob of Paris; and the other is the creation of affignats, which permits the ambitious and the factious to difpofe of all the men and all the property of the nation.

Could the convention be removed from Paris, then it is more than probable that law and order would be introduced, and when affignats can no longer be created, as taxes muft be levied (which cannot be done without a fubmiffion to the laws) fomething like order muft be eftablifhed ; but until one or other of thofe things takes place, it is clear that infurrection will follow infurrection, and the fatisfying of private vengeance will occu-

py

py the intervals between infurrections, as it has done.

When the Jacobins began to fall under the weight of the guillotine, fome people thought that by degrees France would be exhaufted of factious leaders; but that was a great miftake, the number increafes every day, and at prefent the great bulk of the nation is accuftomed to live by diforder, and a confiderable portion of it can live by nothing elfe.

The tyrant had no fooner fallen, than his fuc-ceffors began to bring to light his crimes, and to declaim againft that oppreffion which the promoters of order had declaimed againft all along, but which the friends of Jacobins in other countries denied. It was now that Fouquier Tinvile, the accufer before the revolutionary tribunal, in order to defend himfelf, proved that Robefpierre drew up lifts of victims, and that all thofe who had revenues drawn from the public funds, were profcribed as perfons whofe death would be a public benefit.* The iniquities of the revolutionary

* Much had been faid of courtiers in France, in former times, imprifoning the hufband becaufe they admired his wife. There were fome very difgraceful inftances of fuch things, though they were very rare; but in modern France they were multiplied beyond imagination, and attended with a brutality that added, if poffible, to the crime. The unfortunate women, who folicited for hufbands, fathers, or brothers, not only faw their relations flaughtered without mercy, *after having paid their ranfom at the price of their honour*, but they were themfelves often facrificed to the cruelty of the monfter whofe luft they had gratified. When there were no friends nor re-

tribunal were now unveiled, the cruel oppreffion
of the commiffaries fent into the provinces, and
particularly of Carrier at Nantz, were made
known, and men trembled to hear that their fellow creatures had been confined in prifons under
the moft cruel and moft rigorous regimen that
ever was practifed, or perhaps conceived [*Note* R.]
and that they were dragged to death without trial
or examination.

Men, women, and children, had been drowned and butchered in every method* that their
tyrants could invent, and with thofe circumftances of combined cruelty that revolt nature
[*Note* S.]

All this was brought to light under the idea
that Robefpierre and his agents alone had done it,
but that deceived nobody, for Barrere, Collot
d'Herbois, and Talien, had been fome of his
agents, they were now amongft the rulers, and
were the firft to complain.

It had pleafed the affembly, as we have feen,
to accept of the excufe made by the Jacobin club,

---

* It will be feen in the fragments of the trial of the executioners at Nantz, that are at the end of the work, that
the punifhment of victims was confidered as an amufement.
At Nantz, Carrier caufed an old man and an old woman to
be tied together, naked, back to back; young men and
young women to be tied together in the fame manner, and after
infulting them in whatever manner fuited their favage jocu-
larity at the time, they were thrown into the river. This,
Carrier called *a republican marriage*, by way of derifion.
When Carrier was tried, he found many defenders, and his
punifhment had like to have occafioned a revolution; when
Louis XVI. his queen, and his fifter, were condemned, no
efforts were made to fave them ! ! !

that it was not the club itself, but intruders, who had acted against the convention; and it may please Jacobins in other countries to throw the blame of all the cruelties upon Robespierre; and to suppose that they are over with him, that the rulers of France since that time are men attached to law and order; but this can never be believed, since those rulers have preserved the law of the maximum and the revolutionary government.

The fall of Robespierre disconcerted those who counted upon the vigour of one single party, and one single chief; but the armies were recruited, and the enemies repulsed before his destruction, and that had no favourable effect upon the operations of the latter part of the campaign; on the contrary, it did considerable hurt to the combined powers.

Every change, when things are in a bad state, gives hopes, and this change inspired all the armies with the hope that liberty was now once for all certain; the discussions of the assembly turning against the crimes of Robespierre, seemed to turn in favour of virtue and order; and Talien, the massacring hero of September 1792, was now metamorphosed into a man, who held bloodshed in detestation, so that the French government began to inspire less horror, and those who had to defend themselves against its arms, slackened their efforts. The Dutch began to consider that an alliance was possible with the convention, and that it would not be worse for them to have

Orange for Stadtholder.* They remembered the mortifications of 1787, but they forgot the more recent maffacres in France.

On no occafion, one excepted, have the Jacobins fhewn themfelves *mal adroit* with refpect to turning to advantage the changes operated by unforefeen events, and never did they turn any one more artfully to advantage than the fall of Robefpierre; from that moment did they direct their views to the deftruction of the coalefced powers, by flattering them and feparating them.

The *third ftate*, and the people who had nothing, had triumphed over the proprietors, the clergy, and the nobles, by feparating their interefts, and by holding up hopes to the one, at the expenfe of the other, with the intention of finifhing, by ruining them all ; the fame game was now to be played with nations, that had been played with different orders in their own nation, and the powers at war were to be detached from the coalition, one by one. No more injurious language was heard againft kings in general, as

---

* The Orange party, which had made fuch ftrong efforts for that family in 1787, was now difcontented ; the Stadtholder had not, they complained, given that preference to his friends over his enemies that they merited. This is a very common error, into which moft rulers fall (except the Jacobins). Louis XVI. fell partly for the fame reafon, and James II. of England found fewer fupporters than he would have done, had the conduct of Charles II. been more fevere towards his father's enemies, and more generous towards his friends. It is an odd enough thing that moft governments treat their enemies better than their friends; this is the cafe with minifters as well as kings, and it is one reafon why they have fo many enemies. It arifes from their being actuated more by a principle of fear, than of friendfhip or generofity.

in the times of Briffot and Robefpierre ; the law for putting to death Englifh and Hanoverian prifoners was repealed, and as every thing is judged of by comparifon, the prefent government of France feemed to be mild and humane.

The efforts of the Jacobins in different countries, feconded as they always have done, the convention, and began according to their own term, to *neutralize men's minds (neutralizer les efprits)*. With refpect to the nature of the French government, they had contrived in the convention to feparate the principles of the revolution, from the atrocities of the revolution ; they exclaimed, as all mankind did, againft the latter, and by coinciding with humane and reafonable men in this one thing, led many fuch to coincide with them in the other part of the fyftem.

The feeble defence made by the Dutch was one of the confequences of this ; the negotiations entered into by the king of Pruffia, and the German ftates, arifes partly from the fame caufes ;* others, there is not a doubt, will follow, and provided the plan in view by the convention fucceeds, the whole of Europe will be thrown

---

* The French government being changed, the King of Pruffia had a fhadow of an excufe for changing his conduct alfo. As to the Dutch, their difcontent with the war, added to the efforts made by Jacobin emiffaries, to perfuade them, that France would not do the country fo much harm as its allies had done ; they faw the invafion without either much pain or pleafure ; they have paid pretty dearly for their *fang froid.*

into a ftate of revolution.* The property of thofe who poffefs any at prefent, will be divided as it has been in France, amongft thofe who have none, and the fuccefs of this depends upon one fingle circumftance.

France may make peace with all the nations in Europe, without any fort of hefitation on her fide, for as the whole country is up in arms, it can begin again juft as readily as the municipality of Paris can march againft the convention ; it can likewife employ emiffaries and excite difcontents, while upon its own fide it has nothing to fear and nothing to lofe.†

The taxes, and of confequence the difcontents of people, in other countries, will have been fo much increafed by the prefent war, that it will

* The leaders in France have never varied in the defign of introducing revolution into other countries; this is one thing on which they are all of one mind, and have been ever fince the beginning. The firft convention thought to make conquefts by fpeaking and writing, the fecond by force of arms, and Robefpierre by terror. The plan at prefent is to employ all the different ways at once, arms with one, money with another, emiffaries with a third; by dividing all to triumph over all, and to finifh by robbing each one at its leifure. The fyftem of plunder in Holland is a fpecimen; they knew the guillotine made commercial wealth difappear; therefore a fixed requifition is firft exacted, on pretence of neceffity, with a promife of protection ; another, and another requifition fucceeds, until much more is exacted than could ever have been got by open force at once.

† France is now literally in the fituation of a ragged vagabond, who attacks a well-dreffed man. Its own fituation cannot be made worfe, while every blow given to the enemy does an injury, until he fhall be reduced to the fame fituation of filth and dirtinefs, and then the conteft will become equal.

not

not be difficult to create confusion, and it will not be very difficult to attack them by open force, and one by one.* There is no danger of a new coalition of nations, for some time at least, against France, and perhaps it will even be found possible to turn the arms of the coalesced powers against each other. Recent injuries are most productive of quarrels, and the unfair cecession of one king from the common cause may, with the aid of a little intrigue, bring on new troubles.

The French government, by changing its measures and its identity at pleasure, enjoys an advantage over all other governments, for it can avow, or refuse to avow, any measure that it pleases, as it has already done.

* The taxes in England will be greatly increased by the revolution. To the original taxes before the war, will be added the interest of the money borrowed to carry it on ; and it being impossible to put either the navy or the army on a peace establishment, loans must either be continued in time of peace, or else heavy taxes laid on to pay the increased expenses. It might not be unreasonable to suppose, it will be thus :

Original taxes before the war	16 millions a year.
Interest of money borrowed	3 do.
Expenses of the navy kept up	2 do.
Of the army ordnance and militia	1 do.
Total	22 millions annually.

This is not a very pleasant prospect, and will give our enemies a great handle over us, so that this government must prepare seriously to make a stand against their efforts, and, if possible, get things upon such a footing when a peace is

The thing, then, on which the fate of Europe depends is fimply this ; *Whether the revolutionary government of France, or the power of defending ourfelves againft it, fhall finifh the firft?* that is to fay, Whether the whole of the coalciced powers fhall be reduced to the neceffity of making peace with France before the convention quits Paris, or before the affignats ceafe to fupply the place of regular taxes? This is now the great queftion upon which depends the welfare of Europe, and it muft be confeffed, that after the various methods by which the credit of the affignats have been kept up, it is not poffible to eftimate the duration of that refource, there is even reafon for thinking, that whilft the revolutionary government exifts, affignats will be preferved, and that in fuch a manner as to fupply the place of taxes.

The infatuation of the French prevents them from feeing that their own intereft, and that of the reft of Europe, is the fame ; they want liberty and peace, which they can never have while a few individuals can rule the mob at Paris, and rob the whole kingdom by means of their affignats, It would, therefore, be the intereft of the whole of Europe to come to a proper underftanding upon this fubject, if that were poffible ; but if that is not, there is nothing for it, but for other governments to fet ferioufly about a method of protecting themfelves from an attack, whether by open arms or by difcontents fomented.

The brilliant campaign which the French made laft year tends greatly to diminifh the horror in which their government has been held. Bravery,

very, in all cases, has been considered as a
sort of alleviation of guilt, and though, perhaps, improperly so, it does certainly diminish
the horror in which men hold cruelty. Nero
never did any thing, perhaps, more cruel than
Alexander the Great did, when he took the city
of Tyre, but the one was brave and the other
was only sanguinary; the name of Nero inspires
horror and disgust, that of Alexander does not,
but, on the contrary, carries along with it a certain degree of esteem and admiration. A change
pretty similar has, it is very perceivable, taken
place in Europe since the beginning of the last
campaign. The French arms were then despised,
and their crimes abhorred; people now eye them
differently, their success has operated a change
in their favour; people talk with less disgust of
their crimes, and speak of their government
with rather more respect.

The coalesced powers have neglected much
that they ought to have done, and, amongst other
things, they have neglected to contradict the reports spread about the bravery, discipline, and
order of the French armies.*

Europe is left in ignorance of the truth, and
of a truth so essential to be known and so
easily made known. The French set to work
systematically to spread their false reports of victories, and we set to work to make known our
defeats. The gasconades of Barrere have been

* This neglect is inconceivable, since it might be so easily

copied into all newfpapers in all countries, without either contradiction or commentary: and even thofe who know their falfity have remained filent, when they might with truth have faid, (and without danger of being contradicted) that in no one cafe when the numbers were equal, have the French gained a victory over their enemies; that they have never preferved difcipline nor order, nor abftained from pillage, except when they have been mafters of the country, and when, by a general requifition and diftribution of affignats, the French generals could confider all the wealth and property of the conquered country as being their own ftores, in their own magazines, [*Note* T.] that the private foldier was not permitted to pillage the individual, becaufe the general pillaged regularly the whole country; but that where that could not be done, there was no fort of exaction and vexation that was not exercifed.

Why are not mankind informed of this? Why has pillage and deftruction been allowed to affume the appearance of juftice and order? Wherefore do the combined powers let themfelves be calumniated and abufed? Why has it not been explained, that by mere dint of numbers the French have triumphed over armies fuperior in bravery and in fkill? and why has it not been explained, that the revolutionary government of the French leaves them at all times at liberty to increafe and multiply oppreffion and vexation? That one requifition, which is the title they have chofen to give to robbery, does not preclude them from making another next day, that their

fyftem

fyftem ftill is to continue to take till nothing more remains to be taken.*

The French themfelves require no pofitive teftimony of guilt where there are moral proofs; if then they are to be judged by their own rule, thofe who were cruel and unjuft laft year, muft be cruel and unjuft ftill, becaufe, though men who have been humane may become cruel, men who have once been practically cruel never become humane; and we have feen, that during the whole of the revolution nothing but cruelty and injuftice has prevailed, though the rulers and their agents have often changed; therefore it is in vain that the blame is thrown upon any particular man or fet of men, it remains with the nation, and muft remain with it.

Since the fall of Robefpierre, though Jacobins in other countries have not been lefs active than before, and though they found in him and his party a fcape goat, whom they might load with the enormities which fprung out of their fyftem itfelf, yet they have not had the courage to make an attack upon other governments, in the fame way that they did in the times of the conftituent affembly, and of Briffot's party. They do not vaunt the rights of man, as ufual, becaufe they are fenfible, that the crimes of Robefpierre may be traced to that impure origin, and if they were to ftir up the inquiry it might hurt their caufe; but thofe who wifh the prefent race of men may not be facrificed to wild theories, fhould ftir up

* The expreffions of the French themfelves, before they

that difcuffion, and it fhould not only be proved, but made known in every country, *that the original declaration of rights is the caufe of the miferies of France.* This is the more neceffary, that the enemies of order and government now attack people by the moft infidious method of any, by endeavouring to ftir up difcontent; they cannot now hold France up as they ufed to do, as a model to copy from, but they know that difcontent brings on revolution, and that is all they want.

The language of thofe who praifed the French conftitution as being a mafter-piece, and who admired its authors, are now a little afhamed of their error, fince the guillotine has made fuch ravages amongft their heroes, and fince the fyftem they admired has produced fuch unheard-of fcenes of mifery, diftrefs, and wickednefs; but thofe fame perfons are not one bit lefs fevere on the imperfections of other governments; on one fide *they extenuate much,* and on the other feem *to fet down much in malice;* for certainly take man, infulated from all degree of anger and refentment on one fide, or of favour and good-will on the other, it is impoffible to fpeak with expreffions of indignation againft the eftablifhed governments of Europe, and with expreffions of complacency towards the government of France, yet fuch is the daily practice; let it be granted, that other governments are bad, yet that of France muft be allowed to be worfe, as the end of every government is to make the people happy.

We have already obferved, that the fuccefs of the French arms had diminifhed the horror infpired

ſpired by their crimes, and it is equally true, that with reſpect to their enemies their own cauſe ſeems worſe, becauſe it has been badly defended. The pillaging, murdering ſans culotte holds up his victorious arms, and ſays, there is my title to property, let him who dares diſpute its validity; whilſt his enemies, driven behind mountains and rivers, are employed rather in concealing the ſhame of defeat than in preparing to conteſt his right; and what we have obſerved during the whole of the revolution to take place in Paris, amongſt parties, is on the brink of taking place in Europe, amongſt nations. Strength and power are likely to be where they are thought to be, and the French, victorious, but weak and miſerable, will ſoon have more allies than thoſe who fight againſt them.

As we have traced the origin of Jacobiniſm, but, above all, its rapid progreſs, to cauſes that had long exiſted in the government of France, we may likewiſe find, that its continuance, notwithſtanding the unexampled miſery with which it has been attended, is owing to cauſes that exiſt in other governments, and it would be well for thoſe who are moſt intereſted in the preſent order of things, to conſider what they have at preſent, what riſks they run, and what they may do to enſure themſelves againſt thoſe riſks.

It would be vain to imagine, that thoſe who endeavour to ſow diſcontent in other countries, could meet with attentive hearers, if men were not inclined by ſome general motive to liſten to

We can eafily fuppofe a leading orator, and a few of his friends, to be actuated by perfonal motives of intereft or revenge; we can fuppofe the prefident of a club, and a few of his affociates, to be the fame; but how are we to account for the avidity with which a great portion of the public is fwayed by thofe orators, and that men who are neither ambitious nor vindictive are amongft their followers. We find that this is the cafe, and the following is the reafon.

The exifting governments of Europe, excepting none, *hold abufe, when fanctified by precedent too facred*, and therefore abufes are always accumulating without any hopes of their being diminifhed. The French government is bad, but it is an experiment, and perpetually flatters people with the hope of improvement. Other governments, vaftly more free in themfelves, and vaftly more conducive to individual happinefs, do not offer any hope of improvement, and therefore create difcontent.

It may be faid, that this is not reafonable; perhaps it is not, but it is natural to man. The richeft proprietor in England, will not he be difpleafed if an acre is taken from his eftate? and the pooreft, will he not be pleafed when he fees a profpect of his little property augmenting? It will be no argument with the rich man, that he has got ftill ten thoufand times as much as the poor; no, he thinks not of that, but of what he ought to have. Juft fo it is with us, the miferies of France afford no confolation to an Englifhman, who confiders, that though the abufes in this country are not nearly equal to thofe in France,

yet

yet ſtill there are abuſes, and that he has not the proſpect of a remedy which he might expect.

Upon the ſuppoſition that the legiſlature of this country wiſh ſincerely to preſerve the preſent order of things,* it may be repreſented to them, that, if the deſire of reform is ſo inherent in the breaſts of men, as to make any conſiderable portion of them willing to run the riſk of a revolution, it ought to be carefully conſidered, by what means ſo terrible a thing as revolution is to be prevented.

The error of the firſt aſſembly in France, in rendering all parts of their conſtitution equally ſacred, brought on the deſtruction of the whole. The rotten pulled down with it what was found. The abuſes of the feudal ſyſtem were the cauſe of its total deſtruction, though ſome parts of it were good. The unwillingneſs of the court of France to make a few ſacrifices to the people with a good grace, brought on terrible calamities, that ended in the total deſtruction of the court, and the miſery of the people. A little ſooner, or a little later, ſimilar cauſes produce ſimilar effects in all countries; for the mind of man throughout the world is nearly the ſame. Hope and fear act on all, and muſt always do ſo; therefore, no nation can with reaſon think that it will be exempted from the revolutions, which the paſſions of men bring on, by any other mode than that of preventing the unfavourable action of thoſe paſſions.

There is one reform in this country that will inevitably bring on a revolution when it takes place ; that is, the reform of the reprefentation of the people ; therefore, that reform fhould be by fome means prevented ; and though there are many devices, that may be fallen upon to *retard* the meafure, there is but one to *prevent it.* The houfe of Commons muft fhow that it requires no reform, and then the nation will be contented, but never till then.

Is it not the duty of the reprefentatives of the people, to inquire into what may be done for the happinefs of the people, and to go on with a refolute intention and a firm ftep in the execution of their defign? Is it not notorioufly known by the experience of every day that the code of civil law in this country wants amendment, and its adminiftration wants it ftill more? Does not the whole nation cry out, as with one voice, againft an army of depredators, who, under the pretence of procuring juftice* for individuals, rob them often of their all. A reform in the law would lead to no dangerous confequences, and it would be of infinite utility, and create univerfal fatisfaction; *it would give hope.* We fhould not then fee a few miferable wretches hanged for ftealing trifles, while we fee others riding in coaches, fupported by the fpoils of whole families, and infulting the indigence which they have produced.

* With refpect to the judges of this country, it muft be faid to their honour, that, in no country under the fun are they more equitable, nor more careful to fearch out truth, and adminifter juftice ; but then, tied up by law and precedent on one fide, and tormented by the chicane and fubterfuge of men who act in their courts, they have it not in their power always to do juftice ; nor, when they do, have they any proper controul over the expenfe which that juftice cofts.

When

When evils are complained of, let those who can remedy them inquire into them with candour and attention ; if they admit of a remedy, let it be applied ; and if they do not, let that be proved, and we shall be satisfied ; but it must be owned, that contentment and satisfaction cannot be expected at any lesser price.

Those who enjoy places of power and profit, let them do it with modesty and moderation ; and above all, let them fulfil the duties of their offices; let it be considered that every thing has its price, and that the liberty and happiness which we enjoy, may seem too dear.

Let the vigour of government be preserved ; let it yield nothing to menace, but every thing to justice ; and though we have seen that abstract principles are dangerous in governments, there is one principle that may be adopted without danger : *That when the situation of mankind can be ameliorated by a change, without running any risk of making it worse, it ought to be done, and that it is the duty of rulers to do it.*

Governments, are obliged to employ many forts of means to support their power ; and when they cease to employ any, they soon fall. A bad government that appears eternally struggling to render the people happy by good laws, even if it should not succeed, will find advocates and admirers, it will even inspire enthusiasm in many cases, as we see that of France has done; but a government that seems careless of procuring the

We have feen that affiliated clubs, interfering in the politics and adminiftration of a country, are the ruin of peace, happinefs, and liberty. Let them be forbidden by law under the fevereft penalties; but, at the fame time, let thofe who apply for a redrefs of grievances in a fair, open, and candid manner, meet with attention: let not the power of rulers ftifle public complaint, nor the infolence of office infult or opprefs the individual. The times are changed fince Shakefpeare's days: men do not now rather bear the ills they have, than fly to others that they know not of.

The infolence of office, the law's delay, and the affronts that patient merit of the unworthy bears, are griefs of which the prefent age complains, and which it is not inclined to bear any longer with patience. As this is evident beyond a doubt, let a remedy be fought by amelioration, of which the confequences may be calculated.

Though the fyftem of Jacobinifm, and the reign of Jacobins did not ceafe with Robefpierre, yet its hiftory, as far as relates to the interior of France, may with propriety ftop for the prefent at that period, becaufe the real conduct of the leaders of any party is not known till that party falls; and, as the party which overthrew Robefpierre is yet in the Capitol, though perhaps not very far from the Tarpeian rock, yet it is not time to examine its conduct any farther than to obferve that, though the revolutionary government has continued, and the requifitions alfo, yet neither have been put in execution with the rigour formerly employed. We have already obferved that the true guarantee of the good intentions

of

of the prefent governors of France would be their laying afide that unexampled degree of power fo eafily abufed. We fhall give them their credit for moderation and for good intentions, when they enact laws and eftablifh a conftitution, after having inquired by what means the defpotifm under which France groaned in the time of Robefpierre was eftablifhed. It will not be faid that if Robefpierre's wickednefs made him exercife a cruel defpotifm, that his own abilities or gigantic force made him a defpot. He either muft have found men or things to favour his ambitious views; thofe fhould be fought after; and, furely, it cannot be very difficult to trace his tyranny to the declaration of rights and the infurrections brought about by means of it and of the Jacobin club.

It is by no means with the unfair intention of painting Jacobinifm in its blackeft colours, that we ceafe its hiftory at the fall of its greateft tyrant; although the revolution has gained many partifans by its hiftorian ftopping at the 10th of Auguft, and, therefore, only fhewing its faireft fide. Such partial reprefentations, if done with intention, are unfair; the reigns of Nero and Caligula are not to be felected and given as the reigns of Roman emperors, neither are thofe of Marcus Aurelius and Titus Antoninus to be given under that title. Truth is the object of Hiftory, and whatever tends to difguife that, deftroys its true end.

The parties of Talien and Barrere had been

again, as might be expected. The different partifans of Barrere and Collot d'Herbois, as well
as themfelves, have been banifhed ; and this purification will probably go on till fome new infurrection takes place, of which the fate will depend, as is ufual in all their infurrections, upon
the public opinion with refpect to the ftrength of
the parties. Talien and his friends have now
ruled about nine months ; they have fhewn fome
moderation and much addrefs; they have already
fucceeded in weakening their enemies by the fub-
jection of Holland, and by detaching the King
of Pruffia from the league againft them. They
have been witneffes to vexatious exactions in
Holland, and unexampled cruelties committed
by their armies in Spain. In Holland, where
they were mafters, they have avowed their injuftice ; in Spain, where they expect yet to make
conquefts, they have difavowed their cruelties,
but they have not punifhed them. But the beft
of all their actions is their having punifhed the
agents, and what they call the continuators of
Robefpierre, and expofed the cruelties which
were committed under his reign ; though, until
they have difavowed his principles, and laid down
their power, it will be difficult for us to forget
that they themfelves were of the number of the
tyrant's agents.

More moderate than Robefpierre, and lefs fo
than Briffot and his party, the prefent rulers of
France have co-operated with both ; but all the
three agreed perfectly in their plans of conqueft,
though they differed about the means; they all
agreed in the principle of infurrection and what
                                        they

they call liberty and equality, but they differed as to the lengths to which they fhould be carried In one word, they have all joined in deftroying religion and government, and pillaging property, though they have all differed about the diftribution of power and the divifion of the fpoils. It cannot, therefore, be admitted that Jacobinifm does not reign in France, becaufe of late they have exclaimed againft it; but their doing fo is a proof that the mifery of the country is by themfelves afcribed to the principles adopted by the clubs, and propagated by them. And it affords a reafonable ground of hope that, as their delufion ceafes, their mifery will decreafe, and that that miferable nation may at laft find happinefs reftored, by reftoring order and government, which fhe has fo long facrificed, to a love of theory, and imaginary perfection.

The Jacobins individually having become odious, it will naturally follow that their principles will become fo too; though, from the prefent ftate of things to fo happy a conclufion, there muft be a long progreffion, and many ftorms are to be feared, in fome of which Jacobinifm may triumph, but, in the end, it muft fall; mifery muft at laft get the better of vanity; the provinces of France, muft, in the end, fhake off the yoke of the rabble of the Fauxbourg St. Antoine; and the nation will at laft fee into the abfurdity of putting every thing at the difpofition of a number of intriguing defpots, who by means of a printing prefs and reams of affignats, pillage the nation, and excite maffacre and bloodfhed. Never

did any ſtruggle begun for liberty ſo effectually
retard its progreſs; but the whole human race
may profit by it, and it may be the means of
procuring happineſs for ages yet to come, by
ſhewing the danger of error when ſupported by
enthuſiaſm.

NOTES.

NOTES.

NOTE A.

DECLARATION OF THE KING.

Concerning the present holding of the States-General read to the Affembly of the States at the Seance Royale of the 23d of June, 1789.

IT is the king's will that the three orders of the ſtate ſhould be preſerved entire, as being eſſentially connected with the conſtitution of his kingdom : that the deputies freely choſen by each of the three orders, forming three chambers, deliberating by order (or ſeparately) and having a right, with the approbation of his majeſty, to determine upon deliberating in common, are to be conſidered as forming the body of repreſentatives of the nation. In conſequence of this, the king declares the deliberations adopted by the deputies of the orders of the third ſtate on the 17th of this month ; as alſo whatever may ariſe out of theſe deliberations, to be null and void, as being illegal and unconſtitutional.

His majeſty declares to be good and valid all the powers of deputies verified, or to be verified in each chamber, againſt which no objections have ariſen, or ſhall ariſe. His majeſty orders that communication ſhall be mutually and reſpectively given between the orders on that ſubject.

With regard to the powers which may be contefted,
in each order, and concerning which the parties interefted will do what is neceffary, the king will determine
in the manner hereafter to be ordered, for and during
the holding of the prefent ftates-general only.

The king breaks and annuls, as being unconftitution-
al, contrary to the writs of convocation, and to the intereft of the ftate, fuch reftriction of power, as by dimin-
ifhing the freedom of deputies to the ftates-general, may
hinder them from adopting the forms of deliberation
taken feparately, by order, or in common by the diftinct
will of the three orders.

If, contrary to the intentions of the king, fome of the
deputies have taken an oath rafhly, not to deviate from
fome particular form of deliberation, his majefty leaves
it to their confcience to determine whether or not the
rules which he is about to lay down, agree with, or differ from the letter or the fpirit of the engagements
which they have taken.

The king permits thofe deputies who think themfelves confined by their inftructions, to demand new
powers from their conftituents. But his majefty en-
joins them to remain, in the mean time, at the ftates-
general, and to give their opinion and advice on the
preffing affairs of the ftate.

His majefty declares, that in a future convocation of
the ftates-general, he will not allow the cahiers or orders given to the deputies to be confidered as any thing
more than fimply inftructions confided to the confcience
and free opinion of the deputies chofen.

His majefty having exhorted the three orders to re-
unite themfelves for the good of the ftate, during the
holding of the prefent ftates, and no longer, that they
may deliberate in common upon affairs of general utility, defires to make known his intentions as to the manner in which they are to proceed.

Nothing

Nothing can be treated of in a common affembly that regards the ancient conftitutional rights of the three orders, the form that is to be given to future affemblies, of the ftates-general, feudal or feignorial property, or the ufeful rights, or honourable prerogatives of the two firft orders.

The particular confent of the clergy fhall be neceffary for all regulations that may intereft religion, ecclefiaftical difcipline, or the laws and regulations refpecting regular or fecular orders and bodies.

All deliberations entered into by the three orders, in common, about the contefted powers of deputies, fhall be determined by the plurality of votes ; but if two thirds of the voices in one of the three orders protefts againft the determination, the affair fhall be appealed to his majefty, to be by him definitively determined.

If with a view to facilitate the re-union of the three orders, they fhall wifh that the queftions to be deliberated in common fhall be determined by a majority of two-thirds of the voices only, his majefty is difpofed to authorife that method. The affairs which fhall have been decided in the affembly of the three orders re-united, fhall be a fecond time difcuffed the day following, if one hundred members demand it.

The king wifhes in the prefent circumftances, in order to preferve harmony and concord, that the three chambers fhould begin feparately to name a commiffion, compofed of any number of deputies they may think proper, to prepare the form and the diftribution of the *beaureaus of confidence*, where the different affairs are to be difcuffed.

The general affembly of the orders fhall be reprefented by the prefidents, chofen by each of the orders, according to their ufual rank.

that his majesty should forbid, expressly, any person who is not a member of the states-general, from taking part in their deliberations, whether they are taken jointly or separately.

DECLARATIONS OF THE INTENTIONS OF THE KING.

No new tax shall be levied, nor any old one continued beyond the term fixed by the law, without the consent of the representatives of the nation.

New taxes which may be laid on, or old ones, of which the duration may be prolonged, shall never be done but for the term it has to run, between such time of prolongation or laying on, and the meeting of the next assembly of the states-general.

As loans of money may become the occasion of an increase of expenses, no loan shall be made without the consent of the states-general, except in case of war or other national danger, the sovereign shall have the right to borrow a sum not exceeding one hundred millions ; for the intention of the king is never to put the safety of his empire into the power of any man or body of men.

The states-general will examine with care the situation of the finances, and will demand all the information that is necessary for understanding them perfectly.

A table, giving a state of the revenue and expenses, shall be published every year in a form proposed by the states-general, and approved of by the king.

The sums destined for each department in the state shall be determined in a fixed and invariable manner, and the king submits the expenses of his houshold to that same rule.

The king's will is, that in order to render the sums that are necessary, certain, the states-general do point
out

out to him the regulations neceffary, which his majefty
will adopt if they are fuch as are confiftent with
royal dignity, and the indifpenfable difpatch of public
affairs.

The reprefentatives of the nation, faithful to the laws
of honour and of probity, will do nothing incompatible
with the public faith ; and the king expects that the
claims of the creditors of the ftate fhall be confirmed in
the moft authentic manner.

When the difpofition of the clergy and nobility, already formally announced of renouncing their pecuniary privileges, fhall have actually been realized by their
deliberations, the intention of the king is to fanction it,
and that in future there fhall not exift in the payment
of pecuniary contributions any fort of privilege or
diftinction.

The king wills, that in order to render facred fo
important a principle, the name of *taille* fhall be entirely
abolifhed in the kingdom, and that the tax levied by that
title, fhall be commuted with the twentieth, or fome
other territorial tax ; or that it be replaced in fome other
manner, but upon juft, fair, and equal principles,
without diftinction of rank, birth, or condition.

The king wills, that the right of FRANC-FIEF fhall be
abolifhed as foon as the revenues and expenfes of the
ftate fhall be brought to balance each other.

All forts of property, without diftinction, fhall be
conftantly refpected ; and his majefty exprefsly mentions, under the name of property, tythes, hundredths,
rents, rights, and fervices, feudal and feignorial; and
in general all ufeful or honourable rights and prerogatives attached to lands or fiefs, or belonging to perfons.

The two firft orders of the ftate fhall continue to en-then that all the orders fhould be alike fubjected to them.

The intention of his majefty is to determine, with the advice of the ftates-general, what are to be the employments and places which fhall in future tranfmit or confer nobility. His majefty, neverthelefs, according to the right inherent in the crown, will grant patents of nobility to fuch of his fubjects, as, by fervices rendered to the king or to the ftate, fhall have fhewn themfelves deferving of fuch a recompence.

The king wifhing to fecure perfonal liberty to all citizens in a lafting and folid manner, invites the ftates-general to feek out and propofe to him the beft mode of reconciling the abolition of *LETTRES DE CACHET* with the fafety of the public, and with the precautions neceffary in certain cafes to preferve the honour of families, as well as to crufh fedition in its commencement, and to fecure the ftate againft the effects of criminal correfpondences with foreign powers.

The ftates-general will examine and make known to his majefty the beft means of reconciling the LIBERTY OF THE PRESS, with the refpect due to religion and manners, and the honour of citizens.

There fhall be eftablifhed in the different provinces or generalities of the kingdom, provincial ftates, compofed of two-tenths of members of the clergy, of whom one part will be neceffarily chofen from the epifcopal order, three-tenths from the order of the nobility, and five-tenths from the third eftate.

The members of the provincial ftate fhall be freely chofen by their refpective orders ; and it will be neceffary to be poffeffed of fome property in order to be either a voter or a member.

The deputies of the provincial ftates fhall deliberate in common upon all affairs, according to the cuftoms and practice of the provincial affemblies whom thefe ftates fhall replace.

An intermediate commiſſion, choſen by theſe ſtates, ſhall adminiſter the affairs of the province during the interval of the ſeſſions; and theſe intermediate commiſſions being reſponſible for their conduct, ſhall have delegates choſen by themſelves alone, or by the provincial ſtates.

The ſtates-general will propoſe to the king their views with reſpect to all other parts of the interior organization of the provincial ſtates, and for the choice of the forms applicable to the election of the members of the ſaid ſtates.

Independent of the objects of adminiſtration with which the provincial aſſemblies are charged, the king will confide to their care the adminiſtration of hoſpitals, priſons, depots for mendicants, foundling hoſpitals, the inſpection into the expenſes of towns, the care of foreſts, the care and the ſale of timber, and ſuch other objects as may be advantageouſly adminiſtered by the provinces.

All conteſtations that may ariſe in the provinces where ancient ſtates have exiſted, and all reclamations againſt the forming of theſe aſſemblies, ſhould occupy the attention of the ſtates-general, who will make known to his majeſty the diſpoſitions of juſtice and of wiſdom which it may be proper to adopt, in order to eſtabliſh a fixed rule in the adminiſtration of theſe provinces.

The king invites the ſtates-general to occupy itſelf to diſcover the beſt means of turning the royal domains to advantage, as well as to give their views with reſpect to thoſe which are mortgaged.

The ſtates-general will occupy itſelf about a project conceived a long time paſt of carrying all the cuſtom-houſes to the frontiers of the kingdom, ſo that the moſt unreſtrained and free circulation of merchandiſes, whe-

His majefty defires that the vexatious effects of the taxes on falt, and the importance of that revenue, may be carefully confidered ; and that, at all events, means of foftening the rigour in receiving the faid tax be attended to.

His majefty defires likewife that the inconveniencies arifing from the *droits d'aides*, and other taxes, may be carefully confidered, but without lofing fight of the abfolute neceffity of preferving an exact balance between the revenue and the expenfes of the ftate.

According to the intentions manifefted by his majefty, in his declaration of the 23d of laft September, the king will examine with ferious attention fuch projects as fhall be delivered to him on the adminiftration of juftice, and of the means of perfectioning the civil and criminal code.

The king wills, that fuch laws as he may promulgate during the holding of the ftates-general fhall not fuffer any delay in the enregiftering, nor any obftacle in their execution, throughout the whole extent of his kingdom.

His majefty's will is, that the corvée for the making and keeping in repair high roads, fhall be entirely and perpetually abolifhed in his kingdom.

The king wills the abolition of the right of *mainmorte*, of which his majefty has given an example on his own domains, fhould be extended to the whole of France ; and that fome means may be propofed to him to indemnify the lords in poffeffion of fuch rights.

His majefty will inceffantly make known to the ftates-general the rules by which he means to regulate the *capataineries*, and thereby give his fubjects a proof of his affection by putting reftrictions on what is moft intimately connected with his perfonal enjoyments.

The

The king invites the ftates-general to confider the drawing for the militia in every point of view ; and to confider on the beft modes for reconciling the defence of the ftate with the ameliorations which he would wifh to bring about in the condition of the fubject.

It is the king's will that all rules and difpofitions for public order and the happinefs of his people, which his majefty fhall have fanctioned by his authority during the feffion of the prefent ftates-general ; and, amongft others, thofe relative to perfonal liberty, equality of taxes, the eftablifhment of provincial ftates, never can be changed without the confent of the three orders taken feparately. His majefty places them already in the rank of national property ; and he defires to place thefe, like every other fpecies of property, under the moft facred guard poffible.

His majefty, after having called the ftates-general in order to affift him in great objects of public utility, and in every thing that can contribute to the happinefs of his people, declares in the moft exprefs manner, that he will preferve entire and without the leaft alteration the inftitution of the army, as well as of all autho-rity, police, and power, over the military, fuch as the French monarchs have always enjoyed.

I have given this tranflation complete, as being the only fpecimen that I know of the legiflative talents or difpofition of the court of France, previous to the 14th of July, towards bettering the ftate of the people. A few obfervations muft occur to every one on reading this. To all, the time and circumftances under which this was offered will render its fincerity fufpected ; and it is evident that no fecurity was given for the perma-nence of the advantages that were offered and the con-ceffions propofed. It was, in one word, a half-meafure ; for an arbitrary monarch it was too much, and for a free people too little. The royalifts are attached to this de-king here fays, that when he promulgates a law, during the fitting of the ftates, no delay to the fanction, nor no oppofition to the execution was, to be given ; he there impofed a very hard law, and fet his enemies the example about the veto.   Whoever compofed this muft be accufed of total ignorance of the rights that are neceffary to fecure freedom, and to protect the people againft arbitrary power.   At the fame time that I make thefe obfervations, I think, that if it were poffible for thofe who poffefs power to exercife it with moderation, and to keep ftrictly to what is their right, France might have enjoyed great advantages under their monarchy with thofe modifications, for I do not think they are capable of ever enjoying what we in England call freedom.   I know them well, and I fhall never believe, until I am convinced by experience, that the French have patience or calmnefs fufficient to adminifter a free government, and without a good adminiftration, freedom is worfe than defpotifm.

N O T E B.

A CIRCUMSTANCE little known will prove, that there was no bravery difplayed in the taking of the Baftille.   A number of the fubfcribers to the Lyceum at Paris determined to collect and publifh the facts relative to fo extraordinary an exploit ; accordingly, a great number of witneffes were examined, and it was difcovered at laft, that the governor had opened the door, and let the conquerors walk in.   A debate then arofe amongft the compilers of the hiftory—Shall we publifh a thing that will be difgraceful to the Parifians after fo much boafting and fo many falfities ? or fhall we defift? were the queftions.   Let us go on, faid one fubfcriber, we are fearching for truth, let us find it ; but as all truths are not good to be told, let us not publifh it. The advice was taken, and the latter part of it was the
beft ;

beft; for certainly the conquerors of the Baftille would foon have pulled down the Lyceum, if the truth had been publifhed.

This anecdote, for the truth of which I appeal to M. de la Harpe and M. la Croix, or any of the literary gentlemen who attended the Lyceum at that time, is a proof of the fpirit of democratic deception which pervaded the people of Paris from the beginning of the revolution, and the unanimity with which the French nation joins in exalting its own bravery and deceiving the world. Whilft all orders of nobility were deftroying, an order was inftituted, (compofed of revolted foldiers, fome of the fans culottes of the Fauxbourg St. Antoine, and M. M. Bailly and La Fayette) decorated with a medal, bearing the infcription, " Conquerors of the Baftille." The origin of this was infurrection, and the manner of obtaining it was the teftimony of feven conquerors, which dubbed the eighth conqueror too. As French books of heraldry are all burned, I know not by what regulation M. Bailly and La Fayette were admitted conquerors, as they were at Verfailles on that glorious day. It was by fuch tricks as this that all Europe was juggled by the firft revolutionifts, who were neither conquerors, philofophers, nor well-meaning men; but who, by falfe facts and falfe appearances, contrived to pafs for all the three.

N O T E C.

M. DE LA FAYETTE was the firft who read a project of the rights of man to the affembly on the 10th of July, 1780; the immediate confideration of this

fions, and the affembly adopted that which it liked the beft. Mounier was a literary man and of great abilities, his project was preferred; but, in fact, it was very little different from that of Fayette.

Next to the duty of infurrection, the unlimited liberty of the prefs was the worft of the rights, fedition and calumny are the elements of public and private mifery and misfortune, and it is very unfortunate, that it fhould be poffible fo far to miflead people, as to make them for a moment imagine, that the caufe of liberty is forwarded by fuch rights. A democrat imagined, as the beft method of putting an end to the defpots of Europe, to difpatch a good ftaunch French patriot apothecary to each capital in Europe, where, under the cloak of the law, he might fell poifon, and wait for occafion to fell it to good purpofe. A very grave difcuffion took place, and it was the general opinion of the democrats prefent, that to fell poifon was one of the rights of man on all occafions, and that it was fometimes a duty (*vendre l'arfenic c'eft le droit de toute homme, et l'adminiftrer fur des certains occafions c'eft un devoir*). To fuch a pitch as this did a declaration of rights and duties lead men, by having overturned the ufual ideas of moral right and wrong, and fet the ignorant and ambitious loofe on a fea of error.

N O T E   D.

THE declaration of rights originated with M. de la Fayette two days before infurrection broke out in Paris, and the people were juft full of that new idea of the facred duty of infurrection, when the armed force arriving gave them the fignal for putting the principle in practice. If the famous declaration of rights were out of the reach of criticifm in any other way, ftill it might be attacked upon this principle, that all the

parti

parties fince have equally invoked it, and that therefore it is either fo contradictory in itfelf, or fo difficult to be underftood, that it leads men to oppofe one another, at the fame time that they think themfelves all conforming to the fame declaration.

The confequences of the bill of rights have been terrible, and its origin was vanity. When in England our forefathers infifted upon a bill of rights, they fatisfied themfelves with fixing them upon a folid bafis, without running the rifk of throwing out abftract principles to lead the people aftray. Metaphyfical reafonings are fometimes neceffary to lead people to juft conclufions, but they are very dangerous when thrown out to the people at large, who, in fpite of what may be faid to the contrary, are more interefted in the obedience of laws than the principles upon which thofe laws are founded. It was the vanity of wifhing to appear philofophers that made the firft affembly draw up the declaration in the manner that it was done, or, in other words, that made them adopt this declaration. M. Mounier, though a very clever man, was not exempt from reproach on this head, and it feems probable, that he was led into it by the firft idea given by La Fayette, for the fact is, that though Mounier's project was preferred, all the originality of it was due to La Fayette's firft fpeech on that fubject. Perhaps, alfo, as Mounier had revolt to excufe, having himfelf participated in it, he was led to make the declaration different from what he would have done had he wrote it a few weeks fooner: be that as it may, he was one of the firft to fee and to feel the exceffes to which it led.

<hr>

N O T E F.

of harm, for it was conftrued by the people into a fort
of approbation on the part of the affembly of imbruing
their hands in blood, provided it was not very pure.
The man who had the ferocity to explain himfelf in
fuch a manner, not only muft have had no feeling,
but he muft have been totally ignorant of the terrible
confequences of a mob taking upon itfelf to judge,
whether the blood of any individual man was pure or
not; becaufe, if Barnave was to be credited, murder
was only to be lamented when the perfon murdered was
innocent; now a more dangerous idea never could be
held out to the people, for where does an incenfed mob
ever imagine that its victims are innocent? The affembly certainly participated in Barnave's crime, by not
inftantly fhewing indignation at fuch a principle. The
mafs of the people can only be reftrained from punifhing its enemies by inculcating well upon them, that all
punifhments without a previous, and free, and fair
conviction of their juftice, are equally criminal.

NOTE G.

BERTHIER and Foulon were not more obnoxious
to the people than many other perfons who were never
touched; but the father-in-law, as a monied man, and
Berthier, as intendant of Paris, were acquainted with
fome manœuvres refpecting the monopoly of grain,
that it would have been very dangerous for the party
of the Duke of Orleans to have made known. Perfons
were feen exciting the mob to deftroy the victims, and
certainly the rage againft Baron de Befenval, *who was
not injured by the mob when he was brought* to Paris,
tried and acquitted, was much greater than it had
ever been with regard to Foulon and his fon-in-law.

NOTE

N O T E H.

ALTHOUGH the duke had taken a great many precautions to prevent difcovery, yet as he had feveral accomplices that were imprudent, all he could do was to
prevent punifhment, and there are fome of the creditors
of the unfortunate banker who have got fufficient proofs
of the tranfaction in their hands to lay a claim upon
the fucceffion of the family of Orleans, if things
fhould ever take fuch a turn in France as to admit the
poffibility of it. The manœuvre was not entirely unknown at Verfailles, for the queen was heard to fay,
on being fhewn a perfon who had been ruined by this
bankruptcy, Ah! that unfortunate money of Pinet,
it has largely contributed to our misfortunes. In Paris
it was fpread abroad, that the unfortunate man, having
lent large fums to the Count d'Artois, had blown out
his own brains on account of the flight of that prince,
fo that the democratic party gained doubly by this affaffination; they acquired money and incenfed the
people againft the extravagance of the court, by pointing out Pinet's numerous creditors as the victims of
the extravagance of the Count d'Artois.

N O T E I.

MIRABEAU certainly was, previous to this, in favour with the Duke of Orleans, and he owned, that
having met the Duke on the road, he had obferved to
him, that whether they had a Louis Sixteenth or Se-
venteenth upon the throne, it was all the fame to the
nation; upon which faid he, the duke fpoke to me

With regard to the report laid before the aſſembly by M. Chabroud on this ſubject, it is very clear, that though there was no poſitive evidence againſt the duke, there was much preſumptive proof; from which, however, Chabroud concludes, that the duke was not guilty. It would have been very imprudent to have found the great democratic leader guilty of any at-tempt againſt the ſovereign, as ſuch attempts were deemed honourable and uſefull, and even the cut-throat Jourdan, who had been active, and had cut off the heads of two of the life guards, was protected from juſtice, though accuſed, and an order for arreſting him given; ſo far was this fellow from being puniſhed, that, though one of the loweſt of the people, he afterwards became a general at Avignon. Robeſpierre purged the world afterwards of both thoſe monſters. One argu-ment uſed for the exculpation of M. d'Orleans was, that the Duke de Biron was ſuppoſed to be along with him, and that this latter had never ſhewn himſelf to be of a ſanguinary diſpoſition. The caſe was, that though Biron was a very different ſort of a man, yet they had become allies and partners in moſt of their actions, the one was the tool, the other the knave, and Biron, as he plainly ſhewed ſince, was an enemy to the king; he was one of thoſe eaſy men, who, when they have not a fixed principle of action in their own breaſt, are ready to let themſelves be led away by the deſigning and wicked.

━━━━━━

N O T E K.

SEVERAL different parties propoſed plans for ſaving the royal family; all were rejected by his majeſty as being inconſiſtent with the oath which he had taken, and in danger of producing a civil war. It is not to be doubted but that the fear of being arreſted a ſecond time, and worſe treated than on the former occaſion, weighed

much

much with the king, particularly as after what had happened on the 20th of June, the oath that he had taken
could no longer be confidered as binding.   It was after
the 20th of June, that thofe who had before endeavoured
to perfuade his majefty to depart, doubled their efforts
and perfuafions.   It was propofed to convey the royal
family fecretly to *Compiégne*, to which place a detachment of the army of La Fayette would have been fent
to their protection.   And when the king refufed this
plan another was propofed.   Under the efcort of 1500
of the national guards, of whom they could be certain,
300 Swifs guards, and about 1500 gentlemen, it was
propofed to conduct the royal family to Rouen in
Normandy, where the inhabitants, the troops, and the
commanders, would all be fure to favour the enterprife.   This plan was alfo refufed only a few days before the 10th of Auguft.

No ftep that the king could have taken could be more
unfortunate for the nation than that which he perfifted
in, of remaining till he was attacked; but perhaps he
might have taken one more unfavourable to himfelf.   The
Jacobins have fhewn, on all occafions, fo much energy,
and the other party fo little; the former have been fo
fortunate, and the latter fo unlucky, in whatever they
have attempted, that it is probable the king would have
been led into fome difficulty, that would have terminated
in putting him again into the hands of his enemies, when
he would not have been fo irreproachable as he remained
by refufing to move from Paris.   At all events, the unfortunate monarch would not have been much better,
becaufe he would have been in the hands of the con-
ftitutionalifts, who were not, certainly, able to defend
themfelves within the kingdom againft the anarchifts,
and who were equally inimical to all the combined
powers.   The king's heart is greatly to be praifed for
the refolution of remaining, and his underftanding
merits praife alfo, if he only could have had the fame
refolution when the department of Paris, a few days

NOTE L.

THE difpofition of La Fayette to enter into plots to carry off the king is of very little importance, merely as being a proof of his perfonal ambition, of which thofe who knew much about him never doubted; but it is a clear proof that La Fayette, and thofe who acted with him, were, and had been all along, actuated by perfonal motives, and that oppreffion towards the king only difpleafed them when it came from others, and not from themfelves. What was the difference between the elopement of the royal family now and when La Fayette aided to treat the king with fuch feverity on his return from Varennes; The king had not, on the former period, taken the oath, and now he had taken it. His liberty had been juft as much infringed upon when the people refufed to let him go to St. Clould as it had been on the 20th of June, and perfonally he had been as much infulted, and the queen ftill more. The only difference that can be feen was the pofition of La Fayette and his friends; on the former occafion they were in power, and now they were not; they then ruled, and now they plotted. It is juft what all the Jacobins have done from the beginning to the prefent moment, and when we fee La Fayette acting, fuch a part, we are ready to fuppofe, that if circumftances had demanded, in order to acquire power, he would have entered into the convention and fallen with the Briffotines. La Fayette was never much efteemed in America, but he took great care to receive Thomas Paine, Mr. Barlow, and all the other Americans who came to Paris, at his table, and by that means he had fo many trumpeters. If, therefore, we may judge of him by his friends, he was a republican in his principles, and only affected to be a royalift, becaufe he found it moft likely to fatisfy his own ambitious views.

N O T E M.

SOON after the king came to the assembly, a note from the mayor arrived to inform the president, that he was confined in his own house, and could not come to the assembly.

The assembly answered this note in a style of oriental flattery and adulation, as follows:

" If the first of the constituted authorities is yet
" respected; if the representatives of the people,
" friends to their happiness, have any ascendant over
" them, or preserve their confidence, they beg the ci-
" tizens, and command them, in the name of the law,
" to lift the consign at the mayory, and to allow to ap-
" pear before the eyes of the people the magistrate
" whom the people cherishes."

To this address was added another to the people.

" In the name of the nation, in the name of liberty,
" in the name of equality, all the citizens are invited
" to respect the rights of man, liberty, and equality."

Both these addresses were ordered to be printed and placarded through the city.

A deputation of one of the sections of Paris arrived immediately after.

" We adhere," said they, " to the desire manifested
" by the municipality, for the decheance of the king.
" Receive, legislators, with that declaration the testi-
" mony of our confidence, but dare to swear that you
" will save the republic."

Addreſſes came in from all the ſeƈtions, and one from the municipality of which Huguenin was the orator; the ſame who had harangued the king on the 20th of June.

Another orator arrived, (an artillery man of the national guards) who ſpoke in the name of *the people ;* covered with blood and filth, he offered, as a preface to his petition, to murder the king, if it were neceſſary; and then added, " you muſt know, that the palace is " on fire, and that we will not ſtop the flames until the " vengeance of the people is ſatisfied.   I am charged, " yet once more, *to demand the decheance of the executive* " *power.*"

ˑThe aſſembly had already taken the hint, and now was prepared to do whatever the people ordered, accordingly the following decrees were paſſed immediately.

The national aſſembly, conſidering that the dangers of the country are arrived at their greateſt degree ;

That it is the moſt ſacred duty of the legiſlative body to employ every means of ſaving it, and that it is impoſſible to find any efficacious means of ſo doing, unleſs the ſources from which theſe evils flow are ſtopped :

Conſidering that theſe evils ariſe principally from the miſtruſt inſpired by the conduƈt of the executive power, in a war undertaken in his name againſt the conſtitution and the national independence :

That this miſtruſt has induced different portions of the empire to teſtify the deſire of ſeeing the powers entruſted to Louis XVI. withdrawn :

Conſidering, at the ſame time, that the legiſlative body ought not to augment its own power, and will not do ſo by any uſurpation :

That in the extraordinary circumſtances in which it is placed by unforeſeen events, it cannot reconcile the unalterable duty which it owes to the conſtitution, with its firm reſolution to ſink under the ruins of the temple of liberty rather than to let it periſh, by any other method than having recourſe to the ſovereignty of the people, and taking, at the ſame time, the precautions neceſſary to prevent ſuch recourſe to the people from being illuſive, decrees what follows :

Art. I. The French people is invited to form a NATIONAL CONVENTION ; the extraordinary commiſſion will preſent to-morrow a plan for that purpoſe, indicating the mode and the time for that convention.

Art. II. The chief of the executive power is proviſionally ſuſpended from his functions, until the convention ſhall determine on the meaſures to be taken for aſſuring the ſovereignty of the people, and the reign of liberty and equality.

Art. III, The extraordinary commiſſion ſhall preſent within the day, the new orgnaization of the miniſtry. The preſent miniſters are continued till then.

Art. IV. The extraordinary commiſſion ſhall preſent likewiſe a plan for naming a governor for the Prince Royal.

Art. V. The payment of the civil liſt is ſuſpended until the convention ſhall have deliberated. The extraordinary commiſſion ſhall, within the firſt twenty-four hours, give in a plan for the allowance to be paid to the king during his ſuſpenſion.

Art. VI. The regiſters of the civil liſt ſhall be depoſed on the table of the national aſſembly, after being examined by two commiſſaries who ſhall be named for that purpoſe, and who ſhall go to the houſe of the in-

the roof of the legiflative affembly, until tranquility
fhall be re-eftablifhed in Paris.

Art. VIII. The department fhall give orders within
the day to have apartments prepared in the Luxembourg
for their reception, where they fhall be placed under
the fafe-guard of the law and of the citizens.

Art. IX. Every public functionary, foldier, non-
commiffioned officer, or officer, who fhall abandon his
poft, is declared infamous, and a traitor to his country.

Art. X. The department and municipality of Paris
fhall caufe the prefent decree to be folemnly proclaimed.

Art. XI. Extraordinary meffengers fhall be fent to
the eighty-three departments, with copies of this proclamation; and within twenty-four hours after, they
fhall be obliged to have the fame proclaimed formally
by the refpective municipalities.

The royal family was prefent in the affembly all this
time, and whatever abftract theorifts may think, this
circumftance adds not a little to the indignation which
the conduct of this affembly, which was equally cruel
and cowardly, infpires.

To appeafe the people, the following proclamation
was ordered to be placarded immediately :

*The king is fufpended ; he and his family remain as
hoftages.*

*The prefent minifters do not enjoy the confidence of the
nation ; the affembly is occupied in replacing them.*

The civil lift is fufpended.

N O T E

NOTE N.

IN confequence of the preffure of petitions from all parts, minifters were named according to a feries of arrangements, which minifters were to act as king. The minifter of juftice (Danton) was empowered to place the great feal during the fufpenfion of the king; but the republican party cried out, that the form of a great feal being royal was ufelefs and improper, the decree was annulled, and it was determined that all acts fhould be publifhed without any preamble, and figned by the minifter of juftice, in the name of the nation.

NOTE O.

ON the 14th of July, infurrection againft an hereditary monarch was the theme, but it was not till the 10th of Auguft that it was found that the fame weapon might be turned againft the conftitution of their own making. This confequence had long been forefeen by many perfons, but now became evident to all. Thofe who had any remainder of principle or good intention, were in defpair after the 10th of Auguft; they faw then that all their work was to do over again, and the profpect for infurrection feemed boundlefs; for if the conftitution which had been fo much adored, and to which fo many oaths of fidelity had been taken, could be deftroyed between nine o'clock and eleven in the forenoon, what could be expected to be preferved? The wretched ftate of public credit, and of individuals likewife, rendered the profpect of a fecond revolution a very difmal one.

NOTE P.

THE manner in which the conftitution was done away, is the beft commentary that can poffibly be made on the conduct of the conftituent affembly; the confecration of infurrection, and the right of changing the conftitution, on one hand; and on the other, endeavouring to fetter their followers with regard to any changes of conftitutional articles. Every bad combination in affairs of importance leads to misfortune; and certainly there is no difficulty in tracing the 10th of Auguft to the imperfections of the conftitution. A king with too little power, and infurrection legalized; with a legiflative affembly, compofed of ambitious, intriguing men, who longed for the moment that they fhould be able to throw off the fetters which the conftitution had cramped them with. The reception given to the deputations of thofe who had demanded the decheance of the king, when there was no mob at the door of the affembly, as well as their cruel conduct to him after. The flattering proclamation about Petion the magiftrate, whom the people cherifhed, added to the facility and quicknefs with which the decrees were paffed, all join to prove, that the affembly was as ready to deftroy the conftitution, as the people were to demand its deftruction.

NOTE Q.

BEFORE the maffacre took place, it had been determined on fo decidedly, that three hundred livres had been given to the grave-digger of St. Sulpice, to prepare at Mont-rouge, a mile out of town, a large grave, in which their bodies might be interred.

Manuel

Manuel feems to have been a particularly active agent
in this, and the other maffacres, for he had been to take
M. de Beaumarchais from the prifon of the Abbey,
where he was confined two days before the maffacre,
and had told the *Traiteur* who fent victuals to the prifoners at the Carmelites, to get his bill quickly paid,
for that all the prifoners would foon be difpofed of.

It is clear that Manuel and Petion acted both before
and after this in concert.   It is equally certain, that
Petion and the party of Briffot acted together both before and after this; therefore there can be no fort of
reafon for making a diftinction between them as to criminality.

The bodies of the perfons maffacred in the other prifons, were thrown into the ftone quarries that are near
Paris.   It is fingular enough, that Petion and fuch of
his friends as efcaped the guillotine in Paris, about fix
months after, faved themfelves from the people fent to
arreft them, *in the ftone quarries* near Bourdeaux.

The moft fhocking thing, however, in thefe maffacres,
is certainly the facility with which the inftigators of
them found executioners.   Charles the Ninth did not
every where find obedience when he ordered the St.
Bartholomew; and the murderers of Admiral Colligni
ftarted back with horror, and hefitated, though they
were obliged at the rifk of their lives to obey.   The
murderers of the bifhops and priefts felt no fuch check
in their career; they were not compelled by any force
to be cruel, nor reftrained by any principle from being
fo.   This is perhaps the beft anfwer that can be given
to thofe philofophers who are at fuch pains to fhew
that the human heart is degraded by the fhackles of re-
legious prejudice, and elevated by getting rid of it.
Certainly if there is any difference between murderers,
it is in favour of thofe who acted under the miftaken
influence of religion, to thofe who acted under the

In its proper place it had been mentioned, that the clergy of Paris had been particularly charitable during the severe winter of 1788.   Amongst the priests murdered at the Carmelites, were many of those very men ; amongst their murderers were, very probably, some who had received their help ; and if not, Paris at least contained thousands of persons who had, and who now might have protected them, for the sans culottes run no risk in protecting any persons they pleased ; and it was the indigent of 1788 who were become the rulers in 1792, so that they might be literally said to be murdering their benefactors.

N O T E R.

AMONGST the different accounts of the massacres, none is more interesting than that of M. de St, Meard, formerly captain in the regiment du Roi, who was arrested as editor of a journal.   He was one of the persons who felt what he described, and without following him completely through what he with great propriety calls his *Agony*, nothing can give a better idea of the horror of the scene, than some extracts from it in his own words.

After having been arrested and carried to the mayor's house on the 22d of August, M. de St. Meard had been conducted to the prison of the Abbey, where he remained amidst a number of unfortunate men like himself, confined in what had formerly been the chapel of the prison.

" On the 2d of September," says he, " the door-
" keeper brought our dinner at an earlier hour than
" usual. His distracted looks and haggard appear-
" ance made us presage something sinister. At two
" o'clock he returned, we crowded around him, but he
" was deaf to all our questions, and after he had, con-
" trary

" trary to cuftom, gathered up all the table knives and
" forks, he made the nurfe of the wounded Swifs offi-
" cer, *Reding*, quit the apartment.

" At half paft two o'clock. the terrible noife which
" the people made in the court, and in the ftreet, was
" augmented by the drums, the cannon of alarm, and
" the tocfin.

" We now faw three carriages pafs by, efcorted by
" an immenfe mob of men and woman, who cried fu-
" rioufly *to the force, to the force;* (that was to death).
" They were then conducted to the cloifter of the Ab-
" bey, where they were fhut up along with other
" priefts, and in a few minutes after we were inform-
" ed, that all the bifhops and ecclefiaftics who had
" been confined there were maffacred.

" Towards four o'clock, the piercing cries of a man
" whom they were hacking in pieces with fabres, drew
" us to the window of a fmall tower, from whence we
" faw the body of a man extended lifelefs on the pave-
" ment. Prefently after another was maffacred, and
" fo they continued to go on.

" It is impoffible to exprefs the horror of the deep
" and gloomy filence that reigned during thefe execu-
" tions ; it was only interrupted by the cries of thofe
" whom they immolated with ftrokes of fabres on the
" head. When the victim fell, a murmur arofe, at-
" tended with the cries of *vive la nation*, a thoufand
" times more frightful to us ftill than the horrors of
" the filence.

" During the interval between the maffacres, we
" heard people fay diftinctly, ' we muft not let one ef-
" cape, we muft kill them all, and particularly thofe
" who are in the chapel, where there are none but
" confpirators.' It was of ourfelves that they fpoke,

" At five o'clock a number of voices called M. *Ca-*
" *zotte,** and an inftant after we heard a great crowd
" on the ftairs, the clattering of arms, and the cries of
" men and women. It was the old man whom they
" were dragging along, followed by his daughter ;
" when he was out of the door, that courageous young
" woman threw herfelf on the neck of her father, and
" the people touched with the fight, demanded and
" obtained his pardon.

" About feven in the evening, two men entered with
" bloody hands, and armed with fabres, conducted by
" the door-keeper, who fhewed them the bed of the
" Swifs officer, *Reding.* At that moment I held him
" by the hand, and was trying to comfort him. One
" of thefe men made a motion to carry him off, but
" the miferable victim anfwered, ' Ah, Sir, I have
" fuffered enough, I don't fear death, have mercy upon
" me, and kill me here !' Thefe words prevented that
" perfon from faying any thing more, but his compan-
" ion faid, come along, ; he put *Reding* then on his
" fhoulders, and carried him into the ftreet, where he
" received his death.

" The fame horrors and anxiety continued without
" intermiffion, when next day at ten o'clock, M. *l' Ab-*
" *bé Lanfant,*" continues, St. Meard, " the king's con-
" feffor, and another clergyman, appeared in the tri-
" bune of the chapel, and announced to us that our
" laft hour approached, and invited us to draw near to
" receive their benediction. An electrical movement,
" which cannot be defined, threw us all upon our
" knees, and with our hands joined, we received it.
" That moment, though confoling, was one of the
" moft awful we had yet fuffered. On the brink of
" eternity, and about to appear before the Supreme
" Being, kneeling before two of his minifters, we pre-

* Cazotte, author of *Olivier, le Diable Amoureux, &c.* he
was a virtuous old man, and quite inoffenfive ; he was executed foon after by order of the municipality.

" fented

" fented an appearance which cannot be defcribed.
" The great age of the two venerable men, their po-
" fition, and death hanging over our heads, and fur-
" rounding us on all fides ; every thing joined to ren-
" der that ceremony awful and auguft ; it brought us
" nearer to the Divinity, and gave us courage ; all rea-
" foning was fufpended, and the coldeft and moft in-
" credulous was as much impreffed as thofe who had
" the moft ardour and fenfibility. In one half hour
" afterwards thefe two prelates were maffacred, *and we*
" *heard their cries.*

" What man will read the following details, without
" his eyes being filled with tears, without feeling him-
" felf chilled with horror and difmay !

" Our moft important occupation was to difcover
" what would be the pofition in which we ought to
" ftand, in order to receive death with the leaft pain.
" We fent from time to time one of our number to
" the window of the fmall tower, to examine the pofi-
" tion of the victims which they were flaughtering,
" and to determine after that, which would be beft
" for ourfelves to take. They informed us, that thofe
" who held up their hands, fuffered much and long,
" becaufe the flafhes of their fabres were deadened
" before they ftruck the head ; that there even were of
" thofe whofe hands and arms fell before their bodies,
" and that thofe who placed their hands behind the
" back fuffered leaft. Well ! it was on fuch horrible
" details that we deliberated ; we calculated the ad-
" vantages of that latter pofition, and admonifhed each
" other reciprocally to take it when our turn to be maf-
" facred fhould arrive ! ! !*

" Towards midnight the executions feemed to have
" diminifhed, when an orator in the ftreet demanded

* The defcription of M. de St. Meard goes on in the fame

" attention from the people, and we heard him diftinct-
" ly fay, 'The priefts and confpirators who remain,
" have bribed the judges : behold the reafon why they
" have given over judging.' Scarcely had he finifhed
" when the noife of maffacring began, and the cries
" and agitation of the people became terrible. Three
" of our companions were dragged out, which made
" me feel that my laft hour was at hand.

" At laft, after having fuffered thirty-feven hours of
" an agony, incomparably worfe than death ; after
" having drank a thoufand and a thoufand times of the
" bitter cup, my prifon opens, and I am called. I ap-
" pear. Three men feized me, and dragged me to the
" terrible paffage.

" By the light of the torches I perceived the terrible
" tribunal, which was to give me death or life ; the
" préfident in a grey coat, a fabre by his fide, ftanding
" and leaning on a table, upon which were papers, a
" writing-defk, fome pipes, and bottles. Round the
" table were ten perfons, fitting and ftanding, two of
" whom were in waiftcoats and aprons ; others were
" afleep upon benches. Two men in their fhirts, ftain-
" ed with blood, fabre in hand, guarded the door ; an
" old jailor held the bolt in his hand ; three men were
" then holding a prifoner, about fixty years of age, be-
" fore the prefident. I was placed in a corner, my two
" guardians croffing their fabres on my breaft, inform-
" ed me, that on the fmalleft movement to efcape,
" they would ftab me. A letter from the fection of
" the *Croix Rouge*, in favour of the prifoner, was de-
" livered to the prefident, who anfwered, that demands
" in favour of traitors were ufelefs. The prifoner
" then exclaimed, that's terrible, your judgment is an
" affaffination. The prefident then anfwered, I wafh
" my hands of it, conduct M. Maillé. Thefe words
" were no fooner fpoke, than he was pufhed into the
" ftreet, where, through an opening in the door, I faw
" him maffacred.

" The

" The prefident fat down to write (probably) the
" name of the miferable victim, which, having done,
" he faid—To another.

" Immediately I was dragged before this bloody and
" expeditious tribunal; two of my conductors held me
" by the two hands, and a third by the collar of my
" coat."

The relation of the interrogatories that paft is very interefting, but long; St. Meard was acquitted, partly
becaufe one of the attendants of the prifon was from
the fame province, and protected him, and partly becaufe he defended himfelf with energy and ingenuity,
and even gaiety; but it feems clear, that juftice was
not the reafon, as numbers had been maflacred, againft
whom even being a royalift could not be proved.   As
foon as St. Meard appeared in the ftreet, the populace
having been previoufly informed of the acquittal of a
prifoner, one of his conductors cried, off with your
hats, citizens, behold the man for whom the judges demand aid and affiftance.   When thefe words were pro-
pronounced, the executive power (the murderers) placed
him between four torches, where he was embraced by
all thofe who furrounded him.   All the fpectators cried
out, *vive la nation*.   He was then put under the protection of the people, who let him pafs, accompanied
by three deputies, whom the prefident had ordered to
conduct him home.   One of thefe deputies was a mafon,
the other an apprentice to a barber, and the third a fœ-
derat.   When they had conducted him home, they refufed to receive any money, and accepted only of a glafs
of brandy, faying, that they did not do that bufinefs for
money.

This cruelty, parade of juftice, of humanity, and
difinterefteednefs, is inconceivable; the men who would
have maflacred him, embraced him, and out of veneration were obliged to take off their hats.   It appears

be neceffary; and horrible as this relation is, it may be confidered as a vindication of the tribunal, elfe its author durft not have publifhed it.

The maffacre at the Bicetre was without any form of judgment at all.

═══ ════ ═══

N O T E   O. 2.

THE miferies that have all along accompanied the revolution, rendered it neceffary to find out an object of hatred, on whom thofe who wifhed to rule might throw the blame. A divifion of opinion was natural enough amongft ambitious men, who could not bear rivals in power, the court, however, ferved as an object for the hatred of the people, till it no longer exifted; the parties therefore now from neceffity carried their hatred againft each other to violent lengths, as there was no alternative but that of confeffing that they were all in the wrong, or elfe attributing the mifery to one party only.

The Briffotins wifhed to get the convention removed from Paris; Robefpierre, on the contrary, who felt that all his power was derived from the mob of Paris, and the Jacobin club, was obliged therefore to quarrel with them from neceffity, and inclined to do it from intereft; each employed his means, Robefpierre that of a Parifian mob, and Briffot that of an appeal to the people, both of which prove that infurrection was the principal caufe of the miferies of France.

NOTE P. 2.

SOME extracts from Briſſot's Appeal to his Conſti-
tuents, as they are extremely concluſive in themſelves,
and come from a man who was ſo active a leader, deferve being noticed in a particular manner.

" The laws without execution ; the conſtituted au-
" thorities impotent and difgraced ; crimes unpuniſhed;
" property of every kind attacked ; perfonal fafety vio-
" lated ; the morals of the people corrupted ; no con-
" ſtitution ; no government ; no juſtice.   Such are
" the true features of this anarchy." —

" I was of opinion that all infurrection could not
" but be fatal to the people, and to liberty, ſince it
" could be directed only againſt the repreſentatives of
" the people.

" I conceived that this *doctrine of eternal infurrection*
" muſt draw after it pillage and maſſacres, which muſt
" weary out and difguſt the nation with the republican
" form of government."

" Liberty might ſo eafily have found no other bound-
" aries than thoſe of the world, and now ſhe muſt ſor-
" rowfully confine herſelf within the limits of France."

" You will fee them convinced that the goodnefs of
" laws muſt depend upon the fobriety with which they
" are deliberated upon, and that the refpect for the law
" depends alfo upon the refpect in which the legiſlator
" himſelf is held."

" They are the men who, for the perpetuation of
" their own power, finding it neceſſary to perpetuate
" … have … divided ſociety into two claſſes, thoſe

" cited one of thefe claffes againft the other ; who, in
" order to ruin the latter clafs, wanted to have an army
" compofed exclufively of perfons, all of the former
" clafs, and paid *compulforily* by the latter, and this ar-
" my has been decreed."

" Is it not farther the fad conclufion that muft be
" drawn, when we bring to mind all the ufurpations
" of power, all the violations of law, of which the
" municipality and the fections of Paris have been
" conftantly rendering themfelves guilty fince the 10th
" of Auguft, and which have always remained unpun-
" ifhed ? For which of the laws is it that they carried
" into execution ?"

" When one fees this municipality, in fpite of de-
" crees, fhut the barriers and the play-houfes at their
" pleafure, forbid fuch or fuch pieces, fuch or fuch
" journals, order to their bar the deputies, generals,
" and minifters, enjoin them to difmifs certain fubal-
" tern functionaries, and fend inquifitorial commiffa-
" ries to their houfes to watch over the execution of
" their decrees."

" What do I fay ? No ! it is not in the commonal-
" ty of Paris that the exercife of the national fove-
" reignty refides. *It refides in a club, or rather in a*
" *fcore of thofe robbers who direct that club;* who oblige
" all the authorities that are conftituted by the nation
" to bend under them.

" It is there, it is in that club where the anarchifts
" of the convention domineer. It is there that the
" decrees are fabricated which are to come upon them
" with the force of a command. It is there, that un-
" der the title of petitions or addreffes, orders are fa-
" bricated which are intimated to them. It is in that
" ware-houfe of calumny, that they every day diforgan-
" ize every thing, the miniftry, the adminiftration, and
" the army. It is from thence that the deputies, the
" minifters, and the generals, are called upon to make
                                              " their

" their appearance before them, and humbly bend the
" knee. It is there that they give in their accounts,
" that they make their anfwers to the denunciations
" againft them. It is there that they pay obedience to
" the decrees of the club, who expel or condemn their
" fubalterns. It is there that, occupied in accufing
" the Girondins of governing every thing, of ufurping
" every thing, the leaders of the club, drawing to them-
" felves all authority, govern all, carry off all money,
" bargains, places, commiffions, nominations to tribu-
" nals, &c. &c.

" It is from thence, that the orders go to the revolu-
" tionary tribunal, to remove, to condemn, or abfolve.
" It is there that the *accufer of this tribunal* complains
" that blood is not fhed in fufficient abundance. It is
" there that the jurymen of this tribunal premife very
" foon to bring to the fcaffold the heads of thofe de-
" puties who are enemies to the Jacobins."

" Yes, I declare, from the deep conviction of my
" foul, that as long as there exifts no power able to re-
" prefs the crimes of the leaders of the Jacobins, there
" can exift no convention, no government. All the
" powers are neceffarily with the club. There is the
" legiflative body ; or rather, there is the body above
" the law—above all, the conftituted authorities. *There*
" *is the abfolute power of France.*"

" Bournonville, on entering upon his adminiftration,
" and after having examined the ftate of the expenfes,
" has declared that there was a fum of one hundred and
" fixty millions (about fix millions fterling) of the ex-
" penditure, of which there appeared no particulars.
" Cambon faid to the committee in the roftrum, that
" it was impoffible to bring the expenditure of that de-
" partment to light; that a fponge muft be drawn
" over it."

" ceffive price; battalions, though reduced to a third
" or a fixth, ftill paid for at their full compliment."

" *I am fatisfied that I have fully proved that the anar-*
" *chifts, under the name of the Jacobins of Paris, of the*
" *municipality of the fections, have governed, and do govern*
" *the convention, the executive power, and all the adminif-*
" *trations, and confequently that they govern the whole*
" *empire.*"

" But war with England, with Holland, and with
" Spain, has changed the face of affairs, and it has
" ftopped the courfe of our victories.   Then what has
" occafioned this laft war ? There are three caufes
" of it :

" 1ft. The abfurd and impolitic decree of the 19th
" of November, which very juftly excited uneafinefs
" in foreign cabinets ; a decree which men of know-
" ledge oppofed in vain ; a decree brought to nothing
" by the anarchifts themfelves, who had pufhed it on
" with rage : it was brought to nothing after a fatal
" experience ; but this was done too late, fince the
" mifchief had already been produced.

" 2d. The maffacres of the 2d of September, the
" impunity of which, commanded by the anarchifts,
" has alienated from us all neutral nations.

" 3d. The death of Louis."

" What did enlightened republicans think before the
" 10th of Auguft, men who wifhed for liberty, not
" only for their own country, but for all Europe ?
" They believed that they could generally eftablifh it,
" by exciting the governed againft the governors, in
" letting the people fee the facility and the advantages
" of fuch infurrections."

" But they would profcribe all ftock-jobbing.—
" Why, then, did not Cambon fhut up the exchange
                              " fooner

" fooner, as Claviere has been inceffantly requiring
" fince 1791 ? It was going ftrait to the very fource of
" the evil.   Why, after having himfelf confeffed that
" ftock-jobbing could only be combated by counter-
" ftock-jobbing ; why, after having confeffed that
" ftock-jobbing fo prodigioufly raifed the price of fpe-
" cic, why did they not grant to the executive council
" fome millions for the operations of a bank for raifing
" exchange ?"

" How can you expect, that in this uncertain and
" wavering ftate in which you are, foreign powers can
" confent to treat with a convention, which is every
" day dragged through the dirt ; becaufe it is the loweft
" difgrace to treat with an executive power, which
" is without intermiffion denounced, humiliated, and
" tottering."

" But foreign powers who would treat *with us in the*
" *actual ftate that we ftand in, could they entertain a*
" *fimilar hope?* No, they fay—France is divided by
" factions.   One triumph to-day.   To-morrow it
" will be the triumph of another.   If you treat with
" one, the other will break the treaty.   There is no
" ftability.   Let us wait for that ftability, and then we
" will treat."

" It is madnefs or imbecility itfelf to reckon upon a
" peace, or upon allies, while we are without a confti-
" tution. *There is no making an alliance, there is no*
" *treating with anarchy.* To treat with men, who have
" not the power to arreft the guilty, who infult them
" at their door, or the women, who in fpite of their
" teeth, exercife the police of their precinct, or the Ja-
" cobins, who haughtily fubfcribe their contingent of
" heads to be cut off."

" Anarchifts, robbers ! you may now ftrike ; I
" have done my duty; I have told truths that will

" name; truths that will prove to all France that
" good men have conftantly exerted their whole
" ftrength to open the eyes of France, and to preferve
" her liberty."

N O T E Q. 2.

THE mifcellaneous articles which belong to no part
of the work in particular, but which ferve to illuftrate
the whole, as ferving to make known the ftate of
France, may not be improper, though given without
any regular order.

The decrees concerning the changes in the calendar,
the denomination and divifion of the days and months,
ferved to give the people a romantic fort of enthufiafm,
to make a volatile nation naturally fond of change, admire its reprefentatives, and forget its ancient habits.

The invention of new words, to exprefs meaning,
was often employed to render palatable to the people,
what under its old name would have been too obnoxious. This is of more importance with the multitude
than one is aware of at firft, for ignorant men are governed by founds. The royal power was brought into
contempt by being called the executive power, and
murderers were rendered lefs deteftable by giving to
them the fame title. We have thus feen a perpetual
change of names, even of towns, fections and diftricts;
and this began with the revolution, and continued from
the time that the ftates-general were called a national
affembly, and that the title of provoft of the merchants
was changed for that of the mayor of Paris. By the
laft accounts we have from France, names have perpetually been changing. The great ufe made of names
or epithets, to produce difguft, or excite ridicule, is a

proof

proof that mankind at all times, and in all places, may
be acted upon by this device, though it does not always succeed. M. d'Orleans, for instance, was un-
successful in taking the title of *Egalité;* and the clock-
maker, who called himself *Brutus,* as well as another
citizen, who changed the name of Le Roi for that of
Dix Aout, were only turned into ridicule.

But this changing of names had a mighty effect in
overturning the ideas of the populace, and it is not
to be wondered at, if the great number succeeded against
the small in this contest of ridicule. Sans culotte was
at first an epithet of contempt given to the ragged vagabonds, who collected in groups round the hall of the
assembly, and in other public places. The people were
at first much offended at that, but finding they could
not get rid of the name, they took it up with good hu-
mour, and finished, by enforcing respect to it from
those who at first intended it as mockery.

The different sections at Paris, which had been at
first named after some street, square, or remarkable
building in the section, had their names gradually changed to the section of unity, rights of man, William Tell,
red bonnet, &c. This is something like the names
given in the time of religious fanaticism in England,
Pater-Noster-Row, Amen Corner, &c.

In order to gain to their party, scoundrels of all sorts,
the leading party, even in their first beginning, made
motions in the assembly and in the club, that shewed
such men what a glorious career was opened to them by
this revolution. In the end of the year 1790, when the
revolution was yet very moderate, it was proposed to
call together all the soldiers who had been drummed
out of their regiments *(ceux que avient reçu des cartou-
ches jaunes)* and to form a brigade of them, as being
excellent patriots, persecuted for the love of liberty.
This was too extravagant for that time, but might have

the affair of Nancy, were at laſt reclaimed by Collot d'Herbois and ſuch other patriots; they were ſet at liberty, received a large ſum of money, were feaſted publicly, and finally were to have made a public entry into Paris, on the ſame triumphal car that ſerved for the body of Voltaire when it was carried to the Pantheon. Inſtead of Voltaire's bed and dying apparatus, which had been in this car, twelve benches, elevated one above another, were placed for the galley ſlaves. A deputation of the national aſſembly, the judges of the tribunals, the municipality, and other conſtituted authorities, joined on the proceſſion, in honour of the perſecuted patriots, who, however, were themſelves aſhamed of the affair, and would not mount the car, ſo that the empty benches paraded along, drawn by twelve fine horſes, and preceded by all the magiſtrates of the people. The galley ſlaves, mixing in the crowd, ſhewed that they had more modeſty than the rulers of France. This happened at the ſame time that the cabals for the 20th of June, and 10th of Auguſt, were preparing.

N O T E   R. 2.

Revolutionary tribunal, priſons, Le Bon, &c.

From the things brought againſt the revolutionary tribunal and the commiſſaries, as well as the proceedings at Nantz, it would appear, that though oppreſſion and cruelty altered their form a little, it was not very different throughout France.

At Dijon the Jacobin club had a revolutionary army at its orders, which coſt 250l. ſterling per month; and while the revolutionary ſoldiers pillaged and arreſted people, their wives and daughters filled the galleries of the club to applaud the moſt extravagant amongſt its orators.

Fouquier

Fouquier Tinville proved, that he was obliged to bring before the revolutionary tribunal prisoners according to lists received. As great numbers of people were accused in one block, and with a great many different sorts of crimes at once, as witnesses in their favour were not heard, and as a few hours served to finish proceedings against any number, let it be ever so great, none could escape, except now and then one through protection or favour.

The deputies of Cambray accused Le Bon, the commissary of the convention, who had been sent into that quarter, of having made the streets run with blood : he was accused of keeping a condemned man four hours at the guillotine, while he read dispatches of arbitrary imprisonments, seizing effects of prisoners without giving any account, and of having, by summary methods, put to death numbers of innocent persons.

The Jacobin society of Nimes confessed, that that city had been ruled as rigorously as if Robespierre in person had been there. " Bourdon, judge of the revo-
" lutionary tribunal," say the Jacobins, " has blown
" out his brains, having incurred the displeasure of the
" society for his attachment to Robespierre. The
" mayor, (Courbis) author of Lists of Proscriptions,
" who went each decade with a number of prostitutes
" to dance *farandoles* round the permanent guillotine,
" is arrested, and will be judged."

After the death of Robespierre the Jacobin societies themselves began to denounce his cruelties, although his agents were all chosen from these societies, and the societies were the protectors, the aiders, and abettors of his agents all through France. Talien had reason to call those men camelions in politics, it was a true description, but he should have included himself amongst the number.

N O T E S.

THOSE who had been the agents or accomplices of the cruelties of Carrier at Nantz, were tried before the revolutionary tribunal at Paris.

Different witnesses, Lereque, Perochot, Haler, Joly, and Mainguet, confessed that they had participated in the horrible scenes and cruelties committed on the prisoners. They confessed they had signed orders for shooting and for drowning prisoners without any motive; 162 priests were pillaged of all their effects and stripped naked; their executioners divided the spoils amongst themselves. The most insatiable avarice, unexampled ferocity, and immeasurable ambition, a desire of giving a scope to private vengeance, a singular taste for licentious feasts, are not the only things with which the members of the revolutionary committee are to be reproached; these monsters attacked the virtue of wives and daughters, and, to obtain mercy for fathers and husbands, it was necessary to submit to their sensual brutality. A company of troops, called the company of Marat, composed of the vilest dregs of the people, was entrusted with the power of life and death, and exercised the most terrible and unheard-of cruelties.*

N O T E T.

THE decrees passed in the national convention, which gave their generals and commissaries a power of putting in requisition every article of utility to the republic that should be found in any conquered country, to be

---

* For a full account of these cruelties, see Porcupine's " BLOODY BUOY."

paid

paid for in affignats, was not fufficient. They could not even fpare their ufelefs paper in return for really valuable articles; or rather, as they could not find any pretence for putting the money of the country in a ftate of requifition, the commiffaries were allowed to levy contributions in fpecie, which was done to a very great amount, and exacted with very great rigour all over Flanders and Brabant. The whole of the wealth of the country was by this means at the difpofal of the French army, fo that particular acts of pillage were become entirely ufelefs. It is very extraordinary that this has not been properly explained and made known, as the republic boafts of the refpect for property fhewn by its foldiers, when, in fact, every thing being enregiftered, and at the command of the generals and foldiers, by means of affignats which coft nothing, and which from the nature of things can never find their way back to France, all pillage in detail would have been perfectly ufelefs.

A regular account of their exactions and requifitions would be one of the moft ufeful and curious pieces that the revolution of France has given room for, and it is to be hoped that the opportunity will not be let flip, as it is, perhaps, the only way to convince foreign nations of the injuftice and bad faith of the convention and of French patriots.

To thofe notes which fhew completely the cruelty and injuftice of the revolution, a few extracts from the Memorial of Gregoire on *Vandalifm* may not improperly be added. This report was made at the requeft of the convention.

" The moveables belonging to the nation," fays he, " have fuffered immenfe dilapidation, becaufe rogues, who have always a logic to themfelves, have faid, *We are the nation.* Many of thofe rafcals now have immenfe fortunes, which they have not had the prudence

" It is in the fine arts that the lofs has been the greateft.

" For thefe five laft years whatever was precious in paintings and libraries has been deftroying or fold at a vile price to ftrangers; what the adminiftrators did not fell, were left to be eat by worms, and expofed to the duft and the rain. We have juft now learned, that at Arney the library has been put into hogsheads ! !

" At Narbonne the books have been fent to the arfenal ; and at Fontaine le Dijon the library of the Fuillants has been thrown afide as wafte in the hall of old papers. Some individuals, of whom the tafte may, perhaps, be falfe, and the knowledge limited, inftituted revolutionary tribunals, which profcribed authors and condemned their books ; Horace and Virgil have been condemned not only for acknowledging tyrants, but for having been often printed for the ufe of tyrants, and by the permiffion of tyrants.

" How is it poffible to reftrain our indignation, when, to juftify the burning of thefe books, we are told, that they were badly bound ?

" Many of the libraries of mendicant monks contain editions printed in the firft days of the art of printing ; the Recolets de Saverne is of this number. Books which only fold here for a few crowns, have been fold in London for 125 guineas.

" I pafs now to dilapidations of another fort. Antique ftones, medals, engraved ftones, enamels of Petitot, gems, and morfels of natural hiftory, have often been the prey of knaves. From all parts bitter complaints, well founded and true, arrived. As there are profits to receive on every fale, they take care not to referve any thing, even when it is precious for public inftruction.

" It

"It is also to be observed, that the commissaries are generally traders and brokers, who, knowing the value of articles, reap exorbitant profits by purchasing them at the sales. The better to succeed, they scatter the books, and take to pieces the machines; a tube of a telescope is found separated from its stand; and the cunning knaves know how to put them together again after they have been purchased at a low price. When they are afraid of the competition of people who are judges and men of principle, they offer them money to stay away; and there is an instance, where they beat the person who bid against them.

"At Bretteuil's house a clock *en Malachite* was sold for a trifle, though it is the only one existing.

"The four famous tables in wood of the Autrichienne, (the queen) admirable for their form, the workmanship and the materials, were sold for 800 livres, re-sold for 12,200, and bought back by the nation for 15,000.

"In all quarters pillage and destruction were the *order of the day.*

"At the clocks of the palace the statues of Justice and Prudence of Pilon were broke, and the coat of arms left at St. Nicolas la Chardoneret, the magnificent Calvary by Poulhu, from the designs of Le Brun, was broken; at St. Louis de la Culture a monument, considered as one of the chef-d'œuvres of sculpture, and which cost more than 200,000 livres, was mutilated; at Marly they broke and carried off l'Hypomene, l'Atalante, the figure of the Ocean, and two excellent copies of Diana and the Venus of Medicis.

"At Franciade, (St. Denis) where the national club has with justice struck the tyrants even in their tombs, they

they ought at leaſt to have ſpared that of Turenne, when cuts of ſabres are to be ſeen.*

" · If at Paris and its environs ſuch have been the de‑ ſtructions, what muſt they have been in the provinces ?

" At Nancy, in the ſpace of a few hours, they broke and burned to the value of 100,000 crowns in books and pictures.

" But on the frontiers and the departments of the north the deſtruction is ſuch, that it is impoſſible to find words to deſcribe it.

" At Anet a ſtag in bronze was about to be deſtroy‑ ed on pretence that the chace was a feudal right; it was ſaved on proving, that brazen ſtags did not come under the law.

" At Pont Mouſſon a large picture, which con‑ noiſſeurs offered to cover with louis d'ors as its price, was ſold for forty-eight livres.

" It would require a great portion of indulgence not to perceive wickedneſs as well as ignorance in all this; but if ignorance is not always a crime, thoſe who ſpeak in its praiſe ſhould know, *that it is always an evil:* almoſt conſtantly behind ignorance a contre revolu‑ tionary and evil ſpirit is concealed. Thoſe who ſawed down the *iron tree* in the botanic garden at Montpelier to make of it a tree of liberty, are perhaps the ſame who wanted to cut up the olive trees of the ci-devant Provence.

" No ſooner is a wiſe decree paſſed, than in the in‑ ſtant ariſtocracy endeavours to turn it to its purpoſe.

* At St. Denis, the Weſtminſter Abbey of France, the coffins of all the race of kings were taken up, for the dou‑ ble purpoſe of making lead bullets and inſulting royalty. It is evident, that Gregoire is juſt as violent as thoſe who de‑ ſtroyed the monuments, with regard to royalty.

" If

" If they propofe to convert the bells into cannons, immediately men, ftrangers perhaps, or paid by ftrangers, want to fend to the foundery the collection of ftatues in bronze at the Little Auguftins. The meridian circles made by Butterfield for the globes of Coronelli, and the medals which are at the national library; they calculated that all thefe objects would make the half of a little cannon.

" At Lyons, Caffenet threw into the crucible 800 antique medals of gold.

" To find falt-petre the antiquities of Arles were deftroyed.

" At Bouquier's houfe celebrated pictures were deftroyed, becaufe they reprefented religious fubjects; and at Praflin ftatues of Pagan gods were deftroyed, as being monuments of the feudal fyftem.

" They went farther ftill; men armed with clubs, and preceded by terror, went to the citizens printfellers. A binding or a vignette have ferved as a pretext for deftroying or ftealing books, prints, geographical charts and pictures.

" They even tore the print of the death of Charles I. becaufe they found on it a coat of arms. *Ah! would to God, that after the reality, the engraving art could reprefent to us in the fame manner the heads of all kings, even at the rifk of feeing at the bottom a ridiculous blazonry.*

" Without doubt it is neceffary to fpeak to the eyes republican language, but we fhould calumniate liberty by fuppofing, that its triumph depends on the prefervation or the deftruction of a figure of defpotifm, and when fuch monuments happen to be of excellent workmanfhip, their prefervation, according to the law of the 3d Frumaire, may be ufeful both for cultivating

Such is the maufoleum of Richelieu, one of the mafter-pieces of Girandon.

" The frenzy of the barbarians was fuch, that they propofed to tear off the covers of books with arms, dedications, or privileges, that is to fay, to deftroy them altogether.

" Be affured, that this new fort of fanaticifm pleafes the Englifh. They would pay very dear for your fine editions *ad ufum Delphini*, and not being able to have them, they will willingly pay to have them burned.

" It is, perhaps, the Englifh who have got the memorials, plans, and manufcripts, that are ftole from the depofit of the army and the navy.

" Permit me here to concentrate a feries of facts which is curious and inftructing.

" Manuel propofed to deftroy the port St. Denis, which propofal prevented men of tafte, who loved the arts, from fleeping for eight days.

" Chaumette, who caufed trees to be pulled up, under pretext of planting potatoes, wanted likewife to kill all the rare animals in the mufeum of Natural Hiftory.

" Hebert infulted the national majefty by degrading the language of liberty.

" Chabot faid, he did not like learned men, he and his companions had rendered that name fynonymous with that of ariftocrat.

" Lacroix propofed, that foldiers might mount to any rank in the army, without being able to write.

" Whilft the banditti in the Vendée were deftroying the monuments at Parthenay, Angers, Saumur, and
Chinon,

Chinon, Henriot propofed to renew here the exploits of Omar at Alexandria; he propofed to burn the national library, and the fame motion was repeated at Marfeilles.

" Dumas faid, that all men of genius fhould be guillotined; Robefpierre faid, there ought only to be one.

" In the fections, to confummate the work and dry up all fources of inftruction, it was refolved to deftroy men of genius, of whom the exiftence is fo often tormented by thofe who abufe them, that they may difpenfe with admiring them. All of them were indiftinctly refufed; cards of citizens, and the cry was, *Don't truft that man, he has written a book*. Such men were chaced from the places they occupied; the pride of ignorance was flattered by the perfuafion that patriotifm, fo neceffary in all cafes, was fufficient of itfelf alone, and fo, on pretence of making principle triumph, bring into danger the fortune, honour, and life of citizens, by confiding them to unfkilful hands. This is in what difguifed ariftocracy has completely fucceeded.

" The fyftem of perfecution againft men of abilities was organifed. Deffaulx, one of the firft furgeons in Europe, was imprifoned, who is, befides, at the head of the greateft fick hofpital in Paris, and almoft the only one who raifes young furgeons for the armies. Your committee has fet him at liberty.

" During nine months the celebrated tranflator of Homer, Bitaubé, the fon of a refugee, whom the love of liberty brought back long ago into the country of his fathers, has groaned in a prifon, and whom the tyrant of Pruffia has deprived of his revenues becaufe he is a patriot. Thellaye, Coufin, La Harpe, Vandermonde, Ginquené, Lachabeaulliere, La Roche, Sage, Beffroy, Vigée, and many others, have fhared the fame fate.

" Citizens, if the authenticity is difputed, or the importance diminifhed, of any of the facts which I have mentioned,* although that enumeration is very in-complete, there ftill would remain enough to ferve for evidence of the mifchiefs of ignorance and ariftocracy.

Gregoire adds, " that the republic acquires by its courage what Louis XIV. with immenfe fums could never purchafe. The whole Flemifh fchool, .fays he, has rifen in a mafs, to come and ornament our mu-feums. Crayer, Vandyke, and Rubens, are on the road to Paris.

" The greateft enemy of France could not wifh the country to be going more rapidly to deftruction, than by thofe different facts of crimes, cruelties, and follies, it feems to be."

Two great mafters in the art of painting nature have given a fpecimen of criminality and madnefs, that re-femble ftrikingly the actors on the ftage of the French revolution.

Shakefpeare and Cervantes have painted the progrefs of crime and of folly as we fee them exhibited in France. All the criminal leaders of the French revo-lution feem, like Macbeth, to think, that once ftept into guilt, it is lefs tedious to go on than to return, and the enthufiafts in liberty, like Don Quixote, miftake perpetually every ridiculous excefs for patriotifm. The ftrong are always patriots, and the perfecuted arif-tocrats; and Gregoire, in his report to the convention, fhews as completely that he is mad north-north-eaft as any bedlamite ever was; his memorial is, in itfelf, good and true, but whenever he mentions liberty, crowned heads, or ariftocrats, he is juft as raving mad as the knight of La Mancha was about his enchanters, his knights, and his caftles.

* All Gregoire's facts are not given in this note.

To be confulted in afcertaining facts relative to the revolution.

The Journal de Paris
Courier de Provence
Monieuteur
Logograph
Rabaut's Hiftory
Mounier's Letter

Feuille du Soir & Gazette de
   Leyde
Gazette Univerfel
M. de Montgalliard
M. Peltier, &c. &.

Though, perhaps, none of thefe publications is free from many errors inevitable in relating what is recent, the conduct of the affembly, all remarkable facts and decrees, are accurate; and, in general, the French periodical papers have related things pretty truly, obferving only that they muft be compared together with care.

END OF PLAYFAIR'S

HISTORY OF JACOBINISM.

APPENDIX.

HISTORY

OF THE

AMERICAN JACOBINS,

COMMONLY DENOMINATED

DEMOCRATS.

BY PETER PORCUPINE.

" Hiſtory, who keeps a durable record of all our acts, and exer-
" ciſes her awful cenſure over *all ſorts of ſovereigns,* will not for-
" get theſe events."

BURKE.

PHILADELPHIA:

PRINTED FOR WILLIAM COBBETT, NORTH SECOND

DEDICATION.

TO

Mr. WILLIAM PLAYFAIR,

AUTHOR OF THE HISTORY OF JACOBINISM.

Dear Sir,

I HAVE feldom known a greater pleafure than I now feel, in rendering you my thanks, in this public manner, for your fpirited efforts in the caufe of order and *true* liberty. Your work, Sir, has met with the approbation of all who have read it on this fide the Atlantic, the enemies of mankind excepted; and, as to myfelf, I prefume I could not give a more unequivocal proof of my high opinion of it, than by fubmitting it to the perufal of the people of the United States of America.

The Hiftory of the American Jacobins, commonly denominated Democrats, which I have attempted in the following pages, feemed neceffary to fupply a deficiency, which, undoubtedly, is to be attributed to your want of authenticated materials. I am well aware, that the reader will, at every ſtep, regret that this part of the taſk alſo did not fall to your lot; but, the experience I have had of the indulgence of the public, emboldens me to truſt to it once more, though under the enormous diſadvantage of following ſuch a writer as Mr. Playfair.

I am,

Sir,

Your moſt obliged humble ſervant,

PETER PORCUPINE.

Philadelphia,
10th Nov. 1796.

AMERICAN JACOBINS, &c.

WHEN the Jacobins of Paris fent forth their miffionaries of infurrection and anarchy, their profeffed object was to enlighten the ignorant and unchain the
enflaved. There was fomehitng prepofterous in the
idea of Frenchmen giving liberty to the world; but,
had it been poffible for men in their fenfes to believe, that a club of diftracted Monfieurs, who knew
not the meaning of the word liberty, were calculated for this arduous tafk and were ferious in their
profeffions, fuch credulous perfons muft have been at
once undeceived, when they obferved, that the newly-
enlightened miffionaries were difpatched to thofe
countries alone where the greateft degree of civil
liberty was already to be found. Had the Propagande at Paris been fincere in their profeffions, why
were not their envoys directed towards Ruffia and
Turkey, inftead of England, America, and other free
ftates? The fact is, Briffot and his philanthropic
colleagues wanted to draw as many foreign nations
as poffible within the vortex of their own favage

fyſtem, and they well knew, that where the voice of the people has the moſt weight in public affairs, there it is moſt eaſy to introduce novel and ſubverſive doctrines.

In ſuch ſtates too, there generally, not to ſay always, exiſts a party, who, from the long habit of hating thoſe who adminiſter the government, become the enemies of the government itſelf, and are ready to ſell their treacherous ſervices to the firſt bidder. To this deſcription of men the ſect of the Jacobins have attached themſelves, in every country they have been ſuffered to enter. They are a ſort of fleſh flies, that naturally ſettle on the excremental and corrupted parts of the body politic. It is well known what aid they have received from the diſaffected of ſeveral European nations; but, neither the Malcontents in Geneva, the Patriots in Holland, nor the Reformers in Great Britain and Ireland, were half ſo well adapted to the reception of Jacobinical doctrines and Louis d'ors as the *Anti-federaliſts* in America. This faction was co-exiſtent with the General Government of the Union. Notwithſtanding the neceſſity of eſtabliſhing this government, and its mild and equitable principles, it did not fail to meet with a formidable oppoſition. The perſons who compoſed this oppoſition, and who thence took the name *Anti-federaliſts*, were not equal to the Federaliſts, either in point of riches or reſpectability. They were, in general, men of bad moral characters, embarraſſed in their private affairs, or the tools of ſuch as were. Men of this caſt naturally feared the operation of a government endued with ſufficient ſtrength to make itſelf reſpected, and with ſufficient wiſdom to exclude the ignorant and wicked from a ſhare in its adminiſtration.

However, the *Anti-federaliſts* attracted notice, and acquired conſequence. A hypocritical anxiety for the preſervation of the liberties of the people made up for a want of every real virtue. Some of the ſtates refuſed, for a long time, to accede to the new Confederation, and many individuals, in thofe ftates which did accede to it, remained obftinately oppofed to its principles.

Thus did the Federal Government receive, at its birth, the feeds of a difeafe, which, unlefs its friends difcover more zeal than they have hitherto done, will one day accomplifh its deftruction. It began its career in defiance of a party, organized and marfhalled, and ready to feize the favourable moment for attacking it with open force. We fhall foon fee that this moment was at no great diftance.

The happy effects of the new fyftem, which were almoft inftantaneoufly felt, operated fo forcibly on the minds of the people at large, that the Anti-federalifts began to feel themfelves abafhed. Seeing their numbers daily diminifh, they found it prudent to hide their difcontent; nor would their clamors have fince been revived, had they not been encouraged and backed by the ufurpers in France. The fuccefsful example, the promifes, and, above all, the gold of thefe latter, have emboldened them again to fhew their heads; as the rays of the fun draw the adder from the loathfome retreat, where he has lain engendering and bloating over his poifon.

The French ufurpers, from the moment they had got a firm grafp of the reins of power, loft no time in engaging this defperate faction in their views, which were, to acquire a perfect command of the American government, and force it into the war of Liberty and Equality. Monfieur Ternant, the then ambaffador here, was, befides his being fent by a king, very juftly looked upon as unfit for managing the intrigues of Briffot and his brother regicides. He had ever been accuftomed to live on terms of friendfhip with the officers of government, and to treat their communications with becoming refpect. Citizen Genet was therefore difpatched to fupply his place: a man every way qualified for the miffion he had to execute. Educated in the subaltern walks of the most intriguing court in Europe, he was versed in all the menial offices of corruption; and unencumbered with the family pride of the French Chevaliers, he could visit a democratic club, and give the fraternal buss to its shirtless members, with that kind of cordiality, which gives a zest to flattery, and seldom fails to gain the affections of the grovelling heart. If the Citizen has hitherto failed of ultimate success, we must attribute his failure to the deep penetration and inflexible integrity he had to encounter, rather than to any want of cunning, industry or *liberality* on his part.

The attachment of the Federal Government to a pacific system was well known in France. Genet was therefore instructed, in case he should not be able to shake this attachment either by promises or threats, to apply himself to the sovereign people themselves, whose partiality, it had been represented, and with but too much truth, had received a strong bias in favour of the usurpers. In order to pave the way for acting in the last resort, he disembarked at a point the most distant from the seat of government, that he might have it in his power to act on some part of the people at least, before the sentiments of their government respecting him and his mission were known. He accordingly landed at Charleston, South Carolina, where he remained caballing for some time, and then proceeded to Philadelphia.

The inhabitants of Charleston, and, indeed, of most parts of South Carolina, were admirably disposed for a warm reception of Genet. Not long before his landing, a proposition had been published for a solemn abolition of the use " of all aristocratical terms of *distinction* and *respect*." The levellers had even proposed having an engagement to this effect, printed and stuck up in the market-places, court-houses, &c. for the signature of the citizens. In a state where sansculottism had already made such a progress, the animating presence of the Parisian Missionary was all that could be wanted to complete the farce. The Carolinians had cut the ſtrings of their culottes, and the Citizen pulled them down about their heels.

The frigate, L'Ambuſcade, that brought Genet to America, brought alſo the news of war being declared by France againſt England. The inhabit-ants of Southern climes have never been famous for their wiſdom; accordingly, the people of Charleſ-ton looked upon a prize, which the Ambuſcade brought in with her, as an earneſt of ſucceſs, and an indubitable indication of French naval ſuperi-ority.

No ſooner was Genet on ſhore, than he began to exerciſe his powers, as ſovereign of the country. He commiſſioned land and ſea officers, to make war upon the Spaniſh and Engliſh; he fitted out privateers, and opened rendezvouſes for the enrolling of both ſoldiers and ſailors. The French flag was ſeen waving from the windows in this ſans-culotte city, juſt as if it had been a ſea-port of France. Genet was ſent expreſsly to engage the country to take a part in the war, and ſuch was his contempt for the government, that he did not look upon its conſent as a thing worth aſking for, or thinking about.

The Citizen found more volunteers than he knew what to do with, particularly of the higher ranks: Cap-tains and Commodores, Majors and Colonels, flocked to his ſtandard in ſuch crowds, that had he had a hundred reams of paper in blank commiſſions, he might have filled them all up in the State of Carolina. Whether theſe men of high rank and empty purſes were en-couraged by the confidence they had in the power of the French, or by their own inſtinctive bravery, I know not; but as to the end they had in view, there can be little doubt. For one of them, who was actuated by a love of liberty, there were five hundred who were actuated by a love of plunder. Some of them longed for a dive into the Spaniſh mines, and, in idea,

L'Ambuscade.

already heard the chinking of the doubloons; while others were eyeing the Britiſh merchant-men with that kind of ſavage deſire, with which the wolf ſurveys a herd of fat oxen.

After having remained at Charleſton from the 9th to the 19th of April 1793, the *Sans-culotte corps Diplomatique*, marched off for Philadelphia, where it arrived on the 9th of May.

I avoid mentioning the proceſſions, banquets, &c. that attended the Citizen during his journey; nor ſhould I think it worth while to give an account of his reception at the capital, were I not aſſured that the civilians of the Rights of Man will hereafter quote it as a precedent in the laws of their ceremonial.

The city had been duly prepared for this famous public entry by paragraphs in the papers, announcing the Citizen's arrival at the different ſtages on the road. Expectation was kept on tip-toe for ſeveral days. The beſt penmen among the patriots were at work compoſing congratulatory addreſſes, and their choiceſt orators were gargling their throats to pronounce them. At laſt, on the happy 16th of May, a *ſalve* from the cannons of a frigate lying in the port, gave notice that the Citizen would ſoon be arrived a place called Gray's Ferry, about three miles diſtant from the city. Thither all the patrioticly diſpoſed went, to meet him, and eſcort him to his dwelling. In the evening of the ſame day there was, what was called, a meeting of the citizens of Philadelphia, when it was agreed to appoint a committee to draft an addreſs to him. An addreſs was accordingly prepared, ſubmitted to the ſovereign citizens, at a ſecond meeting, highly approved of, and another committee, conſiſting of about half a hundred perſons, appointed to carry it up.—But I muſt now avail myſelf of their own account of the buſineſs, feeling a total want of capacity to do it juſtice.*

* See the Gazette of *Poor Richard's Grand-Child*, of the 20th of May 1793.

" The citizens aſſembled expreſſing a deſire to
" accompany their committee in preſenting the ad-
" dreſs to the Citizen miniſter, two gentlemen were
" diſpatched to know what time it would be conveni-
" ent for him to receive it, and they returned in a
" few minutes with the following report : " That
" Mr. Genet had expreſſed a high ſenſe of the com-
" pliment intended to be paid him by the citizens of
" Philadelphia ; that he was ſolicitous to avoid giving
" them the trouble of another meeting, and that if
" they would accept the ſpontaneous effuſions of his
" heart, which, however deficient in point of form,
" would not be deficient in ſincerity, as an anſwer
" to the addreſs, he would be happy to receive it
" immediately, leaving to the enſuing day the cere-
" mony of a written reply."——" The citizens teſ-
" tified their approbation of the miniſter's propoſi-
" tion by *reiterated ſhouts of applauſe*."

" The committee, headed by their chairman, and
" followed by an immenſe body of citizens, walking
" three abreaſt, having arrived at the City-tavern,
" were introduced into the preſence, and after the
" *acclamations, as well in the houſe as in the ſtreets*,
" had ceaſed, the addreſs was delivered, at the cloſe
" of which *the houſe and ſtreets again reſounded with*
" *congratulations and applauſe*."

" Citizen Genet, evidently *affected with the warmth*
" *of the public attachment*, thus conveyed, delivered
" an extemporaneous reply, in terms which *touched*
" *the feelings* of every auditor, &c.——It is impoſſible
" to deſcribe, with adequate *energy*, the ſcene that
" ſucceeded. *Shouts* and *ſalutations* were not unat-
" tended with *other evidences* of the effect, which
" this intereſting interview had *upon the paſſions* of the
" parties who were engaged in it.——From the citizens
" in the room the miniſter turned his attention to the
" citizens in the ſtreet, and addreſſed them in a few
" ſhort but emphatic ſentences, from one of the win-
" dows."

In this inftance we fee the fovereign people taking the liberty to act for themfelves, while their fervants, the officers of government, ftand looking on.   What right, I would be glad to know, had the people of Philadelphia, even fuppofing them all affembled together, to acknowledge any man as a public minifter, before he had been acknowledged and received as fuch by the General Government?   No wonder that this infolent miffionary fhould conceive, that that government was a mere cypher ; and many of thofe who afterwards complained of his appeal to the people, fhould have recollected, that they had encouraged him fo to do.

For fome time after the Citizen's arrival, there was nothing but addreffing and feafting him.   It may not be amifs to give an account of one of thefe treats ; the memory of fuch fcenes fhould be preferved, and often brought into view.

" On Saturday laft a *republican dinner* was given
" at Oellers's hotel, to *Citizen Genet*, by a refpectable
" number of French and American citizens.   After
" dinner a number of patriotic toafts were drunk, of
" which the following is a tranflation :

" 1. Liberty and Equality.
" 2. The French Republic.
" 3. The United States, &c. &c.

" After the third toaft, an *elegant ode*, fuited to
" the occafion, compofed by a young Frenchman, was
" read by Citizen *Duponceau*, and univerfally ap-
" plauded.   The fociety, *on motion* [to be fure, *on
motion*] ordered that *Citizen Freneau* fhould be re-
" quefted to tranflate it into Englifh verfe, and that
" the original and tranflation fhould be publifhed.

" After a fhort interval, the *Marfeillois's Hymn*
" was, upon the requeft of the citizens, fung by Ci-
" tizen *Bournonville*, with great tafte and fpirit, the
" *whole company joining in the chorus.*"————— I leave

the reader to guefs at the harmony of this chorus, bel-
lowed forth from the drunken lungs of about a hundred fellows, of a dozen different nations.　Who
would have thought five and thirty years ago, when
the inhabitants of Pennfylvania were petitioning King
George for protection againft the French and their
allies, the fcalping Indians, that in the year 1793,
the people of Philadelphia would carry their complai-
fance to a French minifter fo far, as to ape his outland-
ifh howling in the chorus of a murderer's fong！ But,
let us proceed with the feaft.——" Two additional
" ftanzas to the *Marfeillois's Hymn*, compofed by *Citi-*
" *zen Genet*, and fuited to the *navy* of France, were
" then called for, fung, and encored."

" Before the finging of the Hymn, it fhould be
" mentioned, that a *deputation from the failors* of the
" frigate, L'Ambufcade, made their appearance, *em-*
" *braced*, and took their feats.

" The table was decorated with the tree and cap
" of liberty, and with the French and American
" Flags.　The laft toaft being drunk, the cap of li-
" berty was placed on the head of *Citizen Genet*,
" and then it *travelled from head to head*, round the
" table [juft as the　guillotine has fince travelled
round France] each wearer enlivening the fcene with
" a patriotic fentiment."

" Thefe tokens of liberty, and of American and
" French fraternity, were delivered to the officers
" and mariners of the frigate, L'Ambufcade, who
" promifed to defend them till death."

Thus rolled Genet's time away, in a variety of
fuch nonfenfical, ftupid, unmeaning, childifh enter-
tainments, as never were heard or thought of, till
Frenchmen took it into their heads to gabble about
liberty.

On the very day that this liberty-cap feaſt took place, the citizen miniſter was formally received, and acknowledged in his diplomatic capacity, by the Preſident of the United States. There, indeed, his reception was not quite ſo warm. He afterwards complained, that the firſt object that ſtruck his eye in the chamber, was the buſt of Louis XVI. I never heard whether he ſtarted back or not, at the ſight; but it is certain he looked upon it as an ill omen. He ſaw that he had not to do with a man, whoſe friendſhip ſhifted with the changes of fortune. He ſaw that the Preſident had not been deceived by the calumnies heaped on the unfortunate king; and that, though the welfare of his country induced him to receive an envoy from his murderers, he was far from approving of their deeds.

This ſilent reproof, which muſt, however, be attributed to mere accident, ſtung the inſolent Genet to the ſoul. His reſenting it is a ſtriking inſtance of that overbearing ſpirit which the rulers of the deluded French have ever diſcovered. Becauſe they had killed their king, hurled down the ſtatues of his anceſtors, and dug their rotten bones from the tomb, they had the preſumption to think, that the governors of other nations ought to follow the ſavage example.

But, a cold reception was not the rub that Genet moſt complained of. The Federal Government, informed of his bold beginnings at Charleſton, made no doubt that his inſtructions went to the engaging it in the war. Indeed theſe inſtructions were made known from the moment of his landing; and it cannot be doubted but this had influence on the conduct of the government; for an article appeared in the Charleſton papers, the day after, ſpecifying that a report had gained ground, that the Federal Government *muſt* take a part in the war; and this article made its appearance at Philadelphia, on the very day that the Preſident's proclamation, declaring it the refolution of the United ftates to remain neuter, was firft promulgated.

This wife and determined ftep Genet's mafters had not forefeen; or, if they did forefee it, they were not aware that it would be taken, before their miffionary could find time to make his warlike propofals. This was a moft cruel difappointment to the Citizen, and completely baffled all his projects. In vain did he endeavour to draw the old General from his ground, neither promifes nor threats had any effect on him, and Genet foon found, that he had no hope but in roufing the people to oppofe their government.

A man of more penetration than Genet might have conceived fuch a project feafible, from the violent partiality that every where appeared towards the French, from the little refpect teftified for the opinion of the government, and particularly from the freedom, not to fay audacity, with which its conduct, in iffuing the proclamation of neutrality, was arraigned. Befides, the Anti-federal faction began to appear with more boldnefs than ever. Genet was continually furrounded with them; and, as they fighed for nothing fo much as for war, they ftrengthened him in the opinion, that the people would ultimately decide in his favour.

But, there wanted fomething like a regular plan to unite their forces, and bring them to act in concert. A dinner here and a fupper there, were nothing at all. The drunkards went home, fnorted themfelves fober, and returned to their employments. It was not as in France, where a fingle tap upon a drum head, would affemble *canaille* enough to overturn forty Federal Governments in the fpace of half a night. In America there exifted all the materials for a revolution, but they were fcattered here and

Genet did not judge it prudent to give to the American Jacobins the fame name, that had been af-fumed by thofe in France : that would have been too glaring an imitation. *Democratic* was thought lefs offenfive, at the fame time that it was well adapted to a fociety of men, who were about to fet them-felves up for the watch-dogs of a government, which they pretended was already become *too ariftocratic,* and was daily growing more fo ; but that a Demo-crat was but another name for a Jacobin no one had the folly to deny, when, afterwards, fome of thefe very clubs were known to fend petitions for having their names entered on the regifters of the Jacobin club at Paris.

The Mother Club, in America, met at Philadel-phia on the 3d of July, 1793, about fix or feven weeks after Genet's arrival in the city, during which fpace, it is well afcertained, more than *twenty thoufand Louis d'ors* had been diftributed.

As it is here, properly fpeaking, that the Hiftory of the American Jacobins, or Democrats, begins, it feems neceffary to give fome account of their *conftitution,* as they termed it. This anarchical act fets out with a preamble containing the principles under which the members had united, and it then proceeds to the rules and regulations for tranfacting the bufinefs of the in-ftitution.

" ART. I.

" The Society fhall be co-extenfive with the State;
" but, for the conveniency of the members, there
" fhall be a feparate meeting in the city of Phi-
" ladelphia, and one in each county, which fhall
" choofe to adopt this Conftitution. A member ad-
" mitted in the city, or in any county, fhall of courfe
" be a member of the Society at large ; and may at-
" tend any of the meetings, wherever held."

" ART. II.

" A meeting of the Society ſhall be held in the city
" of Philadelphia, on the firſt Thurſday in every
" month, and in the reſpective counties as often, and
" at ſuch times as they ſhall by their own rules deter-
" mine.   But the Preſident of each reſpective meet-
" ing may *convene the members on any ſpecial occaſion.*"

" ART. III.

" The election of new members, and of the officers
" of the ſociety, ſhall be by ballot, and by a majority
" of the votes of the members preſent. The names of
" the members propoſing any candidate for admiſſion
" ſhall be entered in a book kept for that purpoſe.
" Every member on his admiſſion ſhall ſubſcribe this
" Conſtitution, and pay the ſum of half a dollar to
" the treaſurer for the uſe of the Society."

" ART. IV.

" The officers of the meeting in the city of Phila-
" delphia ſhall conſiſt of a *Preſident,* two *vice Preſi-*
" *dents,* two *Secretaries,* one *Treaſurer,* and one
" *correſponding committee* of five members; and the
" meetings of the reſpective counties ſhall chooſe a
" *Preſident* and ſuch other officers as they think
" proper."

" ART. V.

" It ſhall be the duty of the correſponding com-
" mittee, to correſpond with the various meetings of
" the Society, *and with all other Societies, that may be*
" *eſtabliſhed on ſimilar principles, in any other of the*
" *United States.*"

" ART. VI.

" It ſhall be the duty of the Secretaries to keep mi-
" nutes of the proceedings of the ſeveral meetings;

" and of the treasurer to receive and account for all
" monies to them respectively paid."

Now, what was the object of all this balloting and corresponding and meeting? This we are to look for, they tell us, in their first circular letter: here it is then.

" Fellow Citizen,

" We have the pleasure to communicate to you a
" copy of the constitution of the *Democratic Society*,
" in hopes that after a candid consideration of its
" principles, and objects, you may be induced to pro-
" mote its adoption, in the county of which you are
" an inhabitant.

" Every mind, capable of reflection, must per-
" ceive, that the present crisis in the politics of nati-
" ons is peculiarly interesting to America. The Eu-
" ropean Confederacy, transcendent in power, and
" unparalleled in iniquity, menaces the very existence
" of freedom. Already its baneful operation may be
" traced in the tyrannical destruction of the Constitu-
" tion of Poland : and should the glorious efforts of
" France be eventually defeated, we have reason to
" presume, that, for the consummation of monarchical
" ambition, and the security of its establishments, this
" country, the only remaining depository of liberty,
" will not long be permitted to enjoy in peace, the
" honours of an independent, and the happiness of a
" republican government.

" Nor are the dangers arising from a foreign source,
" the only causes, at this time, of apprehension and
" folicitude. The *feeds of luxury* appear to have taken
" root in our domestic foil : and the *jealous eye of pa-*
" *triotism* already regards the *spirit of freedom and*
" *equality*, as eclipsed by the *pride of wealth* and the
" *arrogance of power.*

" This general view of our fituation has led to the
" inftitution of the *Democratic Society*. A conftant
" circulation of ufeful information, and a liberal com-
" munication of republican fentiments, were thought
" to be the beft antidotes to any political poifon, with
" which the vital principles of civil liberty might be
" attacked : for by fuch means, a fraternal confidence
" will be eftablifhed among the citizens ; every fymp-
" tom of innovation will be ftudioufly marked ; and
" a ftandard will be erected, to which, in danger
" and diftrefs, the friends of liberty may fuccefsfully
" refort.

" To obtain thefe objects, then, and to cultivate
" on all occafions, the love of peace, order, and har-
" mony ; an attachment to the conftitution, and a
" refpect to the laws of our country, will be the aim
" of the *Democratic Society*, &c."

Never did a piece of political hypocrify come forth
to public view under fuch a flimfy difguife as this circular letter. People ftared to fee that there were men
amongft them poffeffed of impudence enough, thus to
invite them to revolt againft the conftitution, under
the pretext of preferving it in its purity.   The Americans can fwallow a pretty comfortable dofe of any
thing that is ftrongly feafoned with *liberty and equality*,
but there were few, above the mere vulgar, whofe
ftomachs did not turn at this.

How *democratic focieties* were to protect the country againft the monarchs of Europe feemed a my-
ftery.   What ftandard were they to raife for the
people to find fhelter under, in the hour of danger
and diftrefs ? Nothing is clearer, than that the combination was intended to operate againft the General
Government, and againft that alone. They fet out
with talking about the dangers to be apprehended from
foreign powers, but they foon come to the point ; the

to combat thefe, that they invoke the aid of their fellow citizens.

Indeed a political club, if it is not intended to
ftrengthen the government, muft be intended to act
againft it. The very foundation of fuch a club muft
imply a fyftematic oppofition to the lawful rules of the
land; it is an act of rebellion, unpunifhable by law
'tis true, but which will ever be punifhed by the abhorrence of all peaceable and honeft men.

No one can read the concluding paragraph of this
letter, without calling to mind the profeffions of the
French and Englifh Jacobins: the former united
themfelves under the name of, " *Les Amis de la Con-*
" *ftitution*" (the friends of the Conftitution), and the
latter, under that of, " *The Conftitutional Society.*"
What fort of *friends* to the Conftitution (of 1791)
the Jacobins of Paris were, their fubfequent conduct,
and the fate of that Conftitution, have fully proved;
and it would be finning againft conviction to fuppofe,
that thofe of England and America exceeded them in
fincerity. The patriots, or *reformers* (call them which
you pleafe) who emigrate from England, throw off
the difguife as foon as their feet touch the fhore.
They tell you, that their intention was to deftroy
" the old rotten conftitution of Britain," from which
they took their name; and there is not the leaft
doubt, but the Democrats would be as candid with
refpect to the American conftitution, were they landed
in France.

As to thofe who placed themfelves at the head of
the Democrats, fpeaking of them generally, they
were very little efteemed, either as private or public
characters. Few of them were men of property, and
fuch as were, owed their poffeffions to fome cafual
circumftance, rather than to family, induftry, or talents. The bulk of political reformers is always compofed of needy, difcontented men, too indolent or
impatient to advance themfelves by fair and honeft

means, and too ambitious to remain quiet in obscurity. Such, with very few exceptions, are those who have appeared among the leaders of the American Jacobins.*

The effects of the institution soon became apparent from one end of the United States to the other. The blaze did not, indeed, communicate itself with such rapidity as it had done in France, nor did it rage with so much fury when it had caught; but this must be ascribed to the nature of the materials, and not to any want of art or malice on the part of the incendiaries. The Americans are phlegmatic, slow to act; extremely cautious and difficult to be deceived. However, such was the indefatigableness of the Democratic Clubs, that I venture to say, without running the risk of contradiction, that more enmity to the General Government was excited in the space of six months, by the barefaced correspondencies and resolves of these clubs, than was excited against the colonial government at the time of the declaration of Independence.

The leading object was to stimulate the people to a close imitation of the French Revolutionists, who had just then begun the career of pure unadulterated sansculottism. Every act or expression that bore the marks of politeness or gentility soon began to be look-

---

* The *Officers*, as they were called, of the Mother Club, and who must ever be looked upon (under Genet) as the chief instruments in founding the sect, were:

DAVID RITTENHOUSE, President.
WILLIAM COATS, } *Vice-Presidents.*
CHARLES BIDDLE, }
JAMES HUTCHINSON,
ALEXANDER J. DALLAS,
MICHAEL LEIB, } *Committee of Correspondence.*
JONATHAN SERGEANT,
DAVID JACKSON, }
ISRAEL ISRAEL, *Treasurer.*
J. PORTER, } *Secretaries.*

ed upon, to ufe their own words, as a fort of *leze republicanifm.* All the new fangled terms of the regenerated French were introduced and made ufe of. The word *citizen,* that ftalking horfe of modern liberty-men, became almoft as common in America as in France. People, even people of fenfe, began to accuftom themfelves to be-citizen each other in as fhameful a manner as the red-headed ruffians of the Fauxbourg St. Antoine.

The news-printers were in fome fort the teachers of this new cant; and it was diverting enough fometimes to obferve their embarraffment in rendering the French political jargon into Englifh. One of them having a wedding to announce, found himfelf at a ftand when he came to the word *citoyenne.* Our good anceftors had not forefeen thefe days of equality, and had therefore never thought of a termination to exprefs the *feminine* of a *free-man.* To fay that *citizen* A. was married to *citizen* B. would have had a brutal found, even in the ears of a Jacobin, and therefore the ingenious news-man invented a termination, and his paragraph ran thus : " On ———— *Citizen* ————
" was married to *Citefs* ———— by *Citizen* ————."*

The *citizens* of France had juft given fignal proof of their patriotic valour, in making war upon the old bufts and ftatues of their kings and nobles, and thofe of America were determined not to be behind hand with them, as far as lay in their power. Lord Chatham's ftatue, erected by the people of Charlefton, South Carolina, as a mark of their efteem for the part he took in pleading the caufe of America, was drawn up into the air, by means of a jack and pullies, and abfolutely hanged, ..ot till it was dead, but till the head feparated from the body. The ftatue of Lord Bettertout, a piece of exquifite workmanfhip, which ftood in the town houfe of Williamfburgh in Virginia, was *beheaded* by the ftudents of that place,

* This article is to be found in the *Federal Gazette,* for the year 1793.

and every mark of indignity, such as ignoble minds can show, was heaped on the resemblance of a man, to whom the fathers of these students had yielded all possible testimony of love and esteem.

The rage for *re-baptism*, as the French call it, also spread very far. An alley at Boston, called *Royal Exchange Alley*, and the stump of a tree, in the same town, which had borne the name of *Royal*, were re-baptized with a vast deal of formality: the former was called *Equality Lane*, and the latter *Liberty Stump*. At New York the names of several streets and places were changed; *Queen Street* became *Pearl Street*, and *King Street*, *Liberty Street*.

Those who were unacquainted with the influence of the Democratic Clubs, were astonished at these marks of political insanity. Indeed, the follies of the French seemed to be wafted over the instant they had birth, and the different districts seemed to vie with each other in adopting them. The delirium seized even the women and children; the former began to talk about liberty and equality in a good masculine style : I have heard more than one young woman, under the age of twenty, declare that they would willingly have dipped their hands in the blood of the Queen of France. A third part of the children, at least, were decorated, like their wise sires, in tricolored cockades. " *Dansons la Carmagnole*," pronounced in a broken accent, was echoed through every street and every alley of Philadelphia, by both boys and girls. Some ingenious democratic poet had composed the following lines :

> " Englishman no bon for me,
> " Frenchman fight for liberty."

This distich, which at once shows the prevailing sentiments, and exhibits an instance of that kind of jar-

Nor were marks of ferocity wanting. At a dinner at Philadelphia (at which *a man high in office* was prefent) a *roafted pig* became the reprefentative of Louis XVI. and it being the anniverfary of his murder, the pig's head was fevered from his body, then carried round to each of the convives, who, after placing the liberty-cap upon his own head, pronounced the word *tyrant*, and gave the poor little grunter's head a chop with his knife.

Never was the memory of any man fo cruelly infulted as that of this mild and humane monarch. He was guillotined in effigy, in the capital of the union, twenty or thirty times every day, during one whole winter, and part of the fummer. Men, women, and children, flocked to this tragical exhibition, and not a fingle paragraph appeared in the papers to fhame them from it.—Much has been faid about the *cruelty of Englifh fports*, and the *humane* French have now-and-then ftigmatized them as barbarians, for the delight they take in feeing a pair of courageous animals fpur each other to death; nay, the charge has been often repeated by Americans, and I muft confefs, that nothing can be faid in its defence ; but I defy both French and Americans to bring me an inftance of cruelty from the Englifh fports, that will bear a comparifon with the exhibition above mentioned.

One cannot think of this exhibition without reflecting on the honours that Louis formerly received on the fame fpot. On the triumphal arch that was erected at Philadelphia, in 1783, was a buft of Louis XVI. with this motto :

MERENDO MEMORES FACIT.
His Merit makes us remember him.

On another part of the arch were the *Three Lillies*, the arms of France, with this motto :

GLORIAM SUPERANT.
They exceed in Glory.

When a reprefentation of this Triumphal Arch was fent to the King of France, what would he have done to one of his courtiers, who fhould have faid to him : " Sira, be not too vain ; depend not too much " on the fincerity of the Americans ; for, ten years " from this day, they will fhake hands with your mur- " derers, and on the very fpot where this arch was " erected, they will murder you in effigy ; and thefe " Lillies, now furpaffing in glory, will they trample " under foot."

It is juft, however, to obferve, that a very great majority of the people of America, abhorred thefe de- monftrations of a fanguinary fpirit ; nor would it be going too far to affert, that two-thirds of the Demo- crats were foreigners, landed in the United States fince the war. The charge that attaches to the peo- ple in general, is, that thefe things were fuffered to pafs unreproved. The friends of order and of huma- nity were dilatory ; like perfons of the fame defcrip- tion in France, they feemed to be waiting, till the fons of equality came to cut their throats ; and if they have finally efcaped, it is to be afcribed to mere chance, or to any thing, rather than to their own exertions.

While the Democratic Societies were thus poifoning the minds of the people, familiarizing them to infur- rection and blood, Genet was not idle. He had fur- rounded himfelf with a troop of horfe, enlifted and embodied in Philadelphia. Thefe were, in general, Frenchmen, and no one can doubt but they were in- tended to act, either on the offenfive or defenfive, as occafion might require. This force rendered his ad- herents bold ; they threw off all referve, and iffued their invitations to rebellion with an unfparing hand. The clubs at a diftance followed the example, and, in fome inftances, improved upon it.

As the Democrats increafed in ftrength and impu-

French ; every one, even of their moſt ſavage acts, was applauded : robbery and murder were called *national juſtice* in America as well as in France. The people, properly ſo called, were fairly cowed down, and things ſeemed as ripe for a revolution here, as they were in France, in the month of July, 1790.

The country was ſaved from this dreadful ſcourge by the haſty indiſcretion of the Citizen Miniſter. The light-headed Frenchman was intoxicated with his ſucceſs, and conceived that the moment was arrived for him to ſet the government at defiance, and call on the people for ſupport. But no ſooner had he expreſſed his intention of " appealing from the Preſident to the " ſovereign people," than he found he had been too ſanguine. He found that the *people of America* were yet more attached to General Waſhington than to the French Miniſter or the French nation. Their love and veneration for their old and tried friend ſeemed to be revived by this inſult ; and though the Democratic Clubs defended the conduct of their founder, they found themſelves too weak to take any decided ſtep in his favour.

When Genet diſcovered that he had been too raſh, he ſtrove to recover himſelf by denying that he had threatened the government with an appeal to the people, and his friend *Dallas*, who, as Secretary of the State of Pennſylvania, had been the bearer of the threat, was prevailed on to deny that it was made. *Dallas* publiſhed an explanation of his contradictory account of the matter, endeavouring to exculpate both the Frenchman and himſelf; but this explanation had no other effect than that which a lie added to an offence never fails to produce.

From this time forward the clubs were a little more cautious in their reſolves. When they met it was by night, and *under lock and key*. Genet became timid, attempted to juſtify himſelf, and ſeemed to tremble for his fate. He ſaw that his reſources decreaſed, and

that the remainder would be wanted for other purpofes than that of nourifhing a neft of hungry Democrats. The vital principle being extinct, the body began to dwindle: the old leaders fkulked off one by
one, and at laft none remained but the mere tools.

Among thefe were the Democrats from England, a
fet of mortals whofe ftupidity is equalled by their obftinacy, and by that alone. They, poor devils, who
had never been fuffered even to fmell the loaves and
fifhes, perfevered with as good heart as ever, after
the feaft was all over; and wondered why others
abated in their zeal. Englifhmen are faid to be
changeable and fickle minded; but when foreigners
lay this to our charge, they fhould make an exception
of one cafe, and that is, *when we are in the wrong.*
No men on earth abandon their errors with fo much
reluctance as the inhabitants on the fouth of the
Tweed.

One *Pearce*, who had had the honour to be a delegate to the *London Correfponding Society*, and who, on
that account, was admitted a member of the Jacobin
club of Philadelphia, propofed a *negro man* as worthy
of a feat. Pearce was a philanthropift, a true equality man, a difciple of Winchefter. He was filly
enough to fuppofe that the Democrats were really
what they profeffed to be, and therefore he forefaw
no kind of oppofition to the introduction of his char-
coal-faced friend, and having an extraordinary degree
of zeal for the increafe of the fociety, took the earlieft
opportunity to propofe him. The club being met and
the doors locked, he rofe in all the pride of confcious
fans-culottifm, and propofed brother Pompey as a
member; but he foon found that the American Democrats did not carry their ideas of equality quite fo far
as he did. " No, no, no," refounded from every
quarter, and when the votes came to be taken, there
appeared but two or three, out of about fifty, in fa-

This refufal, however, loft them the Delegate : he told them, that he had joined the club in the perfuafion that it was compofed of pure Democrats, and that his confcience would not permit him to remain among them a moment, after what he had been a witnefs of that night.

The bufinefs of the clubs was reduced to trifling difcuffions of this fort, when the recall of Genet feemed to forebode their total extinction. Genet's infolence had produced a complaint on the part of the American Government, and this complaint had produced his recal. The corner ftone of the Jacobin affiliation being removed, every one expected the fuperftructure to fall to the ground ; how deceitful appearances were we fhall fee by-and-by, after having made a remark or two on this act of " friendly con-" defcenfion," as it has been termed, of the French ufurpers.

Firft, it muft be remembered, that at the time the complaint was made, the faction, by whom Genet had been fent out, were hurled from their thrones, and another had got poffeffion of them. Robefpierre and Marat were glad of having an opportunity to accufe their rivals of having offended the American Government, and to take to themfelves the credit of healing the wound. Difplacing Genet inftantly, upon application, was a ftep, too, which they knew would render them popular in America, and filence thofe who began to arraign the conduct of the Convention. Thus, by the means of this " condefcenfion," they fecured to themfelves three advantages : it furnifhed them with one more crime to heap on the heads of their rival faction ; they completely fupplanted that faction in the partiality of the people of the United States ; and, which was of ftill greater importance, they purfued the fame treacherous manœuvres, without being fufpected. Thefe were the motives of this act of " friendly con-" defcenfion."

That they did not, in their hearts, difapprove of the proceedings of Genet, is clear from their fuffering him to remain in the United States. When did they forgive thofe who offended them? Had they demanded him, the government muft, and, they knew, would, have given him up; but no fuch demand was ever made, and this circumftance alone fufficiently proves, that, had he fucceeded, a *civic crown* would have been the mede of his machinations.

Fauchet, the fucceffor of Genet, trod exactly in his fteps, but with a little more caution. The Democratic Clubs made not the leaft hefitation in transferring their obedience from one minifter to the other. Indeed, all the difciples of the new-light philofophy are made of the fame commodious kind of ftuff. All that they do is, to afk who directs the ftorm of anarchy, and they inftantly become his ardent admirers, if not his tools. In this refpect no fet of beings, I cannot call them men, ever approached fo near to the herd of Paris, as did the Democrats of America. One day faw the faction of Briffot exalted to the fkies, and the very next, faw the fame compliments, the very fame turgid effufions of patriotic admiration, heaped on their murderers. From the firft affembling of the States General to this very hour, every leader, while he continued fuch, has been the god of thofe wretches who now-a-days ftyle themfelves patriots. I have now a bundle of gazettes before me, publifhed all by the fame man, wherein Mirabeau, Fayette, Briffot, Danton, and Robefpierre, are all panegyrized and execrated in due fucceffion; nor do I yet defpair of living to fee Talien and Louvet added to the lift. The verfatile mob of Paris, who firft canonized Mirabeau and Voltaire, and afterwards fcattered their remains to the winds; and who, after having given Marat's ugly carcafs a place in their temple of fame, and his name to a city, dug him up, put his afhes into a chamber-pot, by way

United States of America; and forry am I to fay, that they are not few in number.*

A circumftance that ftrongly feconded the endeavours of *Fauchet* and the Clubs, was, the difcontents that exifted among the people of the Weftern Counties of Pennfylvania, on account of the excife on whifky. Thefe difcontents were, in fome meafure, done away, or, at leaft, they produced no ferious confequences, before the inftitution of the Democratic Societies: with this inftitution they revived, and affumed a more determined afpect: the malcontents

---

* At the head of thefe we may venture to place *Benjamin Franklin Bache*, a grand-fon (whether in a *ftraight or crooked line*, I know not) of Old Doctor Franklin. This is the man whom the doctor left his books and printing-office to, and good ufe has he made of them. The hiftory of the types of this office would be an amufing performance: it would be curious to trace them from the oppofition of the Britifh Colonial government to as determined an oppofition againft the government raifed on its ruins; from the old faws of hypocritical morality, contained in the pages of *Poor Richard's* Almanac, to the blafphemous nonfenfe of the French Republican Calendar. Thefe types were, indeed, a rich legacy. Their proprietor may, with a trifling change, join in chorus with the highwayman in the Beggar's Opera.

> " See the types I hold!
> " See the types I hold!
> " Let the chemifts toil like affes,
> " My ink their fire furpaffes,
> " And *turns my lead to gold!*
> " And *turns my lead to gold!*

It muft be confeffed, however, that, in one inftance, he did, for a moment, difcover more confiftency than the reft of his fellow labourers. He did defend his friends *Barrere, Collot d'Herbois,* and *Billaud de Varennes,* even after he looked upon them as dead! Of " the three" fays he, " *Barrere* is moft to be regretted."—And why?— " Becaufe *he prefided in the convention when Louis was con*" *demned,* and expreisly declared, that *the Tree of Liberty muft be* " *watered with the blood of the Tyrant.*"—— Thefe are the *humane* and *grateful* Citizen Bache's reafons for regretting the fall of *Barrere!* Would not one imagine that he muft have been fuckled with blood? His friends defend him (God defend me from the defence of fuch friends) by infifting that he is a fool, and the mere cat's-paw of the *fupporters* of his paper. Of the two, I muft confefs, that a *hireling* is lefs deteftable than a *favage,* and as I wifh to excite as little deteftation againft Bache, as juftice will admit of, I leave him to take his choice of the two characters.

had now a rallying point; by means of the affiliation they communicated their pretended grievances to every corner of the Union, from whence they inftantly received affurances of aid and fupport of the clubs. Thus encouraged, they proceeded from one excefs to another, till, at laft, feveral counties were officially declared to be in a ftate of actual infurrection.

To give a detailed account of this infurrection, were it confiftent with my circumfcribed plan, would be of little ufe. That *fifteen thoufand* men were obliged to quit their homes and bufinefs, to encounter a campaign of uncommon hardfhip and toil; that many of thefe peaceable, orderly citizens (citizens in the true fenfe of the word) loft their lives in confequence of the fatigues they underwent, leaving their afhes to be trod on by the vile infurgents; that the expenfes of the armament to a million and a half of dollars, are to be deducted from the fruits of induftry; thefe are well known, and will be long remembered facts, and therefore need no hiftorian. It is to the influence that the Democratic Clubs had in producing the infurrection, and its confequent calamities, that I with to direct the reader's attention.

As foon as the Club at Philadelphia was formed, fimilar ones were formed in the Weftern Counties, compofed entirely of men, who were not only oppofed to the excife law, but to the government which had enacted it. Meffengers and emiffaries paffed continually between the clubs in the Eaft and thofe in the Weft. From this time the *refolves* of the malcontents affumed another tone. Thefe refractory people had hitherto confined their demands to a repeal of the excife law; but they now talked of forcing the government to open the navigation of the Miffiffippi, and complained, in the ftyle of Genet and the Clubs, againft the Proclamation of Neutrality, and, in fhort, againft the whole of the conduct of the Federal Go-

Let any one read their *toasts* and *resolves*, and observe their manner of proceeding, and compare these with those of the Democratic Societies; and then believe, if he can, that they were not both actuated with the same spirit, and had not the same objects in view; namely, a war with Britain, and the destruction of the General Government. During two years had the Western complaints existed: the complainants had often assembled, and had passed resolves without number about their detestable drink; but never till now did they join their cause to that of France: never till now did they wear national cockades, or rally under the *tree of liberty* mounted with a bloody Parisian cap. Will any man in his senses believe that these were mere whims, freaks of fancy, that came athwart their brains by chance, without the least advice or prior instruction from their friends in the East?

Let us hear our old friend *Citizen Fauchet's* opinion on this subject. In giving his masters an account of the breaking out of the insurrection, he says: " In " the mean time *popular societies are formed;* politi- " cal ideas concentre themselves; the *patriotic party* " *unite* and more closely connect themselves, &c."— Then, after giving them a description of the Western people and the nature of their drink, &c. he adds: " Now, as the common dispatches inform you, these " complaints *were systematizing* by the *conversations* " *of influential men, who retired into these wild coun-* " *tries,* and who, from *principle,* or by a series of " *particular heart-burnings, animated discontents* alrea- " dy near effervescence. At last, the *local explosion* " *is effected.* The Western people calculated on be- " ing supported by *some distinguished characters in the* " *East,* and even imagined they had in the bosom of " the government some abettors, who might share in " their grievances or their principles."

I shall not attempt to point out these *distinguished characters in the East;* but let the reader recollect that *Mr. Dallas* was one in the leaders of the Mother,

and then let him read the following extract from another part of *Fauchet's Letter*.

" Of all the governors, whose duty it was to ap-
" pear at the head of the requisitions, *the governor*
" *of Pennsylvania* alone enjoyed *the name of Republi-*
" *can;* his opinion of the Secretary of the Treasu-
" ry and of his systems was known to be unfavourable.
" The *secretary of this state possessed great influence*
" *in the Popular Society of Philadelphia,* which in
" its turn influenced those of other states ; of course
" he merited attention. It appears therefore that
" these men, with others unknown to me, all having
" without doubt Randolph at their head, were ba-
" lancing to decide on their party. Two or three
" days before the proclamation was published, and of
" course before the cabinet had resolved on its mea-
" sures, Mr. Randolph came to see me with an air
" of great eagerness, and made to me the overtures,
" of which I have given you an account in my No. 6.
" Thus, with some thousands of dollars, the Repub-
" lic could have decided on civil war or on peace !
" Thus the consciences of the pretended patriots of
" America have already their prices ! It is very true
" that the certainty of these conclusions, painful to be
" drawn, will for ever exist in our archives ! What
" will be the old age of this government, if it is thus
" early decrepid !"

From the conduct of the democrats prior to the
breaking out of the insurrection, we naturally come to
that which they observed subsequent to that event;
and here we shall find nothing but what tends to
strengthen the charge against them. Immediately upon
the issuing of the President's proclamation, all the papers devoted to the French Minister and his clubs, and
particularly *Bache's,* which might be looked upon as the
mirror of their sentiments, attacked, with all their
malice, both those who issued, and those who were

throats of their fellow citizens merely to fupport the rich creditors of the State ; and, of courfe, that they ought not to obey the fummons to attend. "As vio-"lent means," (fays Bache's paper of the 20th of Augnſt) "As *violent means* appear the defire of high-"toned government men, it is to be hoped that thofe "who derive the moſt benefit from our revenue laws, "will be the foremoſt to march againſt the Weſtern "Infurgents. Let ſtock-holders, bank directors, fpe-"culators, and revenue officers arrange themfelves "immediately *under the banners of the treaſury*, and "try their prowefs in arms, as they have done in cal-"culation. The prompt recourſe to hoftilities will no "doubt operate upon the *knights* of our country to "appear in military array, and then the *poor but in-*"*duſtrious citizen* will not be *obliged to ſpill the blood of* "*his fellow citizen to gratify certain reſentments*, and "expofe himſelf to the lofs of life and of limb to "*ſupport a funding order.*" In the fame paper of the 26th of Auguſt : " The difcontents which have taken "place in the Weſtern Counties, and which have ap-"peared in the form of open hoftility to law, and in-"deed the diſſatisfactions that are to be found in every "part of the continent, may be readily accounted for, "by a reference to the proceedings of our govern-"ment *from its birth.* The bantling fancied itſelf "*ſomething royal*, before it was able to ſtand alone, "and ſince it has been progreſſing towards manhood, "the State dignity, fuperciliouſnefs and manners of a "monarch have characterized its actions. To fupport "itſelf in royal pomp, arofe the funding and banking "fyſtems, *excifes*, &c. Nothing but coronets and "ſtars are wanting, to the ſtockholders. Is this a "land of liberty ? Is this a land where citizens are "*equal ? It would be no wonder* if every citizen, who "is not immediately intereſted in the funding fyſtem, "*ſhould rife up*, and with one word *exclaim againſt* "*its iniquity*," or, in other words, *join the infurgents.*

Such was the language of the democrats, at the very moment that the infurrection wore the moſt threaten-

ing aspect, and such was the effect it had on some de-
scriptions of the people, that it was with the utmost difficulty a sufficient number of men were collected to
make up the quota of the State of Pennsylvania.

Mr. Findley, the ingenious historian of the Western
Insurrection, and a principal actor in it, insists, with a
modesty becoming his country, that the insurrection
ought to be attributed entirely to the irritable *heat of
the weather*, during the dog-days of 1794; and, of
course he wishes us to believe, that it was quelled by
the returning coolness of October and November. It
must be confessed that the insurgents were afflicted with
a sort of canine malady, for they snapped at the hand
that yielded them protection; but, I believe, few people, after what has been said above, will not remain
well convinced, that the insurrection was fomented by
democratic fuel, paid for with French Gold; and that
it was cooled again by the approach of General Washington, at the head of fifteen thousand men.

For the sake of preserving connection, some striking
traits of sans-culottism, which took place prior to the
epoch at which we are now arrived, have been omitted;
but they are too characteristic of the sect whose history
I am writing, to pass altogether unnoticed.

As I have more than once observed, that the Democrats aped the regenerated French in all their follies,
and in all their crimes as far as they were able, it will
be understood, that they made a boast of being atheists
or deists as the Convention changed its creed. When the
faction of Danton seemed to preponderate, and members
exclaimed against the " aristocracy of heaven;" when
the infamous *Dupont* exclaimed: " Oh! shame, Legis-
" lators of the Universe! You have hurled down the
" thrones of kings, and you yet suffer the altars of God
" to remain!" Then the Democrats made an open
profession of Atheism. But when *Robespierre* obtain-

did our good fans-culottes burn incenfe on the altars of deifm, with as much devotion as the ragged groups of *St. Marceau* and the whores and bullies of the *Palais de L'Egalite.*

It has been often obferved, that, however widely atheifm and deifm may differ in theory, in practice, that is in their effects, they are nearly the fame. So it happens now ; for, whether they profeffed the opinions of Danton or thofe of his bloody fucceffor, they ftill teftified the fame hatred of the Chriftian Religion, and perfecuted, with every infult they durft offer, all thofe who had courage enough to ftand forward in its defence.

The firft affault of this kind was on the Reverend Mr. Abercrombie of the Epifcopal Church, Philadelphia. This gentleman had preached a fermon, warning his congregation againft the contagion of French atheifm and deifm. For this inftance of becoming zeal in the difcharge of the moft imperious of all duties, he was attacked in the public papers; accufed of *bigotry,* of being *an enemy to the caufe of liberty,* and of the *French people.* There was not a worthy man in the city, who did not feel an indignation againft the authors of this unprovoked calumny, and who did not regret, that the injured clergyman fhould fee the neceffity of anfwering it. Dreadful times indeed are thofe, when the fervants of the Lord are brought to the bar of the public, for daring to obey the commands of their mafter! For daring to defend him againft thofe, who brand him with the name of cheat and impoftor !*

* About the fame time that this infult was offered to Mr. Abercrombie, a paragraph appeared in the Philadelphia Gazette, publifhed by one Brown, containing a lift of eminent men, who had arifen on " the democratic floor," and concluding with, *Marat, St. Paul,* and *Jefus Chrift.*

I have mentioned this fcandalous paragraph in fo many places, that I fhould not have done it here, had not its exiftence been denied in a pamphlet lately publifhed by a Scotch run-away, whofe name is *Calender,* and who was, it feems, the editor of the gazette at the time. The paragraph appeared in the paper above-mentioned, on the 20th of June, in the memorable 1794.

This pulpit evefdropping having, in fome meafure fucceeded, they caft their fcrutinizing fcowling eyes over the out-fide of the church. Here they found a fmall wooden buft of George II. This buft, like the *Old Stump* at Bofton, had remained very quiet during the American revolution; but could not endure the fiery ordeal of the French revolution. Trifling circumftances like thefe fhow the difference in the influence which thefe revolutions have had on men's minds, in a ftronger light than the moft important events can do, and prove what I have always afferted; namely, that the moderation which marked the American character in the laft revolution, muft not be counted upon, fhould another take place.

The difcovery of the buft was no fooner made, than the Democrats formed the refolution of deftroying it; or, in the language of *Gregoire*, of committing an act of *vandalifm*. They accordingly publifhed the following card, as they called it, in their printer Bache's gazette of the 21ft July, 1794.

" *To the Clergy and Veftry of Chrift Church.*

" Gentlemen,

" It is the wifh of many refpectable *citizens*, that
" you would caufe the image and crown of George II.
" to be removed as readily as poffible. It has nothing
" to do with the worfhip of the moft high God, nor
" the government under which we exift : it has a ten-
" dency to caufe that church to be difliked, while
" *bearing the mark of infamy :* it has a tendency, to
" the knowledge of many, to keep *young* and *virtuous*
" *men* from attending public worfhip : it is therefore
" a public nuifance.

" M."

One is at a lofs which to admire moft, the logic,

vention; *"young* and *virtuous men!"* Canting rafcals! How willingly would you have led thofe *young* and *virtuous men* to cut the throats of their fathers and mothers, and of the minifters to whom they were attached!

In confequence of the democratic *card,* which was rightly looked upon as a threat, a veftry was called, and it was thought more advifeable to abandon the buft to the fury of the *vanduls,* than to expofe the church itfelf to danger. Accordingly, the *barbarians* affembled with ladders, mallets and chiffels. The crown and the projecting part of the buft were chipped off; but the profile, with G on one fide of it and II. on the other, are ftill as confpicuous as ever. All that the Democrats effected, was, a change in the ideas awakened by the fight of the buft. From a monument of well-placed efteem and gratitude, it is become a monument of democratic folly and bafenefs and rancour and undiftinguifhing revenge.

It was eafy to perceive, that they did not mean to ftop here, and therefore few people were furprifed at their next pointing out the propriety of taking the *mitre* from the fteeple.* This demand was not made in fuch direct and pofitive terms, and therefore it was not complied with; but there is little doubt but both mitre and church would have had a tumble long ago, had not the Weftern Infurrection excited a general hatred againft the clubs, and thus rendered them lefs daring and infolent.

At the fame time that we are recording the violences of the clubs againft Chriftian inftitutions, truth requires that we fhould confefs, that but too many of the clergy appeared either contaminated with French principles, or cowardly enough not to attempt an oppofition to their progrefs. All that can be faid in the defence of fuch men, is, that they feared to offend

* 'See Bache's gazette of the 21ft Auguft, 1794.

their congregations, on whom they were totally dependent for fupport. This is furely a very weak defence ; but, I am afraid, it is one that muft often be made, where the paftor is removable at the pleafure of his flock.

But, there were others who were not merely paffive ; who were not afhamed to mingle in the bacchanalian orgies of the civic feftivals, held to celebrate the fucceffes of atheifts over the religion of which they profeffed to be believers, and of which they were teachers. Among thefe the *Reverend Citizen Prentifs*, of Reading, Maffachufetts, and the *Reverend Citizen Doctor M'Knight*, of New York, claim the fcandalous pre-eminence.

Nor were the places dedicated to the inftruction of youth fecurely guarded againft the approaches of fansculottifm. Of this the conduct of Doctor Rogers, a teacher in the Univerfity at Philadelphia, exhibits a ftriking proof. He gave the boys of his clafs a fpeech out of Shakefpeare's Harry V. to get by heart. It was the king's animating addrefs to his army before Harfleur : " Once more to the breach, dear friends," &c. which, in Shakefpeare ends thus :

" Follow your fpirit, and, upon this charge,
" Cry—God for Harry ! England ! and St. George !"

This conclufion the Doctor parodied :

" Cry—God for *Freedom ! France !* and *Robefpierre !*"

All the clafs repeated it with the democratic emendation, except a little Englifh boy about ten or eleven years of age, who boldly faid :

" Cry—God for *Harry ! England !* and *St. George !*"

though a child, certainly poſſeſſed more taſte, more ſenſe, more patriotiſm and more piety than his Reverend teacher.

When the ſweet Warwickſhire bard put this noble ſpeech into the mouth of his favourite hero, he was not bleſſed with the hope, that, hundreds of years afterwards, and thouſands of miles diſtant, it would call forth ſuch a noble ſpirit in a child of ten years of age.

Before I return to take my leave of the Democratic Societies, I truſt the reader will not be diſpleaſed with an account of the civic *fete* of the 23d *Thermidor* (10th of Auguſt, " ſtyle of the ſlaves"), which was celebrated at Philadelphia in 1794.

To ward off every charge of miſrepreſentation, I ſhall confine myſelf to a literal tranſlation of the *Proces Verbal* (Minutes of the proceedings), ſent to the Convention, and which may be ſeen in the French Philadelphia gazette of the 25th *Thermidor*, 12th of Auguſt, " ſtyle of the ſlaves," as the *humane* French Governor of Gaudaloupe calls it.

" At ſun-riſe the *fete* was announced by a *ſalve* of
" 22 guns, in alluſion to the 22d of Sept.—At eight
" o'clock another *ſalve* of 10 guns, at once announced
" the *fete* of the 10th Auguſt, and the hour of aſ-
" ſembling.

" The French and *American* citizens now repaired
" to the centre ſquare, where the order of march
" was to be ſettled on : the greateſt part of the citi-
" zens wore oak-boughs, and little bunches of ears of
" wheat, ornamented with *tricolored* ribbons.

" In the middle of the ſquare there was an obeliſk
" [*made of paſte-board*], decorated with attributes
" of liberty. On the four ſides of the obeliſk were
" *engraven* [engraven on paſte-board mind] the fol-
" lowing inſcriptions :

" To Immortality.

" The French Republic one and indivisible.

" Liberty, Equality, Fraternity.

" Tremble Tyrants, your reign is over.

" A deputation of French citizens then went to
" the French Minister's where the *chiefs civil and*
" *military of the State of Pennsylvania* were assembled.
" A deputy announced to the minister that the good
" people were waiting for their *representatives*. They
" immediately came to the square preceded by the flags
" of the two nations, marching to the noise of drums
" and cannons, and amidst the cries, a hundred times
" repeated, of *Vive la Republique Françoise!* [I will
not disgrace our language by translating the vile accla-
mation]; " and war-like music played, by intervals,
" airs analogous to the transports which burst forth
" from every quarter.

" When every thing was ready, ten guns were fired
" as a signal for the march. Two pieces of cannon,
" followed by French and American cannoneers, took
" the lead. The hatred that we were going to swear
" against tyrants, was written on every countenance.
" The anniversary of the destruction of despotism
" painted on every face patriotism, liberty, and equal-
" ity.

" The *obelisk was carried by four citizens*, two
" French and two American, in red liberty caps :
" these were followed by a French grenadier,
" bearing a *pike* surmounted with a liberty cap."

Now comes the prettiest part of the procession.

" Twelve young *citoyennes* (or she citizens), dressed

What a contrast there was between these little innocent lambs, with their flower-baskets, and the swarthy grenadier with his bloody pike and cap !

" The French Minister, the Consuls, the *chiefs civil*
" *and military of Pennsylvania*, marched in the centre
" of the procession."

Indeed it was diverting enough to see these great personages, the good sober-looking, pot-bellied chiefs of Pennsylvania, come squeezing, and shouldering, and zigzaging along, like so many raw recruits at drill. They were formed into what military men call a platoon, and never did my eyes behold so awkward a squad.

There is a small omission in this part of the *Proces Verbal*, which I shall supply.—Before the procession left the centre square, the *English flag*, which had been brought thither *reversed*, under the flags of France and America, was *burnt* before the obelisk, amidst the triumphant hootings of the brave sons of liberty and equality.—This was by way of retaliation for Lord Howe's victory over the sans-culotte fleet, the news of which had arrived the day before.

" The procession advanced to the garden of the
" Minister François, where there was an altar erect-
" ed to the country, on which stood the goddess of
" liberty.   The flags of the two nations were planted
" on each side of her, while the little she citizens
" were ranged round the altar.

" Patriotic hymns were now sung, accompanied
" with music ; and while the most tender and melting
" invocations were put up, the she citizens made to the
" goddess a sweet smelling offering of the flowers they
" had brought, with which they covered her altar,
" with an innocent zeal peculiar to their age.

The patriotic hymns being ended, an oration was made by a Citizen François,* and then the Miniſter François made another, and then the whole ſwore to be faithful to the Republic. The beſt of this was, three-fourths of the audience did not underſtand a word of what they heard, of what they ſwore to, or even of the oath they took.

" The Miniſter had hardly time to conclude, when " the cries [or howlings] of *Vive la Republique Fran-* " *çois une et indiviſible!* burſt forth from every throat.

" A diſcharge of cannon, a war-like march, and a " roll of the drums, expreſſed the joy of the people, " and ſignified that every heart was glad.—Inſtantly " the ranks broke off, and dances were formed round " the altar of liberty, and over all the encloſure."

Theſe dances were the fineſt fun I ever enjoyed. The patriotic hymns were well enough ; four hundred fellows howling out French bombaſt, without under-ſtanding a word of it, was not a bad ſpecimen of fra-ternal diſſonance ; but to behold fifty or ſixty groupes, promiſcouſly formed, whiſtling, ſinging and capering about they knew not why nor wherefore ; and to ſee the " *chiefs civil and military of Pennſylvania,*" heav-ing up their legs, and endeavouring to ape the light-heeled mounſeers, was a ſpectacle which, I truſt, has been ſeldom equalled.—In one part of the garden you heard the chorus of the bloody

Ah! ça ira, ça ira, ça ira,
Les Ariſtocrats a la Lanterne.

* It is well worthy of remark, that this oration, which was ſent to the convention, contained a high ſtrained compliment to *Robeſpierre,* juſt at the very time that the convention and their mob were hacking and ſhooting and guillotining him.—Had the *virtuous civic feters* known this, they would have curſed him moſt heartily ; as, indeed, they did two months afterwards.—What a

In another :

Danfons la carmagnole,
Vive le fon, vive le fon
Du canon.

While in another,

Alons enfans de la patrie

feemed to iffue from the lungs of twenty infernals.
But what was ftill moft ludicrous, was, to hear all this
uttered, by the greateft part of the chanters, in an
accent barbarous beyond defcription.. But, to proceed
with my tranflation :

" During the reft of the day, public joy was ma-
" nifefted all over the city."—That's a lie. One
half of the people of the city cared nothing at all
about the *fete*, and were aftonifhed and afhamed that
the cannons of the ftate fhould be employed on fuch an
occafion ; and I venture to affirm, that not one-twen-
tieth part of thofe who affifted at it, would have affifted, had they known they were celebrating the anniverfary of the fall of Louis XVI. and the horrid and
cowardly murder of the Swifs guards. This remark
juftice demanded in defence of thofe who attended
through ignorance. With regard to the " *chiefs, civil*
" *and military of Pennfylvania,*" as I have too much
refpect for them to accufe them of ignorance, I leave
them to defend themfelves.

We muft now return to the Democratic Clubs. In
what remains to be faid of them I fhall be very concife.

Though they were inftituted for the exprefs purpofe
of clogging the wheels of government, weakening its
power, and exciting a fpirit of difcontent among the
people, that might acquire ftrength enough to force
it into a war on the fide of France, or totally annihi-
late it ; yet there were three meafures in this continued oppofition, againft which the Democrats made a

bolder ftand than ufual, and called forth more than ordinary exertions; namely, the *Proclamation of Neutrality*, the enforcing obedience to the *Excife-Law*, and the fanctioning of the *Britifh Treaty*. They had entered their folemn proteft againft the two former, and had ufed every means in their power to effect a forcible, and even an armed oppofition to them; and their conduct with refpect to the latter was exactly of the fame defcription. But, of every part of this conduct, their refolves againft the appointment of the man beft calculated to bring about an accommodation; their publifhing the treaty in a mutilated form with their own invidious mifreprefentations; their difpatching runners to all the principal towns, to exafperate the difcontented, and deceive the weak; their difhonourable means of obtaining petitions to Congrefs againft it; the intrigues of Randolph and Fauchet, and the embarraffment and alarm their machinations fpread through the country; all thefe are fo frefh in every one's memory, that it is ufelefs to dwell on them here. Certain it is that they ought not to be forgotten, nor will they be, while *Peter Porcupine's* writings are remembered; and though thefe latter are affuredly not deftined to long life, I hope they will outlive the infernal fect of the Jacobins, and if this hope be to be realized, I fincerely wifh they may fink into oblivion to-morrow.

The Weftern Infurrection and its effects had already rendered the Democrats extremely odious; here their mifchievous efforts touched the pockets and the lives of the people; and their failure in the laft attempt to trouble the peace of the Union, obliged them to hide their heads. The dark caballing clubs do, indeed, ftill exift; but they either never meet, or they dare not publifh their refolves. However, let not the friends of the General Government, of order, of peace and of general happinefs and profperity, imagine that the fect is annihilated. They only wait for a more favourable moment, and fhould the indifcretion or fupinenefs of

arrive, they will obtain an afcendency that will enable them to inflict fignal vengeance for their paft difappointments. From their reign God defend me and mine !

From one juftified by his talents in being anxious about his reputation as a writer, the imperfectnefs of this fketch would require an apology. As this is not my cafe, I fhall make none. However, as publifher of the hiftory of Jacobinifm, I hope I can promife myfelf, that the fatisfaction the reader will derive from the book itfelf, will induce him to excufe the faults of the Appendix.

E N D.